Omer T Gillett

How I Became a Preacher

Omer T Gillett
How I Became a Preacher
ISBN/EAN: 9783337029982

Printed in Europe, USA, Canada, Australia, Japan

Cover: Foto ©Lupo / pixelio.de

More available books at **www.hansebooks.com**

How I Became a Preacher.

A Sequel to

"HOW I BECAME A SAILOR."

BY

OMER T. GILLETT, A.M., M.D.,

AUTHOR OF "SAVE YOUR MINUTES."

CINCINNATI: CRANSTON & CURTS.
NEW YORK: HUNT & EATON.
1893.

DEDICATION.

TO

HARRIET ANN GOODE GILLETT,

who,
for nearly threescore years,
was the loved and loving wife of him whose experiences
are here narrated,

This Volume is Filially Dedicated

by her son,

THE AUTHOR.

PREFACE.

CLOSELY following the publication of "How I Became a Sailor," there came to the author many requests that the hero be carried farther in his career, and that a glimpse of his sailor-life be given.

Those who had known father and his vocation for over half a century, added: "Tell us how he became a preacher."

Compliance with these requests seemed impossible, so meager were the data at my command, until a similar request came from my brother, Philip G. Gillett, accompanied with the statement that he had father's journal of his travels, which he thought would help me. At my request he sent me the journal, and this volume is the result. The book is one of facts which have been collated from every possible source, in addition to the journal; viz., old letters, lectures upon foreign localities, notably Egypt and the Holy Land, and the memory of persons now living, especially that of my mother. More history has been introduced than the journal contained, as have also many truths taken from encyclopedias and reliable works of travel.

"How I Became a Sailor" is not wholly truthful, and that fact demands an explanation.

Samuel's mother did not die in the log cabin in the cornfield near Terre Haute, Indiana; but the sickness was so severe as to break up the family, and Samuel went to work for his living, much as described in the book.

Truth requires me to say also that father had brothers and sisters who are not mentioned in "How I Became a Sailor;" the author's extreme invalidism at the time of writing, and probable speedy death, prompting the writing of a shorter narrative than the whole truth would have demanded.

One brother, Simeon S. Gillett, was a great

assistance to Samuel, doing for him the part which the first narrative assigns to an uncle.

His mother lived to old age, and when mention is made of her in this volume it is in accord with the truth.

Had the publication of a sequel to the first volume been anticipated, conformity to truth would have been observed through the first as it has through the second.

In that case, my father's entire name, Samuel Trumbull Gillett, would have been used.

The author desired to employ the full name in this volume; but at the request of her to whom the book is dedicated, the name was made to conform to the one in "How I Became a Sailor."

Many of the names and characters in this narrative are fictitious.

If, however, the person mentioned was at any time commander of a vessel, or higher in rank than a captain in the United States Navy, the name is correctly given.

Names of representatives of our Government in foreign lands are also given correctly. So is that of Lieutenant S. H. Hopkinson, who died near the Island of Milo. Likewise that of Mr. Mooner, the generous sailing-master of the *Lexington*, who so befriended father during a long sickness on shipboard. Mr. Mooner has probably, long ere this, passed to his reward, but the kindness he did my father is gratefully acknowledged to-day by the son.

Many copious extracts are taken, verbatim, from father's journal. These, it is hoped, his old friends will recognize from the style.

Quotations from literature of a date more recent than that of the occurrences narrated, the author has freely made.

O. T. GILLETT.

COLORADO SPRINGS, 1893.

CONTENTS

CHAPTER I.
Orders—Too Late—A Familiar Face—"All is Well that Ends Well," 15

CHAPTER II.
The Fresh-water Sailor—At Sea—Meditations, ... 21

CHAPTER III.
Seasickness—The Azores—Gibraltar, ... 27

CHAPTER IV.
Nelson and Trafalgar, ... 37

CHAPTER V.
Gibraltar, ... 42

CHAPTER VI.
The Dear Old Flag, ... 50

CHAPTER VII.
Port Mahon—The Crippled Fruit-girl—The Gambling Priest—A Knock-down Argument, ... 56

CHAPTER VIII.

The Cochlins—Letters from Home—Malta—A Little
Mythology—Milo and the Pirates, ... 63

CHAPTER IX.

Temple of Minerva—Stormy Weather—Scio—English
Pride—Smyrna—An Encounter with Greek Pirates, 73

CHAPTER X.

Pirates again—The Austrian Captain's Story—Shall I
"do right?"—The Ruins of Troy, ... 83

CHAPTER XI.

Captain Booth Sick—Sail for Malta—Mount Ætna—
Tunis, ... 91

CHAPTER XII.

A Pleasant Quarantine—The Cochlins—Fourth of July—
A Race—Death of Captain Booth—Farewell Lieutenant Breese—Lieutenant Rumage—Algiers—
Malta, ... 100

CHAPTER XIII.

Syracuse—Catacombs—Ear of Dionysius—Fountain of
Arethusa—Grave of Archimedes, ... 109

CHAPTER XIV.

Scylla and Charybdis—Palermo—The Sirocco Wind—
Rome, ... 119

CHAPTER XV.

Leghorn—Story of Leopold—Pisa—Duomo Baptistery—
Leaning Tower—Campo Santo, ... 129

CHAPTER XVI.

Off for Florence—Banditti—"Make Way for my Masters"—Palace of the Pitti—Garden of the Boboli—
Royal Gallery—The Grand Duke—Sufferings—
Prime Minister helps us, ... 139

CONTENTS.

CHAPTER XVII.
An Equinoctial Storm Yellow Fever—Gayety—Sickness—Homeward Bound—Smallpox—Stormy Passage—America!......................151

CHAPTER XVIII.
Marriage-bells—Examination Victory!..........163

CHAPTER XIX.
Pleasing Orders—Crying Babies—Docking the *Delaware*—Aground—Gayety—The Suicide—A Fatal Fall—Visitors from New York,..............166

CHAPTER XX.
Distinguished Passengers—A Perilous Night—An Enjoyable Calm—Cherbourg—To Paris in a French Diligence,............................177

CHAPTER XXI.
Paris—Cemetery of Père-la-Chaise—Ney—Jardin des Plantes—Versailles—St. Denis—Royal Gallery of the Louvre—Fish Market—Notre Dame—Pantheon—Disappointment,..................189

CHAPTER XXII.
Again at Mahon—Changes—A Tragedy—A Rascally Trick which takes us to Naples—Divine Service in a Grand Church,......................198

CHAPTER XXIII.
Naples—Tomb of Virgil—Grotto of Posilipo—Grotto del Cane—Lake Avernus—Lazzaroni—Ascent of Vesuvius—An Eruption,....................207

CHAPTER XXIV.
Pompeii and Herculaneum—Museo Borbonico—Statues of Peace and War,....................219

CHAPTER XXV.

Stromboli—Scylla and Charybdis again—Burial at Sea—Egypt—Alexandria, ... 228

CHAPTER XXVI.

Off for Cairo *via* Canal—The Nile—Desolation of Egypt, ... 238

CHAPTER XXVII.

An Egyptian Landscape—Alma Dancers—A Nocturnal Songstress—Milk, Whisky, and Chickens—A Sad Sight—The Nile Proper—Goshen—The Pyramids—Bulak—Warm Reception—Cairo—A Mad Doctor, . . 251

CHAPTER XXVIII.

Grand Cairo—Tombs of the Califs—The Citadel—The Mamelukes—Tombs of the Mamelukes—The Governor's Reception—Must I Smoke?—The Harem—View from the Citadel—On, and Prophecies about it—Joseph's Well, ... 262

CHAPTER XXIX.

Mehemet Ali—Palace of Ibrahim—A Wise Dog—The Slave Market—A Syrian Home—Dinner at the Harem, ... 275

CHAPTER XXX.

Off for the Pyramids—Donkeys and Sour Grapes—Site of Battle of the Pyramids—Description—Ascent—View from the Top—Remarks—A Foolish Race, . . 286

CHAPTER XXXI.

Interior of the Pyramid—Hard Work—Dinner in a Tomb—Also, a Nap—The Sphinx—A Taste of Desert Travel—Tomb of Psammetichus—We purchase Human Flesh and Bone—Site of Memphis—Mene's Great Work, ... 299

CHAPTER XXXII.

A Bible Lesson at the Birthplace of History—Floating down the Nile—Egyptian Darkness, and a Surly Arab Boatman—Stopped at the Gates of Cairo—Noise opens them—A Party to Mr. Gliddon—Farewell to Egypt, ... 310

CHAPTER XXXIII.

Jaffa—Off for Jerusalem—Robbers—Ramleh—Plain of Sharon—Valley of Elah—The City of the Great King, ... 321

CHAPTER XXXIV.

Approach to Jerusalem—Remarks about the City—Our Quarters—The Recent Capture of the City—Death of Mrs. Thompson, ... 336

CHAPTER XXXV.

Church of the Holy Sepulcher—Empress Helena, and Finding of the True Cross—The Moslem Guard—Stone of Unction—The Ædicula—Impressions at the Sepulcher—Place of Apparition—Chapel of the Armenians—Mount Calvary—Impressions—Other Localities about the Church, ... 347

CHAPTER XXXVI.

Via Dolorosa—Site of St. Stephen's Martyrdom—Tomb of the Virgin Mary—Garden of Gethsemane—Mount of Olives—Magnificent View—Remarks about Sacred Places in Sight, ... 359

CHAPTER XXXVII.

Mount of Olives, and Impressions received there—Bethany, and Tomb of Lazarus—King's Dale—Pool of Siloam—Moloch—Tophet—Valley of Slaughter—Gehenna, ... 372

CHAPTER XXXVIII.

Hill of Evil Council—Mount Zion—Tomb of David—Bethlehem—Church of the Nativity,.........386

CHAPTER XXXIX.

Stones from Solomon's Temple—Pool of Bethesda—Mosque of Omar—Jews' Quarter—Visit to the Governor—Oriental Justice—Missionaries—Farewell to Jerusalem—Accidents,................395

CHAPTER XL.

Mount Carmel—Prophecies about Palestine and the Jews—Tyre—Sidon—Beirut—Smallpox—Cholera—Homeward Bound,...............406

CHAPTER XLI.

Home and Friends—Perfect Happiness—Conversion—Shall I preach?—Promotion—Camp-meeting—"I yield,"........................419

CHAPTER XLII.

My Wife's Distress—Licensed to Preach—Resignation as Lieutenant—Join the Indiana Conference—Become a Chaplain in the Navy—Resignation,....430

How I Became a Preacher.

CHAPTER I.

ORDERS—TOO LATE—A FAMILIAR FACE—"ALL IS WELL THAT ENDS WELL."

> I love the sea! I love to be
> Where ocean billows foam!
> No other freedom is so free
> As when the seas we roam.

THE thirteenth of May, 1827, was Sunday. In common with my associate midshipmen attached to the receiving-ship *Fulton*, and not at that hour on duty, I was attending divine service in the Bethel connected with the navy-yard at Brooklyn, New York. With me—I think with the others also—it was a pleasure to go to Church. Though not a professed Christian, I remembered early teachings, and the requirement for us acting-midshipmen to attend service once on Sunday was gladly obeyed.

There was quite a company of us connected with the *Fulton*, where we were doing light duty on full pay, and waiting for orders to active service.

We all earnestly desired to get to work, being enthusiastic sailors in spirit, and desirous to see the reality. Every one, therefore, hoped for orders. The chaplain of the navy-yard preached that morning from the text: "Be ye also ready; for in such an hour as ye think not, the Son of man cometh."

It was a splendid text, and, I suppose, a splendid sermon; but so anxious was I to get sailing orders, my mind would wander in spite of an honest effort to listen. Something unexpected was to come, the text said; to me that was "orders," and from that thought I could not escape.

In the midst of the sermon and of these thoughts, Captain Budd, commander of the *Fulton*, entered the church, and called me from the room.

"Mr. Trumbull," said the captain, when we were out of the building, "there are orders for you in the commodore's office. You are to report at once on board the *Lexington*. She sails in an hour, or less, for the Mediterranean, and you have not a minute to lose. So hurry up!"

Scarcely taking time to thank Captain Budd,

I dashed off at full speed toward the *Fulton*. "How can I get aboard the quickest?" was my thought. It was necessary that I go on the *Fulton* to get my things, and no boat was at my disposal.

Captain Budd kindly solved the dilemma by calling after me as I ran:

"Take my gig, Mr. Trumbull, and hurry!"

"Hurry!" No need for that injunction. I ran as only a Hoosier can. I was the first Hoosier in the navy, and I doubt if any of those who followed me ever obeyed orders with more velocity than I. Gladness gave me wings, and I *flew* to the gig, the crew of which rowed me to the *Fulton* in quick time.

As we were crossing the water, I thought of the text—the first clause of it—"Be ye also ready." For the reception of orders in the usual way, I was fully prepared; but I was not ready to be called from church and sent away in such a precipitous manner. Though *semper paratus* is the sailor's motto, upon which I had endeavored to act, there were many little things I wanted to get before sailing. Now there was no opportunity, and I must go without them. In a very few minutes all my belongings were packed, when a boat set them and me on shore.

Having been on the *Fulton* about six weeks, many pleasant friendships had been formed; but there was no time for farewells. The truth was, most of my friends were still in church. In short order, I bade adieu to the few on board, and off for the *Lexington* I hastened. I knew the vessel was lying in North River, opposite New York City. Hailing a carriage—as it was Sunday, I was peculiarly fortunate in finding one quickly—we drove as speedily as possible to Fulton Ferry, upon which we crossed East River; thence across New York City to the bank of North River.

There, as I expected, was the beautiful sloop-of-war *Lexington*; but, contrary to expectation, she had weighed anchor, and was sailing proudly down toward the bay. The sight was to me most distressing. She was off for the Mediterranean, and I was left behind!

The Mediterranean!—the cruise which, of all others, I longed to take! Rather than send me to the *Lexington* by some other vessel, the Government would assign me to other duty! Keener disappointment than was mine at that moment I had never experienced. In desperation I cried to the driver:

"Go to the Battery as fast as you can drive!"

What good going to the Battery would do was not to me very clear; but it was in the direction the *Lexington* was sailing, and therefore I wanted to go.

Down the river we went, as fast as two good horses could take us, on the street bordering the river. The noble ship was but little in advance. She was "so near, and yet so far!"

In my anxiety to get nearer I leaned far out of the carriage—so far that the driver refused to proceed unless I seated myself properly.

We had almost reached the Battery when I saw something which caused my heart to leap with joy.

"Stop!" cried I; "stop!"

The driver complying, I alighted, and approached a gentleman who was passing upon the sidewalk. It was Lieutenant Samuel L. Breese, first lieutenant of the *Lexington*, whom I knew by sight. I knew the ship would not sail without him, and I was happy. Lifting my cap, I said:

"Lieutenant Breese, I am ordered to report for duty on the *Lexington*."

"Where are your orders, sir?"

"I had not time to get them, sir. Captain Budd told me they were at the commodore's office, but that I had no time to get them, as the ship was on the point of sailing, and I had not a minute to spare. He called me from church to tell me this."

"I suppose the commodore was at church?" said the lieutenant.

"Yes, sir, he was," I replied.

"I see it! The commodore knew we were to change our anchorage, but his clerk did not, and supposed we were off for good. The ship is to anchor a mile or so down the harbor. What is your name?"

"Samuel Trumbull."

"Go back to the navy-yard, Mr. Trumbull, and get your orders. You can report to-morrow for duty."

I was delighted with Lieutenant Breese. With a happy heart I watched the *Lexington* as she came to anchor. The sound of the cable as it passed through the hawse-hole was sweet music indeed, and the grace of movement with which the ship responded to the restraint of her cable was most pleasing.

I went back in the carriage to the navy-yard, paying the driver a good fee, for he had earned it. Monday morning I procured my orders from the commodore's clerk; did what shopping I wished to do in Brooklyn; bade my shipmates in the *Fulton* good-bye; and in one of the ship's boats was rowed away to the *Lexington*—a much more pleasant and dignified way than racing across town in a carriage.

CHAPTER II.

The Fresh-water Sailor—At Sea—Meditations.

THE *Lexington* did not sail till the 19th. As I came on board of her on the 14th, there were five days in which to get acquainted with my shipmates. I was prepared to be pleased with everything and everybody.

Of the officers, only one besides myself was taking his maiden voyage. That was a young acting-midshipman named Perkins, from one of the States bordering the chain of great lakes. Being green hands, we early became intimate. Perkins was a little fellow, full of fun, a great joker, and, what is somewhat uncommon with jokers, able to enjoy the fun when the laugh was upon himself. Acquaintance proved that he was a little boastful. He professed great love for the sea, though he admitted he had never seen salt-water till he came to the navy-yard to report for duty, only a few weeks before.

"I am a first-rate sailor, Trumbull," he said to me; "for I have been on the lakes so much."

"I wish I were," was my reply; "but I am not, and I expect to be terribly seasick."

"If you are, I will take care of you. I am used to the 'bounding billow,' though not the kind seasoned with salt—the same genus, if it is a different species. So I am *healthy* when it comes to seasickness."

The 19th at last came, and we were to sail. Arrangements for departure began early in the morning.

I had read something about the sailing of ships—about the friends being present in great numbers to bid sad farewells to those whom they feared never to see again. There was some of this with us, but not much; for we had said our good-byes to the loved ones weeks or months before. I had spoken mine from the lower deck of the Ohio River steamer *Rainbow*, over a thousand miles from New York Harbor. Most of the crew and officers were likewise from home—though few so far as I—and to them and me the sailing was a longed-for occurrence. To the old tars, it was no novelty. To us all, it was a matter of business; and we were delighted when the anchor hung at the bow, and sails filled with a favoring breeze were urging us to the ocean. To the ocean! I had never yet fairly seen it, for but little of it is visible from New York Harbor; but our majestic ship is bearing us proudly to its broad surface. As we passed the Narrows the forts on either side gave us a parting salute, as a wish for a prosperous voyage.

Perkins and I were alive to everything that occurred.

"I suppose," said Perkins, "that long, low point of sand on the right is Sandy Hook."

"I expect so," said I. "Look at the lighthouse! How glad I am to see Sandy Hook! I have heard so much about it."

"So am I glad to see it. When we have fairly passed that, we are at sea, are we not?" asked Perkins.

"I believe so," was my reply.

I did not want to talk; the situation was too impressive for words. I think Perkins took the hint from my brief reply, for he was silent.

About eleven o'clock we passed Sandy Hook, and were on the Atlantic. The Atlantic! How constantly it had been a factor in the dreams of my boyhood! "The name," said I, to myself, "is based on the fabulous personage, Atlas. Atlas upheld the world; and how nearly does this ocean hold the good and great things of this world! Its waters, with the aid of the great Mediterranean Sea, lave the shores of the countries where civilization was first cradled, and where, in later centuries, it has attained its robust manhood."

Byron had the idea, when to the sea he sang in his "Childe Harold's Pilgrimage:"

> "Thy shores are empires, changed in all save thee:—
> Assyria, Greece, Rome, Carthage, what are they?
> Thy waters wasted them while they were free,
> And many a tyrant since; their shores obey
> The stranger, slave, or savage; their decay
> Has dried up realms to deserts. Not so thou—
> Unchangeable save to thy wild waves' play;
> Time writes no wrinkle on thine azure brow;
> Such as Creation's dawn beheld, thou rollest now."

The ocean is ever the same, and to this great Mediterranean Sea it is affording us a kindly passage. In the lands bordering this great midland sea we will study the wonders of the past ages—the wonders of nature, and the wonders of art; and, above all, we will walk the paths which the feet of the Savior trod.

Thus did I meditate till called to go on duty. As I walked the deck, I thought of what a wonderful thing is power and authority. Here was I, a young, eighteen-year-old boy, fresh from the frontier of Indiana, with little knowledge of this world and its way, yet, through the authority which my position as a midshipman gave me, I was temporarily in charge of the deck of this great ship—subject, of course, to those higher than I in rank, yet temporarily in charge of the deck.

"How great is this ship," thought I, "yet it is under *my* control! And how great is the sea! Far as the eye can reach, its immensity and grandeur extend." While thus thinking, the curtain of night fell over the sea and the ship, and the heavenly firmament became studded with stars. I further thought, "How wonderful are the heavens!" and I repeated, as I paced the quarter-deck: "The heavens declare the glory of God, and the firmament showeth his handiwork." "When I consider thy heavens, the work of thy fingers, the moon and the stars which thou hast ordained; what is man, that thou art mindful of him?"

Then I further thought: "As I, a weak worm of the dust, am superior to this great ship, because of some trivial authority, so art thou, O Maker of the universe, superior to all these earthly and heavenly wonders, for thou didst make them. Thou art the embodiment of authority. By thy word were they created. As the wonders of the universe transcend in magnificence and grandeur this frail vessel, which is but a spot on the vast ocean, so do thy might and power surpass those of thy servant man."

Such were my thoughts the first day and evening on the sea. I cried with delight:

> "The sea! the sea! the open sea!
> The blue, the fresh, the ever free!
> Without a mark, without a bound,
> It runneth the earth's wide regions round."

The weather thus far had been favorable. A gentle breeze, sufficient for fair progress, yet not strong enough to roughen the sea, had blown steadily all day. With deepest gratitude to God for his many mercies, I sought my hammock, first committing myself to the care of Him who holdeth the seas in the hollow of his hand.

CHAPTER III.

Seasickness—The Azores—Gibraltar.

CONTRARY to my fears, I was able to be up next morning. Seasickness I confidently expected. Not so, however, with my friend Perkins, the fresh-water sailor from the Northern lakes. We had a good breakfast that first morning at sea, to which Perkins and I did ample justice; after which we went on deck. The morning was glorious, though the sea was a little rough—quite rough, I thought at the time.

Soon Perkins leaned over the gunwale. Why he did so did not occur to me. My wits were sharpened when the captain, in passing, said:

"Ah, Mr. Perkins! feeding the fishes, are you?"

"I suppose it does look that way, Captain, but I'm not seasick; only a little nausea from something I ate. I'm quite a sailor," said Mr. Perkins.

"I'm glad you are," said Captain Booth; "but it looks a little suspicious."

Perkins again took a lean over the side. As he seemed very sick, I went to his assistance.

"Can I help you?" asked I.

"No, thank you. I'm not sick, only my stomach feels badly. I think it is the potted mustard I ate. Mustard, you know, is an emetic."

"Seasickness is an emetic this time, Mr. Perkins," said I.

"No, sir!" replied he, with indignation. "I tell you it is the mustard, and nothing else. My uncle is a doctor, and I know something about medicine."

The poor fellow braced up while saying this; but the sickness soon regained the ascendency, and I helped him off to bed.

"This is worse than seasickness," said he. "I know a little medicine, and I am poisoned. Won't you please fetch the surgeon?"

That I quickly did. The surgeon knew Mr. Perkins as a joker, and was very grave.

"Are you seasick?" asked he.

"O no, Doctor! Worse than that! I think I'm poisoned with potted mustard. I'm a good sailor, and won't be seasick; then I'm posted about medicines. I'm poisoned! The mustard gets the poison from the tin pot."

The doctor saw proper to agree with Mr. Perkins, and said:

"I believe you are right. How lucky you threw the poison from your stomach!"

Perkins was almost too sick to reply, but managed to say:

"Yes, sir; but, Doctor, there is a terrible lump in my stomach. Being informed about such things, I know that a lump comes with cancer of the stomach. Do you think that poison has started a cancer?"

"Cancer is usually of slow growth, taking years to come; but that mustard was very bad, and I do believe you are right! I am glad you thought of it. I'll give you cancer medicine," said the surgeon, happy in the thought that he had something good to tease this joker about, when he got over his seasickness.

The sea, during this talk, had grown much rougher; and, by the time the cancer remedy was administered, the doctor had another patient in the person of myself. Though the evil hour for me had not come so promptly as for Mr. Perkins, it came with equal intensity. I was so miserable I feared I *would die;* when it got a little worse, I feared I *would not;* and that, I understand, is about the best description one can give of seasickness. The ship was rolling badly. I thought that if the motion could be stopped for a moment I would be all right. That, of course, I knew could not be. But I thought, in my misery, that the course of the ship might be changed for a few minutes, so as to go across the waves, and change the rolling to a pitching motion. I was foolish enough to ask the surgeon to request the captain to make such a change for my benefit. This request the doctor enjoyed; for it gave him as good a joke on me as the cancer scare did on Mr. Perkins, and Dr. Adair was not the person to forget such a thing. A seasick sailor is considered legitimate game by his messmates; and, when Dr. Adair told in the forecastle of our fears and requests, much fun was had at our expense.

When—while convalescing—we first entered the forecastle, our attention was drawn to some rhymes which an unconfessed wag had written and pinned up for the amusement of the company. This is the way he touched up Mr. Perkins:

> "I'm not seasick! No! Not seasick!
>   My stomach's badly flustered.
> It acted as an em-e-tic –
>   That awful potted mustard!
>
> It must be cancer, Doctor, dear!
>   I'm poisoned from the tin!"
> "You're right! And I must give, I fear,
>   Strong cancer med-i-cine."

This was for my benefit:

> "Dear Doctor, tell the captain
>   I'm feeling very bad;
> If he would turn the ship around,
>   I would be very glad.
>
> 'T would stop this everlasting roll—
>   It makes me deathly sick;
> I surely will throw up my soul!
>   *Please* ask him to be quick!"

I was much teased by these lines and the merriment they caused. So was Perkins. His happy faculty of enjoying a joke on himself came to the rescue, and helped him through. I tried to follow his lead in this, with only partial success.

But I have been anticipating, and will return to the narrative.

The fresh-water sailor and myself were sick nearly a week, for the weather soon became very bad. There were head-winds day after day, and our progress was not at all gratifying. We passed quite near to the Azores Islands, but did not stop. These islands are unfortunate in not having a good harbor; otherwise they would have many callers, who now pass as we did.

I viewed these islands with great interest; partly because they were *land*—we had seen no land for nearly three weeks, and the monotony of the voyage was thus broken—but mainly because they were a foreign land. It was the first time I had ever seen any country which did not belong to the United States, and I gazed at these nine islands with much interest. They are only eight hundred miles from Portugal, to which they belong; and that implied that our voyage was nearing its end, and that erelong we would see the coast of the Old World.

Soon this hope was realized; for on June 21st, "Land, ho!" was heard from the masthead. How that cry did ring through the ship; and how it thrilled us, especially us new hands! Immediately the entire crew crowded to the deck, and many climbed into the rigging, to confirm the truth of the cry. Every glass on the ship was brought into use. Little could be seen with the naked eye, but the glass assured us that the coast of Spain was not far distant.

Spain! I did not care much for Spain as a country, but for Spain as a part of Europe I cared very much. The sight of her coast *clinched* the fact that *I*, the poor, fatherless boy from the wilds of Indiana, had crossed the Atlantic Ocean! Until I came to Brooklyn to report to the naval authorities, I had never seen a person—an American, I mean—who had crossed the ocean; and now I had done it!

Our ship's course had been well laid for the Straits of Gibraltar, and in a few hours we saw the coast of Africa on our starboard bow. The sight of Africa also impressed me, but not so deeply as did that of Europe; for the view of Europe came first, when the mind was in a more impressible mood. Moreover, great as was Africa, it was *not* Europe.

Surgeon Adair was very kind to Mr. Perkins and me, the two youngsters among the officers. He talked much with us, and always taught us something.

There was plenty of time to talk, as we were beating up the Straits of Gibraltar to an anchorage in the Bay of Gibraltar, or Algesiras, for it took us three days.

"Boys," said the doctor, "you must post yourselves thoroughly on every point we visit, and learn all you can about it. Read about it, and question every one who knows more than you about it."

"All right, Doctor; as we have nothing to read, we will commence on you with our questions," said I; "for you have been here before, and are posted."

"All right; go ahead."

"How wide is this strait?" I asked.

"At this—the west—end, it is twenty-four miles; at the eastern, it is fifteen; and it is thirty-six miles long."

"I suppose," said Mr. Perkins, "that the

island we see on the larboard bow is the Rock of Gibraltar?"

"What you see is the rock, but it is not an island. It is connected with the mainland by a low, sandy isthmus, about nine hundred yards wide near the rock, and only ten feet higher than the water. This low isthmus is called the neutral ground. You know England owns Gibraltar, and Spain owns the mainland."

"Yes," said Mr. Perkins; "and I suppose that was made neutral in a treaty of war?"

"That is it, exactly. When you get closer you will see that there is a large bay—eight miles long, by four miles wide—on the west of the rock. The anchorage is not the best, and the protection from southwest winds only partial. This is the Bay of Algesiras, or Gibraltar. The town of Algesiras is on the west side of the bay, and Gibraltar is on the east, right at the western base of the rock. This western side of the rock presents a gradual slope, interspersed with abrupt precipices, as you can see from here. The southern side presents a rather steep slope near the top, which terminates in a precipice, succeeded by a rocky flat; again, a precipice and a flat; the face of a third precipice is washed by the waters of the sea, and is called Europa Point, being the most southern point of Spain. The north and east sides present an abrupt, precipitous wall, thirteen hundred feet high. The substance of the rock is a gray, dense, calcareous formation, known as primary marble. Strata, from thirty to fifty feet thick, and with a dip of thirty-five degrees to the horizon, are visible on the north face."

"How high is the rock?"

"It is 1,439 feet high at the highest point, and with Cape Centa, just across the strait on the African coast, forms the eastern boundary of the strait. Do you remember what the ancients used to call these capes?"

As we did not, the doctor said:

"They called them the Pillars of Hercules, and they were supposed to limit the possibilities of navigation toward the west—to pass them was considered dangerous. The western limits of this celebrated strait are Cape Spartel on the African coast, and Cape Trafalgar on the Spanish side."

"Cape Trafalgar!" cried I. "Was n't it here that the battle of Trafalgar was fought?"

"It was, indeed. Look at the water!" said the doctor.

"I do n't see anything in the water," said Perkins.

"This is the water in which the great battle of Trafalgar was fought; is n't it, Doctor?" I asked.

"The very spot."

Evidently the fresh-water sailor was not posted about Trafalgar and Nelson. He confessed as much, and asked the doctor to give him a history of the battle.

"All right, the next chance we have for an hour's talk," said Dr. Adair.

CHAPTER IV.

NELSON AND TRAFALGAR.

THAT same evening the doctor gave us the talk about the great naval battle of Trafalgar. He said:

"To understand about this battle, which was fought right where we are to-day, one must know about Nelson, the greatest admiral England has ever had, and perhaps the greatest naval commander the world has produced. You boys just entering the navy must learn all about Nelson.

"Horatio Nelson was born in 1758. He was of good family, a fortunate thing for him, as it assisted him to 'get a start' early in life. Physically, he was of little account, being a small, delicate child. But his attenuated body was fired by a soul of intense spirit.

"When only thirteen years old he entered the royal navy, being sent to a ship commanded by his uncle. This uncle was soon made comptroller of the navy, in which position he rapidly advanced his nephew; for, in those days, promotion was largely a matter of personal influence at court. No matter how great responsibilities were placed upon the shoulders of young Nelson, he was always able to maintain his position with credit. In 1793, while engaged in the sieges of Bastia and Calvi, in the island of Corsica, he lost an eye. Not long after, when in an assault against Teneriffe, he lost his right arm.

"Little things—such as the frail body already mentioned, the loss of an eye and an arm—did not daunt the spirit of Horatio Nelson, and he soon was intrusted with the command of a fleet. He caused his own indomitable spirit to pervade this entire fleet, and, as a result, the stupendous victory of the Nile was placed to England's credit and his own. We can not follow him through all of his wonderful achievements—you must read of them, boys— but come to Trafalgar. It was in 1805, when the French Revolution was in progress. France and Spain were working conjointly in naval matters against England. They had a large and powerful fleet, much larger than that of England; but they had no Nelson, and they knew it. Fearing him, they avoided a conflict, and he chased them half around the world. Finally he caught them in these waters. Yes, this one-eyed, one-armed, frail little man, with comparatively small fleet and force, caught the combined navies of France and Spain, and he whipped them. Whipped them? Ay! He practically annihilated the navies of France and Spain! But his life was the forfeit.

"Let me tell you how he was killed. It was his desire to fight this battle at close quarters. His own ship, the *Victory*, did not fire a gun till after fifty of her crew had been killed, and her mainmast shot away. It was his aim to break the enemy's line, and he reserved his broadsides until they would do the greatest possible execution.

"To break the line, the *Victory* ran on board the *Redoubtable*, one of the enemy's vessels, and, just at that moment, the *Victory's* tiller-ropes were shot away.

"At such close quarters was the fighting done in this battle, that, at one time, four ships, two belonging to either side, lay as close together as though moored in compact tier, all their bows lying the same way. The English vessels in this tier were the *Victory* and the *Téméraire*; the French and Spanish were the *Redoubtable* and another, the name of which I have forgotten.

"While thus in absolute contact, the officers of the *Victory* ordered the guns of the middle and lower deck depressed, lest the shot pass clear through the enemy's vessel and injure the *Téméraire*, which lay upon the farther side of said vessel.

"Now, fire in one of these vessels would have been about as bad for either of the others. So, on the *Victory*, the fireman of each gun on the lower deck stood by with a bucket of water, which, after the firing, he dashed into the hole made in the enemy's side by the ball from his gun. As these lower-deck guns were in actual contact with the enemy's side when fired, the wisdom of this action is evident.

"How was Nelson killed? By a shot fired from a rifleman in the rigging of the *Redoubtable*. That was a mode of warfare he abominated, and never allowed his men to practice. He believed it to be barbarous and cruel, and wholly inefficient, as the picking off of a few men could never decide the issue of a naval engagement. As we know, these vessels were sandwiched one beside the other, very closely; in fact, so closely that Captain Harvey, of the *Téméraire*, though killed on his own vessel, fell upon the deck of the *Redoubtable*.

"The *Victory* was equally close to the latter ship on the opposite side, and a marksman in the rigging of the *Redoubtable* would be practically above any one on the deck of the *Victory*.

"A man, so placed, shot down upon Nelson. The ball struck him in the left shoulder, about the location of his epaulet.

"It reached the spine, probably, and in a few short hours—but not till the victory was assured—Nelson was no more. Among his last words were these: 'Thank God, I have done my duty.'"

Dr. Adair loved to talk, and we boys were glad to listen. So, evidently, were many other of the officers, and, ere he ceased, he had quite an audience. Mr. Perkins said:

"Doctor Adair, we thank you. You have given us—me at least—much valuable information, and all, I know, have been interested. Nelson was 'most as good as John Paul Jones."

"Jones was a fine officer, and I am glad, my boy, that you stand up for your countryman. No man could handle slender resources better than many of the naval heroes of the Revolution, and perhaps they could have handled an immense fleet equally well, but possibly not. Certain it is that, of those who have commanded great navies, none has done better than Horatio Nelson."

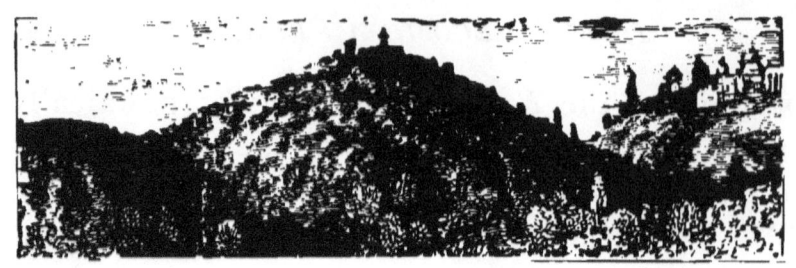

CHAPTER V.

GIBRALTAR.

THERE is a strong current constantly flowing through the Straits of Gibraltar from the Atlantic to the Mediterranean. It is strong enough to keep a ship from passing from the sea to the ocean unless there is quite a strong breeze blowing. This current was in our favor. There was a strong wind indeed; but it was dead ahead, and we were three days in beating up the straits.

On the evening of June 23d, about eight o'clock, we dropped anchor in the Bay of Gibraltar. The wind blew violently in the night, shifting from the east to the southwest. To such a wind this harbor is much exposed; the anchorage is poor, and our anchor dragged so much that the ship almost went on shore. In the morning the wind lulled, and those of the officers not on duty prepared to go ashore to

THE ROCK OF GIBRALTAR.

visit the town. Alas! I could not go. An eruption had come out on my person during the night. I showed it to the surgeon, who was not certain what it was. To my extreme sorrow and disgust, he quarantined me for three days. That meant that I could not go on shore, save on duty, till the three days were passed, and if, perchance, I should be sent on duty, it would be only to the literal shore, beyond which I must not go. Of course, I had to submit, and tried to do so gracefully; but I was boiling internally with indignation at the doctor's decision. Think of it!—within a cable's length of [the soil of Europe, and not allowed to put foot upon it; at the base of the Rock of Gibraltar—of which I had read so much—and not permitted to inspect its wonderful fortifications!

Upon the second day of my imprisonment, to my great delight, I was ordered to take a boat and a crew, and bring off to the ship some stores which had been purchased. Mr. Perkins had leave of absence for the day, and was to go ashore with me in the boat. So to the shore we went, and from the boat I sprang with feelings of intense delight. Europe! Yes, my foot trod the soil of Europe!

"Now, Trumbull," said Mr. Perkins, "I will attend to loading this boat, and you slip up in town and see what you can see."

"No, thank you, Perkins. This eruption is still out, and I can't go."

"That eruption's all bosh! I know something about medicine, and it amounts to nothing!"

"I'm on duty, Perkins, and must not leave the boat. It would not be right."

Memory reminded me of the time I left the quartermaster in charge of the deck of the *Fulton*.

"That's so," said Mr. Perkins; "it isn't just the thing; but you need not go out of sight of the men, and I will stay right here and watch them."

"Thank you, Perkins; I think I will not go. I want to do right."

Just then the quartermaster appeared, and told me a heavy box, up near the business part, was to be brought down. Wasn't I glad? Duty now took me where, by mounting for a moment the box, I had a good view of the immediate surroundings. Many of the fortifications I could see; they were large and numerous. I was strongly impressed with the strength of the place, from a military standpoint.

The streets were narrow, crooked, and crowded with carts, mules, jacks, and people from every quarter of the globe, but mostly Jews and Spaniards.

Though to me interesting, it was not a pleasing sight, for the inhabitants were a hard-looking assortment. There are said to be some fine English citizens in Gibraltar, but I saw none of them. The architecture of the town was not pleasing; for the best buildings—good enough to make a fair show when along with other similar ones—were sandwiched among miserable, one-story shanties, belonging to the natives. So much did I see in about three minutes; by which time I returned with the men, when Mr. Perkins started off for a ramble. He told me about it in the evening, after he had gotten back to the ship.

"Well, Sam," said Mr. Perkins. "I have had a fine time. Sorry you could not go, too."

"So am I, George."

To my delight, we two "middies" had gotten hold of each other's first names.

"Yes, I had a big time. I climbed clear to the top of the Sugar Loaf."

"Sugar Loaf! What's that?"

"The top of the rock. It's over fourteen hundred feet high, and hard climbing much of the way. And monkeys!—you should see the monkeys."

"What! in a cage?"

"No sir-ee. They are Barbary apes. They got across the strait from the Barbary States some way, and are wild. Not exactly wild, either, for the English Government protects them. They won't allow a gun fired on the rock; so the apes are really very tame. And there are lots of rabbits, partridges, pigeons, and woodcocks."

"What do they live on, George?"

"They live on the rock."

"I mean what do they eat? The rock is as bare as a baldheaded man."

"O, in the crevices there is plenty of verdure, which you can't see from here."

"O dear!" said I. "I can see nothing from here but that eruption. But it itches, and that's a sign it's getting well."

"And there is a cave, Sam! Yes, there are several. We went in the biggest, called the Hall of St. Michael. It starts in a thousand feet above the sea. There are many rooms, some quite large and beautiful, with stalactites and lots of passages, some quite narrow, so one can scarcely crawl through them. The passages lead downward, and we went down about five hundred feet. We could have gone farther, but the air got too foul. You could hear the sea roar, Sam; so the cave must connect with the sea. And we saw the big reservoir that holds ten thousand tons of water."

"What is that for?"

"To supply the garrison and ships with

water. There are no springs on the rock, and all the rain possible is caught and carried to this and other reservoirs. And every house has a cistern for private use."

"The guns, George!—tell me about the guns. Is it true that there are 1827 of them—one for each year of the Christian era?"

"There are a lot of them; but I think that report is a little doubtful. The place is wondrous strong. Fortifications everywhere. They point in every direction. Some at the sea-level, some five hundred feet up in the rock."

"Is it so," I asked, "that the guns are put into some of these natural passages that honeycomb this rock?"

"Perhaps in some, but surely not in many. There are hundreds of guns mounted in passages in the rock; but the passages are mostly artificial, blasted out of the solid stone. It would be a hard place to capture by assault, if manned by a strong garrison."

"Talking about Gibraltar, boys?" said Purser Jackson, who joined us at this point in the talk.

"Yes sir," said I, "that is, Mr. Perkins is; I am listening. You know I have seen nothing."

"Too bad! Are you posted on the history of this rock?"

"Not very well. Tell us about it, please."

"The little I know is soon told," said the paymaster. "You know this rock and the high hill, or mountain, opposite on the African coast—Apes Hill it is named—were called the Pillars of Hercules by the ancients, and were supposed to be the end of the world. The Phœnicians and Carthaginians knew about it, probably. From implements of war, found in some of the caverns of the rock, it is proven that the Romans did. In these caves were also found skeletons of African animals, which are found in no other part of Europe. So, many believe that this used to be part of Africa, and that what is now the neutral ground was the original site of the strait. Be that as it may, the first positive knowledge history gives us of this rock is that the Saracens fortified it in 711. They were commanded by a general with a long name, part of which is Tarik, and it was called Gebel Tarik, which means Hill of Tarik. The word Gibraltar is a corruption of this.

"The Saracens held it for six hundred years, when the Christians of Castile captured it, about 1309. In 1333 the Moors drove the Castilian Christians out, and held the place against all assaults, till the Spaniards took it in 1462, with the help of a renegade Moor. During all these centuries the place had been made stronger and stronger, till it was supposed to be impregnable.

The Dutch and English proved this to be a mistake, by capturing it in 1704.

"By this capture the English became masters of Gibraltar, and such they have ever remained. But they have had to fight for it. France and Spain gave the rock little rest. In 1779, when England was busy with our Revolution, and also at war with France, Spain determined to have Gibraltar. She left no stone unturned (except Gibraltar; she could n't turn that).

"Starvation by siege almost gave the Spanish success. But the English fleet, under Admiral Rodney, vanquished the Spanish, and revictualed the fortress. Again the English fleet did that thing. At one time the Spaniards constructed floating batteries—ten of them—with sides of porous timber seven feet thick, which would stop the balls. So they would if the balls were cold. But the English fired red-hot shot, which nestled comfortably in the inflammable timber, and burned every one of the ten batteries. They were completely annihilated. In this single attack with the floating batteries the Spanish loss was two thousand in killed alone. This entire siege lasted three years, seven months, and twelve days, and the entire loss of the English, in killed, was only 333.

"I have told you but little, boys, and you must read that siege up in the histories."

CHAPTER VI.

The Dear Old Flag.

CAPTAIN BOOTH had hoped to find some American men-of-war at Gibraltar, but was disappointed. Our stay was, therefore, not long, and by the time my quarantine had expired, we were weighing anchor, bound for the Balearic Islands. Of course, I saw little of Gibraltar. Dr. Adair said:

"Too bad, Mr. Trumbull, to have kept you from seeing this interesting place more closely. You could have gone safely, for that was only an herpetic eruption."

"I don't know what that means, Doctor," I replied; "but the second syllable describes my fix exactly, for I was in a pet at your decision. I don't want to be her pet any more, if that is the way Dame Fortune treats her favorites."

The doctor laughed so heartily at my dissection of his big name for the eruption, that I had to forgive him, and told him so.

"I am glad, Mr. Trumbull," said he, "that there is to be no eruption in the friendship between us."

"No, indeed, Doctor; I could n't afford that."

Favoring gales rapidly wafted us from the straits toward the east, through the blue waters of the historic Mediterranean. We "paralleled the convexity" of the coast of Spain, passing the islands of Iviza and Majorca, and, on the 26th of June, dropped anchor in the harbor of Mahon, in the island of Minorca.

We were glad to see the Stars and Stripes floating from the masthead of the United States schooner *Porpoise*.

Glad! We were all glad; but Perkins and I, who had never before met the dear old flag away from home, made an exhibition of ourselves in our glee.

"Hurrah for the Red, White, and Blue!" cried the fresh-water sailor, waving his cap high in air, after which he gracefully threw a back somersault. My part was to second the "hurrah," and turn a handspring, which was the utmost my acrobatic ability would allow. We were heartily laughed at, but it was in the way of indorsement; for the flag was dear to every heart on board.

"Boys, did you ever study Latin?" asked Dr. Adair.

"Yes! Of course we did! But it's United States we're dealing in now!" cried Perkins.

"That's all right, boys! Stick to your colors. But when the superfluous energy has escaped, I want to show you something."

We cooled off pretty soon, when the doctor said:

"I want you to translate this Latin sentence for me."

Taking a pen he wrote: "*Qui crudus tibi lectus, albasque spiravit.*"

The officers were all on deck, and, while we were puzzling over the sentence, gathered about us.

"*Qui*," said I, "means 'who,' and is the subject of the sentence, and *crudus*, I suppose, agrees with it."

"And *spiravit* is the verb, and it means 'to breathe or to blow,'" said Perkins. "*Tibi* is the dative of *tu*, and means 'for thee.'"

"But what does *crudus* mean?" I asked. "I am too crude to say."

"Good for you, Sam! That is a good hint. *Crudus* means 'green' or 'raw.' Now," said Perkins, "let's understand the verb *est*, which means 'he is,' after *crudus*, and it will help. This will be the order: *Est crudus qui spiravit*— 'He is green who breathes.'"

"But *spiravit*, George, is in the perfect tense.

'He is green who breathed,' must be right; but that *que* at the end of *albasque* means 'and;' it should connect *lectus* and *albas*. *Albas* is the accusative plural of *albus*, meaning 'white;' but the *lectus* stumps me, for it is the form of the nominative case, singular; but I do n't know what it means; and *que* can't connect an accusative and a nominative."

"No, it can't; but *lectus* probably is from *lego*, which means 'to read'—participle, you know—and to be rendered 'read,' with the pronunciation of the past tense. Sam, could *albas* mean books? The leaves are white, you know!"

"Rather liberal; but what could you make of it?" I asked.

"He is green who breathed, having read the books for thee."

"No, George, you have left the *que* out. Now clouds are white as well as leaves, so let 's take some of the other meanings of the words, and let 's suppose that the subject of *est*, understood, is 'wind,' also understood. Then we would have, 'It is a raw wind, which blew white clouds for thee'—No, that won't do! I 'll give it up; *lectus* is left clear out."

"So will I!" said George.

"Boys," said the doctor, "you have done well; for, though you have not translated the sentence, you have shown that you know something of Latin. Take this pen and jot down some of the meanings of the words to help you a little. Write out the sentence in Latin first, and then put the meaning of each word under it, just for convenience. I will tell you what meaning to take from those you have mentioned."

George took the pen, and this was what he had after following the doctor's directions:

"Qui—crudus—tibi—lectus—albasque—spiravit."
"Who—raw—for thee—read—white—and—blew!"

"That's done," said Perkins; "what next, Doctor?"

"Please read rapidly the meanings you have put down."

Mr. Perkins read quickly, and the meanings made him say:

"Hurrah for the red, white, and blue!"

Every one saw it in a second. Perkins sprang on a coil of rope, and cried:

"Three cheers for the 'Red, White, and Blue!'"

We gave them with a will. Then Perkins grasped the doctor's hand, exclaiming:

"Doctor, you're a darling! I swear eternal admiration and friendship!"

Seeing and hearing that something unusual was occurring, the whole crew drew near to have a hand in the fun. Captain Booth explained all to them. Many knew nothing of Latin—perhaps none of those before the mast—but all knew the spirit which endeared his flag to an American, and they insisted on three more cheers, which we all gave with a will.

This absurd Latin became a byword in the ship—every one knew it; and if "three cheers" were wanted, these words were called out, when the cheers would follow with a will.

CHAPTER VII.

Port Mahon.—The Crippled Fruit-girl.—The Gambling Priest—A Knock-down Argument.

THERE is a pretty good harbor at Mahon, which is a town of some ten thousand inhabitants. It seemed as though a fair percentage of these had come out to meet us in little boats. By the time our anchor dropped we were surrounded.

To sell anything possible was the boatmen's aim, but especially fruit. The fruit was very fine and very cheap, so much buying was done. The Balearic Islands belong to Spain, and the Spanish language was what we mostly heard from the boatmen, who called their wares at the top of their voices. Above all, however, was the shrill voice of an English child, or, perhaps, an Irish. I was glad to hear the loved tongue from a stranger, away in this foreign land, and I speedily hunted out its owner. It was a fair-haired little maid of perhaps twelve years. She was trying hard to reach the ship's side, but stronger boatmen kept her away. It was an unfair battle, and Captain Booth, who also had been attracted by the voice, ordered the rude boatmen back in a manner so peremptory, that they speedily obeyed, and the little girl came alongside with her boat. Then we saw that what we had supposed—if, perchance, we had noticed—to be a pair of small oars, was a pair of crutches, and that this child had but one leg. It is needless to say that her entire stock was sold out in half an hour. She was the "leading merchant" for three reasons: First, she spoke English, and was a member of the great Anglo-Saxon family; second, she was a most pleasing child, with light hair and blue eyes, and her clothes, though much worn, were clean; third, she was a cripple. Either was sufficient to sell her cargo; combined they were a power.

Several of us were ready to go ashore. As no boat was at our immediate disposal, we hired this little girl to row us to the dock. I wanted to row for her, but she would not permit. Her skill in handling the boat reminded me of my dear little sister, Faith, and made me very sad. All my sympathies went to the child.

Soon we were ashore, and on our way to see the sights. After going a short distance, I remembered that I had left my pocket-knife in the boat, and ran back to get it.

The child was talking with a man, evidently an Irishman, and giving him—though most reluctantly—her money. I heard the man say:

"Oi want it all! Give me ivery cint."

The child obeyed, while the tears streamed down her face. Had I been near enough I would have struck the brute; but I was a hundred feet away, the man's talk having been loud. I ran to the little cripple and asked:

"What's the matter? Who is that?"

"It's my father," sobbed the child. "He took all the money, and mother is sick."

I was fighting mad; but if that was the child's father, what could I do? Very little. I gave her what money I could spare, saying:

"Don't let your father know you have this."

"Thank you, sir, I won't; and I'll bring you some fruit for it to-morrow."

"No, I don't want you to. You may have that, and welcome."

"But mother says I must not beg; though father tries to make me by whipping me."

"You didn't beg."

"Mother would say there was not much difference. So I will bring the fruit."

I rejoined my associates, and went about with them to see the town, telling them, meanwhile, of the brutal father taking the money from his crippled daughter. We were all indignant, but we could do little to help the child.

We found the people of Mahon very friendly, especially toward the Americans. They dislike Spain, and little would be needed to cause all the inhabitants of the Balearic Islands to revolt. England used to be in authority here, and then the place was strongly fortified. Ten thousand soldiers were kept here all the time. Now, under the Spaniards, there are but five hundred, and the fortifications are going to decay and ruin.

The prevailing religion is Roman Catholic. There are several nunneries, about as many monasteries, and a very fine cathedral. The morals of the people are fearfully low. Vices the most flagrant are flaunted in one's face, especially that of gambling. We went to the cathedral. It is magnificent. The organ is next to the largest in the world. Mass was being said, in which Dr. Adair took part, for he is a devout Catholic.

Later in the day we went into the largest gambling-house in the city, to see how they did it. There, in disguise, was the very priest who officiated at the mass we had attended. Dr. Adair was grieved and horrified.

"Alas!" said he, "there are hypocrites the world over. Even among the twelve disciples there was one Judas."

"And the man he is playing with is the little crippled girl's father!" said I.

"Is it possible? The priest has all the money, and the game is about to end."

Just then the Irishman left the room, and Dr. Adair and I followed him. We dogged his steps clear to his home, and followed him in. There was the little cripple, and there was the sick wife. The house was shabby, but clean. Dr. Adair introduced himself as the surgeon of the United States ship *Lexington*, and me as a midshipman.

"We saw," said he, "this little lame girl at the harbor this morning, and I heard that you, madam, were sick. What can we do for you?"

"I would be grateful, sir, for some advice about my disease, but I fear I can not pay you."

"I want no pay. Tell me about your sickness."

She did; and the doctor saw that the trouble was not serious in itself, but aggravated by starvation. He obtained quite a history of their desperately poor condition ere he ceased. Then he turned to the man, and gave him such a talking to as he, perhaps, never had before. He drew a vivid, verbal picture of his frail but faithful and intelligent wife, slowly dying of starvation; of his darling daughter, earning money on the harbor among the rough men—the tender child, with but one leg. Then he portrayed to the man his own true position. But the man got mad, and attacked him. Dr. Adair was a powerful person, and promptly knocked the Irishman down. Up he sprang in a fury; aimed a terrific blow at the doctor, who warded it off, and knocked him down again. This time the man lay quiet for a moment.

The wife was greatly alarmed, but the doctor said:

"He is not hurt, madam. Pardon me for what I have done. Mild measures would do no good with him."

Soon the man got up, completely subdued, when the doctor finished his picture, showing him how he had starved his wife, and beaten his crippled child for not begging money for him to gamble, after having squandered all that she earned honestly. The man wanted to deny the gambling, but the doctor said:

"We saw you at the table with the priest; so you need not deny."

Then he appealed to Cochlin's (such was his name) manhood; showed him how gambling would beat him every time, and be his ultimate ruin. Cochlin promised to reform—a promise he kept while we staid in port, seeking work at once.

Next, the doctor sought the priest, to whom he painted another picture. He told the priest all that the reader knows, and showed him that he was taking the life from these people by winning from this man the crippled child's earnings.

"They are good Catholics," said the doctor, "and it is a shame for you to treat them so. Gambling is a grievous sin, but for you to win from your parishioners is heinous."

The priest, at heart, was a kind man; but he had allowed the gambling propensity to possess him, and he knew not the full significance of his actions. He declared he would never gamble again, and the next day paid back to Cochlin all he had won from him. Moreover, he promised to look out for Cochlin, and keep him straight.

CHAPTER VIII.

The Cochlins—Letters from Home—Malta—A Little Mythology—Milo and the Pirates.

WE remained in Mahon till the 24th of July, nearly a month. There is a Spanish navy-yard here, and the *Lexington* needed some repairs. Hence the delay. While here, we learned more about the Cochlins. Mrs. Cochlin was an English woman; Clara, her daughter, an only child, was thrown from a buggy when but four years old. Her knee was hurt, and " white swelling " set in. Amputation became necessary in a year or so. All this occurred in England.

Cochlin was a ship-carpenter, and a good workman. He came to Mahon in 1824—three years ago—to work in the Spanish shipyard. He was naturally a kind husband and father, but the demon—a love of the gaming-table— captured him soon after reaching Mahon, and he sank to the level in which we found him. Dr. Adair had taken the only means to reach this man; namely, by physical violence. That he was reached was proven by his going to work and caring for his family. Ere we sailed, they were on the way to comfort. The priest had also called a halt in his course. He took an interest in the Cochlins, and watched the father very closely.

On the 17th of July the United States frigate *Iowa* majestically sailed into ⁎port

We gave her a salute with the guns, to which, of course, she responded, and just as she dropped her anchor, Doctor Adair cried: "*Qui crudus tibi lectus albasque spiravit!*" That meant three cheers, and we gave them with a will.

The *Iowa* was direct from Boston *via* Gibraltar, and we knew she had a mail on board.

Letters from home! We were all on the alert for letters. Mostly from relatives they would be; but I looked for none from a relation, though I hoped most earnestly for one from a person who would some day bear to me a peculiar relation. Yes? There it was!—my first letter in a foreign land, and from my Harriet, who had promised to share with me my lot in life.

Having gotten our letters, we sought as perfect retirement as the ship afforded, that we might read them. It was a "feeling" time, and the faces of the ship's crew—such as had letters—were a pleasing study. A happy smile upon one, which perhaps grew to an audible laugh. There is a lieutenant, who, with his handkerchief, wipes away a tear; and there is an ordinary seaman who does the same with the back of his hand. No tears in mine, though! But that is a sacred topic, and I will not speak of it.

On the 24th we left Mahon, bound for Smyrna, by the way of Malta. Our course took us along the coast of Africa, and was especially pleasing, as we could see the site of the old city of Carthage. I gazed with keenest interest and a spyglass at the historic spot, remembering the hours I had studied Carthage with a Latin dictionary. I liked the spyglass way the better.

On the 2d of August we were off the port of Valetta, the capital city of Malta. This port is one of the finest harbors in the world, and is strongly fortified. It is in the northeastern part of the island. To reach it, we had passed the little island of Gozo, which lies but a half mile from the northwestern coast of Malta. Purser Jackson told me something about it as we sailed past.

"It looks very barren in places, you see," said the purser.

"It does indeed," I replied. "And it seems to be divided into fields by stone fences or walls, and I see some windmills; at least I think they are mills."

"They are; they are to grind the grain which is raised on the island. Naturally, the rock—for such it is—is barren, but the inhabitants bring soil in ships from the Island of Sicily. This they spread on the rock, and from it raise fine crops."

"Is it possible! What a way to farm! It is better on Malta, I suppose."

"Somewhat. Malta is a kind of porous limestone. Owing to this porosity, the water which falls as rain is absorbed and retained by the superficial part of the rock. This water the rock parts with gradually under the persuasion of the warm sun, and it keeps the superjacent vegetation in a constantly flourishing condition. The soil, however, is scant, and it is supplemented by soil brought from Sicily."

"How far is it to Sicily?"

"About fifty-six miles. We could see it if it were not cloudy. With the aid of this soil, Malta raises fine crops of grain and vegetables—including sugar-cane—and especially mules and asses. The animals are very fine, and—"

"Cats! How about cats, Mr. Jackson? Don't Maltese cats come from here?"

"I can not say as to that; but, my boy, that is the Port of St. Paul off our starboard bow."

"Is it named for Paul the apostle?"

"Yes, it is where St. Paul was shipwrecked."

"Why, no!" said I, "that was in the island of Melita."

"So it was, but the Melita of the Scriptures is the Malta of to-day."

I was deeply impressed. My mother had taught me deep reverence for the Scriptures and the actors therein, especially the Apostle to the Gentiles. This was the scene of that wreck of which I had so often read in childhood. This was the place where they had "cast four anchors out of the stern, and wished for the day!" (Acts xxvii, 29.) There was the coast upon which St. Paul landed, where the viper fastened on his hand. It was the first time I had seen land which the Bible worthies had trod.

Seeing my abstraction, Mr. Jackson was quiet. When I came to myself and surroundings again, he said:

"Malta is the key to the Mediterranean. It is central, capable of successful defense, and able to resist quite a siege, owing to the productiveness of the soil. England did wisely in securing possession here. She has established an arsenal and a dockyard, and made

Malta the headquarters for English influence in this great sea. The religion is Roman Catholic, but, considering that the flag of England floats here, there is very little religious liberty."

The *Lexington* did not enter the harbor, but lay off the mouth of it till morning, in the meantime sending a boat in to see if there were any American men-of-war in port. She brought back word that there were none, but that the pirates were very troublesome in the Archipelago, and that several merchantmen, bound for Smyrna, desired us to convoy them to that port. That we agreed to do, and early next morning got under way, with six vessels under convoy.

It was a lovely morning, and as the sun rose we could see, on the northern horizon, the Island of Sicily, distant from us about fifty miles; and nearly as much farther north we could make out, in the sunlight, the celebrated Mount Ætna, with the smoke rising from its crater. It interested me much, and I thought of the Cyclopes—the one-eyed fellows, who forged the thunderbolts of Jove in this their workshop, Mount Ætna. But the Cyclopes were ugly, grimy old chaps; so we left them, and speeded on our way to the island of Cerigo, which was the birthplace of Venus, or rather the place where she took to the shore after she had risen from the foam of the sea. Hastened! Not exactly, for we experienced many calms, and did not reach Cerigo till the 10th, getting a glimpse, in passing, of Cape Matapan, the most southern point of Greece. It was but a spot above the horizon. How strange that I, the frontier boy, should be in these mythological regions, and should see a Greece-spot! I mentioned this latter point to my fellow-midshipmen at mess, and they took my dinner from me, making me go hungry till supper.

Venus was said to be handsome; but her taste was queer, or she would never have gone ashore at Cerigo. It would have been better to foam a little longer; for Cerigo is a barren rock, some seventy miles in circumference, a great resort for pirates, and under the sheltering hand of Great Britain. These last two attractions it did not enjoy in Venus's time. In lieu thereof, the inhabitants took the lone female in and built her a temple, the remains of which are said to be still visible.

We had no use, this trip, for Cerigo, save as a landmark to help us find the Island of Milo. This we did on the next day, the 11th. Five boat-loads of pirates, about thirty in each boat, and in one boat a cannon on a pivot, had, likewise, found it but a few hours before our arrival. The pirates also found an English brig in port, with thirty-three thousand dollars in gold and silver on board. This they, of course, appropriated, and speedily departed for parts unknown. With the hope that, perchance, we knew where the rogues had gone, Captain Booth put a large force of men, fully armed, on board of a schooner—one of our convoy—and sent her to the Island of Cephanto, whither the pirates were supposed to have gone. We hoped thus to decoy the pirates from their hiding, that they might capture the schooner, or try to, when the men on her would turn the tables and take the pirates. But the rascals were too sharp, and the schooner came back without seeing anything suspicious.

On the evening of the 11th, the day of our arrival at Milo, the frigate *Iowa* also came. Of this we were glad. That same evening, our fourth lieutenant, Alexander H. Hopkinson, died of yellow fever, after a week's illness. He was a fine man, an able officer, and his death cast a gloom over the crews of both the *Iowa* and the *Lexington*. The next day, a company from the two ships buried Lieutenant Hopkinson with naval honors, the chaplain of the *Iowa* officiating. The grave is near the seashore, in a pleasant spot some two miles from the principal town, called, as the island is, Milo.

This island is a barren rock, some hundred

miles in circumference. The inhabitants are of Greek descent, and all pilots, whom the pirates fear. In this vicinity "might makes right." As was said of Ishmael, in Genesis xvi, 12, "His hand will be against every man, and every man's hand against him," so may it be said of his descendants, who are numerous about the Eastern Mediterranean.

The Greeks and Turks are equally unsatisfactory. All are unprincipled and cruel, and they submit under coercion only. They are against every one else. But they all let the people of Milo alone; for these people are expert pilots, and they possess too much valuable knowledge to make it wise to anger them. Their town—Milo—is built on a high hill, or rock. They built up there to escape the plague, which was fearful at times in its ravages, but from which this altitude affords them exemption. There is little room for a town on this pinnacle-shaped rock, and the streets are so narrow a man can stretch his arms across and touch the houses on either side with his hands; they are as "crooked as a ram's-horn," and filthy in the extreme.

Some Turkish prisoners were murdered here most brutally, while we lay in port, by some of the inhabitants of Candia. The Candiots go armed, and commit depredations at will, there being no power which can successfully contend with them.

Greece is at present demanding independence. The Turks object. While we were at Milo an English frigate arrived, with the news that France, England, and Russia favored Greece, and that if Turkey did not acknowledge Greece's independence in thirty days they would unitedly declare war. As the Turks have two hundred vessels fitting out at Alexandria, such a war would make things lively in the Mediterranean.

CHAPTER IX.

Temple of Minerva—Stormy Weather—Scio—English Pride—Smyrna—An Encounter with Greek Pirates—Their Vessel Destroyed.

WE sailed from Milo for Smyrna on August 12th, with a convoy of three vessels. To my delight, we skirted the coast of Greece, being only about three miles from the land. We could see quite distinctly, with the naked eye, objects upon shore, and were especially interested in a temple of Minerva. This sight took me, as Carthage had done, back to the old school in Indiana. I remembered that Minerva—or, as the Greeks called her, Athene—was the best of all the mythological gods and goddesses. How could she be otherwise, when Zeus, the greatest of the galaxy, was her father, and Thetis, the wisest—the goddess of wisdom, indeed—was her mother?

Zeus, because Uranus and Gæa—Heaven and

Earth—advised it, swallowed his wife, Thetis. It is a good thing to get wisdom in any way one can, and the advice of the combined Heaven and Earth must have been very persuasive. Still, it was a strange thing for a husband to swallow his wife; but Zeus did it. It was an innovation on established customs; and as the time was coming for Athene to be born, and as she must now be born of Zeus as well as Thetis, another innovation was necessary. So Zeus got Vulcan, the blacksmith, to split his head open with an ax, when out from his brain sprang Athene, a fully developed woman, clad in full armor. No wonder Zeus's head ached before she got out! Anybody who would swallow his wife deserves to have headache; and ought to have his head split, too. Athene was good—in fact, she was perfect. As no god of the male sex could be found to mate her appropriately, she was doomed to single blessedness. Thus was virtue rewarded.

I was called abruptly from these reminiscences by a squall striking the ship. It was the commencement of a long and violent windstorm. As this wind—called *Levanter*—at times continues for two or three months, the prospect was not pleasing.

After the squall was a temporary lull, during which we spoke the United States ship *Warren*,

Captain L. T. Rearney. Captain Rearney came on board the *Lexington*, and staid long enough for us to write some letters. He was convoying three American brigs, bound for home, through the pirate-infested waters, and these brigs would take any mail we had to send. Such an opportunity was not to be neglected, and we improved it.

We spoke, about the same time with the Americans, an Austrian man-of-war, with a convoy of thirty sail, mostly Austrian. It was a beautiful sight, so many sail all following their big leader. It reminded me of a hen and chickens. Now, if anything goes wrong with the hen—say something that causes her to cackle instead of cluck—the chickens will be frightened and scattered. Every living thing in the Archipelago was frightened that night, and the three fleets in the vicinity were sadly scattered. The wind was fearful! We close-reefed the topsails; still the good ship careened so as to alarm many, especially the fresh-water sailor and myself. In the morning, the ships in sight were in deplorable condition; for the rigging had been roughly handled, and, upon some of them, was torn into shreds. Progress was impossible against this wind. So we put back to Milo, where we found several French vessels.

The wind continued, and in a week the *Iowa*

came into port. She had made a most determined effort to reach Smyrna, but failed. We sailed on the 24th, with her and a large convoy, and, on the 26th, were off the beautiful Island of Scio, which lies seven miles off the coast of Asia, at the entrance of the Gulf of Smyrna. Scio was much observed; for it is the place where, but two or three years before, the Turks had perpetrated a most brutal and indiscriminate massacre of the Sciotes, simply because they were at war. Twenty-five thousand were killed with the sword; forty-five thousand were sold as slaves—some make these numbers larger—very few escaping. The beautiful island was left desolate, though, as liberty is gained, the Sciotes are returning to their homes.

We found that vessel—dear to every American—"Old Ironsides" (*Constitution*), also the *Ontario*, at anchor in the Gulf of Smyrna. Two English "seventy-fours" were also there.

As we approached, the American ships gave us a full salute, but the English were silent. Of course, to the saluting vessels we returned the honor. England will never die of modesty. As is known, she aspires to be "mistress of the sea;" and her custom has been, in saluting the ships of other nations, to return a smaller number of guns than they have fired in her honor. All nations, save America, have tamely submit-

CITY OF SMYRNA.

ted to this indignity; but the Yankees would have none of it. The Revolution had proven us the peer of England, and we demanded gun for gun. We got them, too, until lately, when, owing to the remonstrances made by the others at the discrimination, England ceased to salute the "Stars and Stripes" at all, preferring to be silent rather than meet us on a par. No other place can she meet us. If, perchance, it should become necessary to salute Britain with guns charged with ball, so much of the Revolutionary spirit remains that we will see that she has shot for shot.

However, though we do not exchange salutes with the English navy, we are on good terms with her; and the English officers told us that the English and French were concentrating in the Archipelago, with the hope, in case war was declared with Turkey, that they could force a passage through the Dardanelles and reach Constantinople. As the answer of the Turks is due on September 16th, we are all on the *qui vive*.

Smyrna is the chief city of Asia Minor, and of great importance commercially. It is one of the oldest cities in Asia Minor, being especially in repute as the birthplace of the poet Homer, and near the location of the city of Troy, about which Homer sang so beautifully in the "Iliad." It is one of the seven cities to which our

Heavenly Father—through the Revelation of St. John the divine, on the Isle of Patmos—sent a special message. (Rev. ii, 8–11.) The town is built without much beauty—mostly one-story buildings. There are about twenty mosques. The town is divided, by the character of the local inhabitants, into Greek, Armenian, Catholic, and Protestant portions.

We remained at Smyrna till September 12th. I hoped, while in this part of the world, to have an opportunity to visit the ruins of the city of Troy. One company went; but, being on duty, I could not join it. I put the time in, while at Smyrna, in hard study; for the time for our graduation was coming in a few years, and I wanted, as all did, to pass high among those of my date.

The 12th found us *en route* for Milo. On the way, we passed through the Straits of Silota, formerly called Salamis, where the Greeks and Xerxes fought a memorable battle. How much of the world I was seeing!

We arrived at Milo on the 14th. The American consul met us just outside the harbor, and told us that on the 11th, when off the Island of Cerigo, the American brig *Cherub* had been attacked by pirates and robbed of about forty thousand dollars' worth of coffee, sugar, and tea. We hurried into harbor, and came to with the larboard anchor, where we learned that the brig *Cherub* was from Boston, in command of Captain Loring. When off Cerigo, an hermaphrodite brig had captured her. It was early in the morning. The vessels had come together in the darkness of night, and the morning light had revealed to each vessel the proximity of the other. Escape for the *Cherub* was impossible. The pirate—which was a swift sailer, with four guns and a hundred men—ran alongside the American and fired a volley of musketry, demanding that a boat be sent them with the ship's papers. The papers were examined, the cargo transferred, and the *Cherub* released.

We sailed at once for Cerigo, to capture, if possible, this brig, and recover the cargo. Much as we desired to hasten, we made little progress, for the winds were dead ahead. It was, on the second day, blowing a gale, and we furled all sail, and ran back before the wind to Milo.

On the 18th, Captain Loring came on board, and told Captain Booth that some of his cargo was on sale in Milo, having been brought in a small vessel from Carabosa, a little village on the western end of the island of Candia. We made prisoners of the four men composing the crew of this little vessel, and hastened off for Carabosa. Favoring winds bowled us along famously, and on the 22d we were off the little port.

Lieutenant Breese went at once, with a boat's crew, to the castle to confer with the authorities. Soon after his departure a sail was descried from the masthead. We saw from the rigging—that of a brig forward, and a schooner aft—that she was an hermaphrodite, and probably the very one we were after. She was towing another vessel—a Genoese brig, we soon learned. As they were bearing down for Carabosa, we remained still till they were quite near. Then we made all sail in pursuit. It was an exciting time, especially to us youngsters—Perkins and me.

A shot was fired across the bow of the brig, but she kept right on. However, she cast off her tow. Just at this moment a shot was fired accidentally across the bow of the tow. She hove to at once; but as we pursued the pirate, she took the opportunity to show a clean pair of heels, and escaped.

The pirate was making all effort to reach a port near the castle, but the *Lexington* was speedy enough to prevent it. So the pirate tacked, and made for the shore, as we thought, preferring to risk the rocks than capture. We watched to see them go to pieces; but the rascals knew that coast, and slipped in between a couple of ledges of rock, and were temporarily safe, coming to anchor in a small cove, though one but poorly protected from a high sea. We ran as close as we dared, and fired a number of shot, but they fell short of the mark.

We now stood off the shore, with our main topsail to the mast; and cleared away the boats, which we manned and armed well, and sent off to capture, if possible, the brig. It was a dangerous expedition; but I was anxious to go, and the opportunity was fortunately given me.

We pulled away for the rocks, behind which the pirate could be seen, and worked our way through the passages between them. When we emerged from the rocks the pirates opened fire. We were within long musket range, and at a distance for a cannon-ball to do much execution. Bullets pattered all about us, several struck the boats, and one took a piece out of my cap. Our only chance was to board; but the pirates had put up a netting, which made that almost an impossibility. They were a hundred strong, with four cannon, which they were evidently holding in reserve; for these Greeks are shrewd fighters. But we were enthusiastic, and would have tried. Some one cried out,

"Qui crudus tibi lectus albasque spiravit!"

when we gave three cheers, and bent to the oars. Just then we were signaled from the ship to return, which, of course, we had to do. It was well we did, as the sequel proved.

We found Lieutenant Breese on board when we returned. He had found the authorities anxious to help him, but able to do little, as the pirates were stronger than the Government. There were six piratical cruisers with headquarters at Carabosa, and they were practically in authority. We were after the one which captured the *Cherub*.

A council of war was now held, at which it was decided to go as far as possible next day toward the rocks, and try to sink the brig with the *Lexington's* guns. So we got very close to the breakers next day, and fired some shots; but they did little harm, for a heavy sea was setting on shore, with much wind, and we had to haul off. We determined to man the boats on the morrow, and board at all hazards. The wind blew hard all night, and next morning nothing of the pirate was to be seen. She had gone to pieces on the rocks.

CHAPTER X.

Pirates Again—The Austrian Captain's Story—
Shall I "Do Right?"—The Ruins of Troy.

EVEN while we were viewing with satisfaction the destruction of this vessel, which our shot could not effect, but which we had driven into a position where the waves did it for us, a brig, with another in tow, was seen approaching. Of course she was a pirate with a prize, and we gave chase. She ran toward shore, and, apparently, right into the breakers, through which she and her tow safely passed. This put the vessels in the snuggest of harbors, with a barrier of rock towards the sea so high that we could see only the tops of the rigging.

Manning the gig, we sent Lieutenant Breese to ascertain certainly her character. On the gig approaching, the pirates hailed her in good English:

"Boat ahoy!"

"Ay, ay, sir."

"What do you want?"

"We want to examine your papers, so as to know who you are."

"We don't carry papers. We are pirates, and as such we defy your authority. Go back to your ship and tell your commander that if he knows what's healthy he will leave these waters, and let us alone."

This bold speech gave Lieutenant Breese the information he wanted, so back to the ship he came. We ran the *Lexington* as close in to the rocks as we dare. There were the two vessels in their snug little cove, though from the deck we could see only the rigging; the shore was lined all about with armed Greeks, ready to help their friends.

We fired a broadside, which did the vessels no harm, but made the men perched about the rocks hunt shelter in a hurry.

We could do nothing; for boarding was not to be thought of in that cove surrounded with sharpshooters. So we sailed away, leaving the pirates to continue their nefarious customs.

Some time after that we spoke an Austrian brig. As we were becalmed within a fourth of a mile of each other, her captain came on board the *Lexington*. He said:

"It was this ship that ran a pirate and her

tow in behind the rocks on the west end of Candia, about two weeks ago, wasn't it?"

"Yes, it was the *Lexington*, and it was hard not to capture her after she was cornered," said Mr. Breese.

"Yes, but we were mighty glad to see you sail off."

"You! What had you to do with it, and what do you know about it?"

"My vessel there was the tow, and we were all prisoners on the pirate. When your gig came to speak us, the pirates made all arrangements to blow you out of the water. They proposed to kill you every one. I begged hard for your lives, but no use. They said you must die. Then I saw that you had no arms in your boat, and I begged harder, and they let you go back because you had brought no arms."

"Well, captain, you did us a good service, and I thank you."

"Yes, and you did us a good service when you sailed away, and I thank you," said the Austrian.

"How is that?"

"Those Greeks are desperate and cruel men, and they meant to hang us prisoners if you killed one of their number, on either ship or shore, or if you did their vessel any harm."

"Do you think they would have done it?"

"Done it! Yes! They were in earnest. They got the ropes ready. I tell you, it was a serious time with us. Your sailing saved us."

Such are the samples of work we did that season on the *Lexington*. Actual captures of the pirates are few, but the vessels of war do an immense service in protecting commerce. We were kept on that service all the fall and winter, spending most of the time at Smyrna. I did much study, and went to all the balls that were respectable, for I loved to dance. Smyrna was not a gay place, but we made it as gay as we could.

I fought a hard battle with my conscience while at Smyrna. Dancing, card-playing (not for money), social wine-drinking, and theater-going were among the usual amusements of naval officers. My parents had taught me to consider them wrong. Should I do as my associates did, or should I do right, and be singular? I decided to do right; but by sophistry persuaded myself that wrong was right. "Everybody does these things in the navy, and that makes it right." "Your parents did not know you were to be a naval officer when they taught you that a simple dance or a social game of cards was wrong." "Circumstances alter cases," and "when in Rome do as the Romans do," came to my mind as arguments. The stability of the last thought was shaken by the following: "When among cannibals, do as the cannibals do."

"You are already singular, Trumbull," I said to myself. "You don't use tobacco in any form, and you don't swear. Now, if you do not dance or play whist, you will be avoided by your associates." I wanted the arguments in favor of the dance and card-table to prevail; and I tried to believe that they did, though I knew that, if these things were wrong in one place, they were in another. Wanting to be persuaded, I argued that I was. However, I compromised by deciding that I would never drink any alcoholic beverage from over a bar, and that I would never play for a stake. These last I kept faithfully; but a social glass of wine I learned to take, and I became most fascinated with the ball-room. [It is with pleasure that, in reviewing this journal after many years, I interpolate the statement that I never was intoxicated in my life, that I was never profane, that I never gambled, and never used tobacco.]

Thus did I twist my motto, *Do Right*, to suit my pleasure, and imagined that in so doing I was consistent—at least, I tried to believe that I was.

We had one trip that winter which I much enjoyed. It was to convoy the American brig

Delos, bound for Constantinople, to the Dardanelles. We saw the reputed tombs of Ajax and Achilles. They amount to little, so far as appearance goes, being small mounds; but the association with the names of these old heroes gave them interest.

We had a close view of the Island of Tenedos, and the little harbor which was headquarters for the Grecian fleet during the siege of the city.

There was a good view of the Plains of Troy from the topsail-yards. So, 'way up there, Perkins and I perched to see that about which we had read so much. The plains are properly so called. They are quite extensive, covered with stones and underbrush, with here and there the dwelling of a Turk.

"Just to think, Sam," said George, "that those plains are where that great battle was fought! Do you believe there was such a battle?"

"O yes, George," said I. "I believe it, with modifications. I believe there was such a city and such a siege; but, of course, the gods did not fight with the men—some on one side, some on the other—as the 'Iliad' has it."

"But the 'Iliad' is fine; is n't it?"

"Yes," said I. "And to think that poor, old, blind Homer had to peddle his literary wares, or beg for a living, on the streets of Smyrna and other neighboring cities!"

"Too bad, too bad!" said George. "But posterity has done him justice. And I love to think of the battle of Troy as he has so beautifully described it. All the characters I love to accept as realities. And now, as I sit perched 'way up here on the topmast-yard, I am in mind seeing those worthies before me. Just to think that this is the place where Paris and Menelaus fought their duel!"

"And where," I added, "the great Achilles fought so ably, and where he refused to fight till the Greeks settled his quarrel with Agamemnon."

"Achilles had the best of that quarrel," said Mr. Perkins. "I always liked Achilles."

"I did n't always," I said. "When the brave Hector proposed that, on the eve of their duel, each agree not to do violence to the person of the one vanquished, I rather admired his reply: 'I make no covenants with thee. There is no agreement between wolves and sheep. Show thyself a warrior, if thou canst.' Now, Hector was a foeman worthy of even Achilles's steel; and it was most revolting for Achilles, after slaying him in honorable warfare, to fasten his body to his chariot and drag him about the walls by the heels. The magnitude of his victory does not in the least justify it."

"And the wooden horse, Sam!" said George.

"The famous wooden horse pranced—no, that word won't do—the wonderful horse was exposed on that plain, and through the walls of Troy it was dragged! Yes, Sam; that is the place."

But the winds wait for no one, and soon they wafted us from this view which we so much enjoyed.

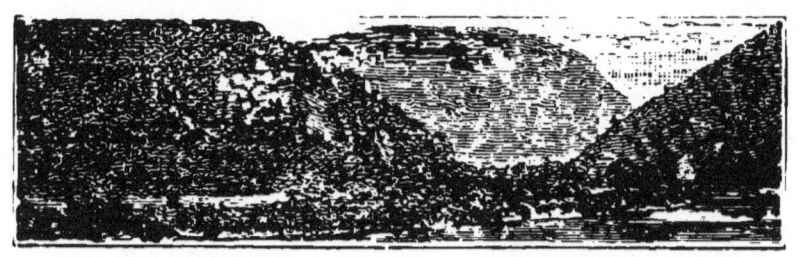

CHAPTER XI.

CAPTAIN BOOTH SICK—SAIL FOR MALTA—MOUNT ÆTNA—TUNIS.

ON May 21, 1828, the United States frigate *Iowa*, Captain John Downes, arrived from Port Mahon.

A report was spread on the 26th that the plague was prevailing in Smyrna. Captain Downes ordered all communication between the American vessels and the shore to cease. Accordingly, we hoisted a quarantine flag, the first the *Lexington* had ever flown.

Captain Booth, our commander, had been for some time sick, and at this time was expected to die. Temporary command was given to Lieutenant Breese.

The able and unremitting efforts of our competent surgeon got Captain Booth in condition to start with the *Lexington* for Mahon.

We sailed for that port on May 28th. The 6th

of June found us off the harbor of Valetta, on the island of Malta. We had a fine view of the city of Valetta. It is a beautiful city. The houses are of white stone, very elegant, square-roofed, and built on the hillside, so that one tier shows above the others most pleasantly.

We anchored in quarantine harbor, and Captain Booth left the ship, going for residence to the lazaretto, which was very large and comfortable for the sick.

The United States ship *Delaware*, seventy-four guns, Commodore Crane, hove in sight on the 12th of June, and lay off the harbor some time. She sent in a boat, with orders for us to proceed for Mahon by way of Tunis.

We started next day. The wind being ahead, we stood over toward Sicily, off which we lay becalmed for two days. As Mount Ætna was in active operation, the time passed quickly; for it gave us pleasant occupation to watch the dense volume of smoke.

"The Cyclopes have a good big fire, Mr. Trumbull," said Purser Jackson.

"Indeed they have. I guess they are forging some thunderbolts for Jove."

Great volumes of sulphurous smoke were being impelled toward the zenith. They assumed most fantastic shapes, and our lively imaginations gave to these shapes most weird signification, and to us entertainment, of which it seemed we would never tire.

"What do you see in that?" I asked an officer who stood near me.

"I see an example of the laws of nature. Too much heat down there; too much gas formed, and it has burst out. What do you see?"

"I see an example of God's power. To me God is greater than nature."

"Going to preach, hey? Well, adieu. I am not in the mood for a sermon."

The man meant it for a rudeness; but I remembered that "a gentleman will not insult me, and no other can." To me, the volcano was an exponent of my Maker.

By night it was more beautiful than by day. We brought Captain Booth out on deck to enjoy the sight, as well as the fresh air. The heavens were lit up most beautifully. The reflection of the subterranean fires from the dense smoke they had ejected from the crater was indeed gorgeous. It did the sick man good.

The ruins of the old city of Agrigentum were in plain view. With a spyglass we could see them quite well, and thought we could distinguish the remains of the temple of Jupiter. It was a most enjoyable calm.

The sirocco wind came to our relief, and we

came to anchor in the Bay of Tunis on the 17th. The ruins of ancient Carthage, once the "rival of the mistress of the world," are near by. A party was organized to visit the site of the former great emporium. Another party was to go to visit the Bey of Tunis, as the local monarch is called. Fortunately, I was permitted to join this last party. Mr. Perkins came to me and asked:

"Sam, where are you going?"

"To visit the Bey of Tunis."

"Why, I thought we were in the Bay of Tunis."

I laughed at this answer till I cried, and George stood by and wondered where the laugh came in. When I told him, he was too much teased to laugh, but begged me not to tell. But it was too good to keep. However, to pay the boy for the teasing, we took him into the party.

We left the ship about 9 A. M. The American vice-consul accompanied us. His dragoman was with him. Just what he—the dragoman—was along for, we did not at first know; but we found out, to our gladness. He was a pompous personage, much after the similitude of a drum-major. Like the latter, also, he marched at the head of the column. He was in the service of the bey, who assigns such a man to every representative of foreign governments as a bodyguard. Civilization is at a low ebb in all the Barbary States, and the people hate Christians. Hence the bodyguard. Hence, also, the brace of silver-mounted pistols and the big saber—about three feet long—which he carries. This last is to cut the head off of any one who interferes with his charge.

We, of course, left the ship in boats, which passed from the bay into a narrow canal, about one and one-half miles long. Upon one side of this canal is a long row of small boats, drawn completely out of the water, and sheltered from the sun by covers—sheds, I suppose, they are. The boats are gaudily painted with crescents all about, in honor of Mohammed. That of the bey was especially conspicuous from its brilliant coloring. On the other side of the canal was the "Castle," so called. It was rather a battery, and a poor affair indeed. The guns would do; but the carriages were so old and rotten that the danger anywhere near them would be about as great at the discharge as was the danger at the muzzle, for they would surely fall at the recoil. But the castle, or battery, was half-moon shaped, and that covered a multitude of lesser defects.

It is thirteen miles from the castle to the city, so we hastened on our way. Having traversed the canal, we passed abruptly into a lake, some twenty-five miles in circumference. It is supposed to occupy part of the site of old Carthage, the land having sunken after an earthquake. The lake is very shallow. A decided current flows from the bay into it, but no other water enters, and it has no outlet. Evaporation, under the intensely hot sun, is rapid. As the water ever goes, and salt ever comes from the sea, the water of the lake becomes a saturated solution of salt. If, perchance, a drop falls on one's clothing, an incrustation of salt marks the spot.

"What is that?" asked George, of me.

"I don't know. It looks like a skeleton stuck on a pole."

Sure enough it was. The guide explained that, after execution, the bodies of criminals are thus exposed as a warning to others.

Leaving the ghastly sights—there were many such skeletons—we went to the home of the American consul. The greeting his pleasant wife gave us was most refreshing, and the comfort of his civilized—ay, Americanized—household was indeed pleasing. It carried us, in thought, across the sea to our own loved firesides. Yes, it did! Though why I should say firesides is a puzzle; for it was "hot as blazes," and the cool drink Mrs. Heap gave us did us a *heap* of good. Mr. Heap was from home. He was in France.

Mrs. Heap, her seventeen-year-old daughter (Perkins could see nothing else), and her two younger children, had been shut closely in the house for several days. A mob was amusing itself in the streets of Tunis. To kill Christians was to them a pleasant pastime. Hence, most of the Christian residents had flown to the shipping in the bay.

From Mr. Heap's we went for a stroll about the city. Then it was good, as we reached the crowded streets, to see that dragoman clear the way of Moors and beggars. That big saber encircled his head in a manner to us most pleasing; but for the fellow in the dragoman's field of vision, most alarming. Thanks to his energy and stentorian voice, we walked unmolested. It was a good thing, for the filth was all we wished to contend with. The streets are narrow and dirty, and swarm with beggars, like those of Smyrna; but the Turks dress better than the Moors.

We went first to the square in front of the citadel. A few soldiers were drilling after the Moorish style. The bey has recently introduced the discipline of European armies into his own— at least, he has tried to—but they do n't like it; and, as the bey was away, they came back to their first love, the Moorish style.

This square was the place of execution, as well as a drill-ground. There was a large stone, hollowed out into the shape of a mortar. Upon this stone the victim lays his head, when a burly executioner decapitates him at a single blow, with much such a saber as our dragoman carried. After exposure for several days in the most crowded part of the city, the bodies of these poor victims are placed in the lake on stakes, as we had seen. The wish to make crime heinous is most laudable, but the means are most revolting.

Next we went to the palace. I never saw a palace before, and I was not particularly charmed. It is composed of very fine materials, especially the mosaics. The marble columns and floors are very fine, and the ceilings glitter with gold and azure and purple. But it seemed to me that the workmanship by which all this was put together was poor—all but the mosaics; they were fine. Then we went to the harem. The harem was much the same, only it was neater. Its glories were departed, for the ladies had gone—probably to the bey's country seat.

From there the dragoman cleared the passage for us back to the house of the American consul, where we enjoyed an excellent dinner, cooked and served in Yankee (everything American is Yankee over here) style, too. O, but it was good! So were the wines and fruits—especially figs and dates, which grew near.

Bidding Mrs. Heap farewell, we hastened back to the ship, which we reached at nightfall, well pleased with the day's enjoyment. At daylight next morning we weighed anchor, and bore away for Port Mahon.

CHAPTER XII.

A Pleasant Quarantine—The Cochlins—Fourth of July—A Race—Death of Captain Booth—Farewell, Lieutenant Breese—Lieutenant Rumage—Algiers—Malta.

WE arrived at Mahon after a speedy passage, and went into a quarantine of fifteen days, as is common with vessels from the Levant. Quarantine is usually dreaded; this time it was most enjoyable.

We lay alongside of a small island, which we had all to ourselves. While there, the ship's rigging was overhauled, the hold stored afresh, and the ship painted within and without. We officers passed all our spare time on the island, swinging our hammocks under the trees. "Sailors on shore" has become almost a proverb, and is an abundant incentive for the caricaturist. But we were n't so clumsy as these pictures indicate; and we had lots of fun, playing ball, pitching quoits, and foot-racing. In the last, Perkins was the victor. There was a fine bathing-place. I was, all through my boyhood, a perfect water-dog, and enjoyed this immensely.

One moonlight evening, a boat from town approached, by a roundabout way, our little island. The occupants asked to see Doctor Adair and Captain Trumbull. I knew at once who it was, for I could not prevent the Cochlins from calling me captain. It teased me, but they would do it. The doctor and I, with several of the dignitaries of the ship, were disporting ourselves with the intellectual game of leap-frog; but we answered the call, and there were the Cochlins. So anxious had they been to see us, that they had stolen by night into the quarantine harbor. All had gone well with them. Cochlin really had the propensity to gamble knocked out of him, and was earning and judiciously using good wages. Clara had an artificial limb, which, though rude, was a great improvement on the crutches; and she seldom sold fruit in the harbor—never unless her father accompanied her. The priest, they told us, had proven a good friend. He, also, had abandoned the gaming-table. We were indeed glad of this stolen visit and of this good news.

The Fourth of July occurred while in quarantine. We hauled off to the middle of the harbor, and observed the day as a holiday. At noon we fired a salute of twenty-one guns in honor of the day. Every mess had a big dinner, and every one was gay. The backset was, many of the crew got very drunk, and much fighting occurred among them.

On the 6th of July, having ridden out our quarantine, we took *pratique*,* and in twenty-four hours were making all sail for Gibraltar. Captain Booth, who had been much improved by a sojourn on shore while at Mahon, was with us.

The 8th of July, 1828, is a day long to be remembered by me. We were then between the Island of Majorca and the Straits of Gibraltar. It was my watch on deck, and I was pacing back and forth as duty demanded, the vessel meantime making good speed on her way, when the commander—Lieutenant Breese—came on deck, and said:

"Mr. Trumbull, you will please put the ship about immediately."

I knew we were to be put to that test sometime—Perkins and I—but when? and would Perkins or I be first?

The maneuver having been executed, I touched my hat to the commander, when he was so kind as to speak favorably of my suc-

---

*Legal release from quarantine, giving permission to communicate with the shore.

cess. I tell you it was a proud moment for me! I was as proud as the boy with his first red-top boots; proud as the doctor who saws his first leg off—or, rather, who saws some one else's leg off for the first time.

While on this passage we fell in with a celebrated English packet—bound also for Gibraltar—noted for her fast sailing. For a day, nearly, we were together; but in getting around some of the capes on the Spanish coast, the wind did not just suit her. We forged ahead, and soon had run her down the horizon. She came into Gibraltar twelve hours after our arrival. We knew the *Lexington* was a fast sailer, but she did more in that contest than we supposed she could.

Captain Booth was removed on the 21st to the American ship *Bingham*, of Philadelphia, for passage to America. Ere her departure, however, he died. His remains were brought back to the *Lexington*, from which he was buried in the Gibraltar cemetery with military and naval honors, in which the English forces joined.

I made many visits to the Rock of Gibraltar this time, and became familiar with it, making especial study of the fortifications.

We sailed for Mahon on August 1st, reaching there on the 6th. The United States ship-of-the-line *Delaware* was there at anchor. **The** commodore was aboard her. We passed close under her stern, giving her a salute of thirteen guns, which she returned with seven, at the same time parading her band in full uniform on the poop, and playing "Hail Columbia."

Lieutenant Breese here left the *Lexington*, Lieutenant James Rumage succeeding him. Several midshipmen from the *Delaware* also joined us.

On the 12th we weighed anchor for Malta, by way of Algiers, where we were to leave orders for the American consul. As we entered the harbor of Algiers a cannon-ball came flying toward us. It passed over us, striking the water a fourth of a mile beyond, and, after a succession of beautiful skips, resting beneath the waves; but its passage had been too close to be beautiful. We hastened to show our colors, which we had delayed too long to do. We were probably mistaken for a Frenchman; hence the shot.

We saw little of Algiers, for we staid but half an hour—not anchoring. The consul came off in a boat for his papers. We saw, however, that the harbor was good, and well defended with strong fortifications; the walls of the city not very high or strong in themselves, but strengthened by watch-towers, and the houses square and compactly built.

The consul having gone, we filled away, and made all sail for Malta, running the coast of Barbary down in a style that did us all good. On August 17th we dropped anchor in the quarantine harbor. Having satisfied that custom, we came around into the *pratique* harbor amid lovely strains of music, which were wafted over the water from the town of Valetta.

This was the third time the *Lexington*, during this cruise, had been in Malta. Yet we had not as yet set foot on the shore; for we had not before had *pratique*.

Many of the citizens came on board to inspect the ship. Being freshly painted, she presented a fine appearance. To avoid these visitors, Purser Jackson and I got leave for the day, and went ashore. There was much to be seen. The language in most common use is the Arabic, a tongue which, to me, is not pleasant. Valetta—population 70,000—is the chief city. Its harbor is good, and so defended as to make this the next to the strongest place in the world.

We went first to the Saint Antonio Gardens. They are very fine, being kept in perfect order by the governor.

"O, this is fine!" said Mr. Jackson. "It is glorious, after so long a time at sea, to get among the flowers."

"Yes, it is, and I am tempted to pluck one," I replied, "though against the rules."

It was not necessary. The gardener came along, and was evidently impressed with our uniforms, for he gathered us each a fine bouquet. To the catacombs we did not go, though they are said to be very fine. "Fine!" thought I; "what a word for such a place!" It is like a doctor's successful surgical operation, though the poor patient dies soon after.

We went to St. Paul's Creek, at the mouth of which is said to have occurred the shipwreck. I was much interested. A cave is also near here, said to have been the residence of Paul while on the island. A statue of the saint has been carved out of the solid rock at the entrance of this cave, the sight of which fills every good Maltese with awe. I surely shared with them a deep respect for the memory of the apostle, as I gazed upon the statue. This vicinity is all regarded as sacred, and the dust from the sides of the cave is esteemed a sovereign remedy against all contagious diseases. Every house has a supply of it, and he is indeed an infidel who does not carry a portion about his person. The Maltese instance, in proof of its efficacy, the exemption of the island from the plague. They say the

ISLAND OF MALTA (ST. PAUL'S BAY.)

island is not only exempt—that might be chance—but it is exempted by the virtue of this dust.

Nearly all the soil—more than I supposed at my first visit—has been imported from Sicily; yet there is enough to render the island very productive. The armory is most interesting, having three thousand stands of arms and three hundred coats of mail, which belong to the Knights of Malta.

Our stay at Malta was very short; for the morning of August 24th found us in the harbor of Syracuse. I was much interested in Syracuse; for it was visited by the Apostle Paul after he had left the Island of Melita, or Malta. Here he had remained three days. (Acts xxviii, 12.) As every one knows, the Island of Sicily is a triangle. Syracuse is near the southeast angle; north of it, and near the coast, is Mount Ætna; farther north, at the northeast corner, is the Strait of Messina, separating Sicily from Italy. In this strait the ancients believed a dangerous whirpool—Charybdis—to exist, and on the Italian coast is the famous headland, Scylla, which the old navigators greatly dreaded. Away off to the west, near the northwest angle of the island, is the city of Palermo. All these points of interest we were to see, and hence we were glad to visit Sicily. Moreover, we expected a mail-bag for the *Lexington* was waiting our arrival at Syracuse. It was there, and we were happy. I received two letters—one from my dear brother Simeon; the other from—no matter! It was a good letter.

CHAPTER XIII.

Syracuse—Catacombs—Ear of Dionysius—Fountain
of Arethusa—Grave of Archimedes.

IMMEDIATELY after dinner on the day of our arrival at Syracuse, a company of us, having obtained leave, left the vessel in one of the ship's boats, and went to the city; to Syracuse!—once, one of the great cities of the world; now, a disgrace to her former greatness. We entered by the western gate. The walls presented a sorry aspect. They were crumbling to pieces. Those walls, which were the terror of Rome in her day of power; those walls, which so abundantly resisted the Roman arms; those walls, from which the genius of Archimedes flashed reflections of the sun's rays with mirrors, and thus burned up the enemies' ships; those walls, from which huge engines—the product of the same mighty genius—grappled such ships as ventured too near, lifting them from the water and dashing them to pieces against the rock,—those walls were crumbling. We passed through the gate, only to see a repetition of the same desolation. The streets were narrow and crooked, and swarming with beggars, who plied their vocation in a manner one would expect from the decayed and falling condition of the houses. Old statues and images—elegant in themselves, and significant of former grandeur—were lying where they had fallen, or, perchance, rolled to one side a few feet, covered with rubbish. This was new Syracuse. For it we had little use. So, procuring a guide and horses, we went to old Syracuse—formerly known as Ortygia—to visit its ruins. Our guide was a big, strong native, who spoke English well enough for practical purposes. Having mounted, he said:

"Catacombs, gentlemen. Come see catacombs."

"What are the catacombs?" asked one of the party, desiring to quiz him.

"Dead men live in catacombs."

The poor man never understood why we laughed at this reply. Having ridden a mile and a half, we alighted and entered the catacombs.

"They very fine, very fine!" said the guide.

The same adjective, I noticed, they used over

in Malta. They were dark as Egypt; so torches were lit. They are subterranean, or, rather, sub-rock, passages beneath the site of the original town of Ortygia. The walls, ceiling, and floor are solid rock—part of the foundation of the island. These passages, as every one knows, are the burial-places of the ancient inhabitants. They are fifteen feet from floor to ceiling, from ten to twelve feet wide, and bordered with niches about large enough to receive a human body—some large, for adults; others small, for children. Large rooms are excavated every twelve or fourteen feet. These are for the use of families. They are provided, also, with niches, from fifteen to twenty in number, owing probably to the number of persons in the relationship. It is said that there are forty-two miles of these sepulchral passages. That, I somewhat doubted; but, rest assured, I did n't try to find out; for half a mile was enough for me. That much I wanted to see; but no more, thank you. There was little to remind us of death, had we not known of the object of these passages. Those of us who went farthest found, by searching for them, a few skulls and some finger-bones; but most of the bones had been carried away, either by living man or by the wind, as for centuries it had passed over the dust of these ancient generations. It was, indeed, a dark and gloomy place. Yet hither, during the reign of the tyrant Dionysius, had the persecuted fled for shelter; and here were they gladly domiciled, though at that time, as the guide said, "dead men lived there."

The famous Ear of Dionysius next engaged our attention. The approach to this stupendous monument of the ingenuity and cruelty of that tyrant arouses feelings of horror mixed with curiosity. A more intimate acquaintance intensifies these feelings. Appearances alone would imply that one was approaching a freak of nature; but the smoothness and regularity of the walls, as also the close resemblance to the human ear, disprove this impression. Upon reaching the interior, the iron staples anchored in the walls, the chains and balls attached thereto, confirm the impression that human devices are here seen, and that their prime object has been one of torture. Its extreme length is one hundred and fifty feet, and its height eighty feet. The interest in this work of diabolical intent centers in a chamber which constitutes the focus of the ear. It is, however, sixty or seventy feet above the floor, and to be reached only by a rope, with which one must be hoisted. We sailors were not to be daunted by such a necessity, though the rope *did* seem a little small. Up we would go, for we knew all about ropes.

"Come, guide, you go up first," said one of us.

"O no, I not go up. You go up. Dionysius old tyrant, but Ear very fine."

So up we were hoisted, one at a time. Then we saw why our big guide did n't want to come. This rope, small at first, was fearfully chafed in places, by friction upon the rock. It was liable to break any time, and it made us tremble to think that we had hung over that dizzy height by that frail support. And it made us tremble again to think that we must be lowered by the same weakened line. But there was no use to cross this bridge till we came to it. We went merrily to the investigation of this chamber. Its acoustic properties are what make it wonderful. Sounds are intensified and transmitted with startling distinctness. The softest whisper can be heard distinctly across the chamber. The sound produced by tearing a piece of paper at a distance of two hundred feet, was carried into the Ear and to us in the chamber, so intensified that we heard it distinctly. The voice of ordinary conversation was uncomfortably loud, and the report of a pistol was painful.

Around this chamber were many staples, with chains and iron balls, for the confinement of prisoners whom the tyrant suspected of not favoring his wishes. Connecting with this acoustic chamber—by a hidden passage—was another room in which Dionysius used to conceal himself and eavesdrop, that he might learn who were his enemies. Such were speedily executed. Lest the existence of this secret room be learned, and the object of this Ear be divulged, all workmen engaged in its construction were put to death upon its completion. Well was this monster called " The Tyrant of Syracuse!"

Then for the descent. With fear and trembling we made it, holding, instinctively, our breaths, lest the least jar should break the cord, and we be precipitated to the stone floor beneath. We all made the descent safely, however. I suppose they will keep using that rope till some one is killed.

Near this Ear are the quarries from which were taken the stone for the pillars to the temple of Jupiter. The statement that the space made vacant by the removal of these stones, is now used as a ropewalk, may give some idea of the magnitude of these quarries.

The remains of a theater and amphitheater are to be seen a little west of the Ear, and near by these remains are excavations in which were kept the bulls for the bull-fights, with a subterranean passage from the excavations to the amphitheater.

Some of the pillars of the Temple of Jupiter

are still standing. They are stately and imposing, well repaying the visitor for inspecting them.

Some of the pillars from the famous Temple of Minerva now adorn the cathedral in the new city of Syracuse. They also are worthy of inspection in their new location. The guide pronounced them very fine.

"Now," said the guide, "I take you to very fine fountain—Fountain of Arethusa."

It was indeed a fine fountain, situated in Ortygia, near the seashore. It bursts from the ground with the volume of a small river.

"Very fine fountain, indeed, gentlemen," said the guide; "very fine water."

We tasted it. It was brackish and disagreeable. We grasped the guide and dragged him to the water's edge, saying:

"We are going to put you in for lying to us."

The big fellow was so scared—they can not resist a uniform—that we let him go; but he told us no more lies.

"Fountain," said he, "comes from river Arethusa, in the continent, long way off—thousand miles—water from river go down into ground, run under the sea, and come up here. Fine river and fine fountain."

"O yes! that's all very fine; but no more of your lies!" said one of us.

"No lie, gentlemen. All true! Cup lost in river far away on continent come out here in fountain."

The guide spoke what he believed to be true; for the legend is that the River Arethusa in Greece, and this spring, are connected, that they rise and fall synchronously, and that a goblet cast into the river made the wonderful journey, and was recovered here.

We visited the grave of Archimedes.

"Very fine grave," began the guide; but we shut him up in short order, for, to some of us, the ground that held the dust of this great mathematician and original thinker was almost sacred. We wanted none of the guide's fine comments.

The grave, as such, was not fine. It was scarcely to be distinguished from the other graves in the vicinity. Only a mound of earth indicated it, and nothing of the cylinder and sphere, which, at his dying request, marked for a time his resting-place, was to be seen. I mentioned its absence, when Mr. Perkins said:

"What about the cylinder and sphere, Sam? Tell me; I'm not informed."

"The relations," replied I, "that these two geometrical figures bear to each other, are a big mathematical problem, which Archimedes was the first to solve. It was a thing he was proud of, and he asked that a cylinder inclosing a sphere should mark his grave."

"Dear old man!" said George; "too bad that his great enthusiasm for his loved science—mathematics—should have hastened his death!"

"How was that?" I asked.

"Why, don't you remember? Just at the moment the city was captured, Archimedes was studying a problem, the diagram for which he had drawn upon the sand at the shore. As the soldier dashed up to make him a prisoner—having instructions to bring him in safety to the conquering general—the old man not knowing what had happened, cried out to the soldier, 'Don't spoil the picture!' This enraged the soldier somewhat; but when Archimedes refused to go till the problem was solved, the brutal Roman struck him down."

"The miserable wretch! I didn't know that," said I. "Let's think of something more pleasant about him; for instance, when he thought, just as he was entering the bath, of the great truth that a body immersed in water loses as much weight as the displaced volume of water weighs. The great discovery so impressed him that he leaped from the water, and, forgetting to dress, dashed home, exclaiming, 'Eureka! Eureka!' I have found it! I have found it!"

"Yes, that is very funny, Sam," said George. "I am glad we have that to think about."

With deep reverence for this worthy man's memory, we boys—the rest had already gone—left his grave, and sought the ship.

The 27th of August found us coasting along the eastern shore of Sicily, bound for Palermo.

CHAPTER XIV.

Scylla and Charybdis—Palermo—The Sirocco Wind—Rome.

COASTING along the eastern shore of Sicily was most enjoyable, owing somewhat to the beauty of this most fertile island, but largely to the presence of Mt. Ætna. Its ever-changing smoke gave us constant enjoyment by day, and the flashes of light made night duty a positive pleasure; therefore I walked the deck with Perkins during his vigil. As my watch followed his, he returned the compliment; and we talked about volcanoes, and Scylla and Charybdis, which we were approaching.

"Why," asked Mr. Perkins, "are volcanoes like wild young men who spend the night carousing?"

"Something about sparks, I suppose. Let's see: because they do a lot of sparking," I answered.

"Pretty good, Sam, but not just it."

"Then you had better tell."

"Because they scin-til-late."

"Ah! Bright enough for even me to see it—or, rather, to recognize it, for I have heard it before. Now, let me give you an old one: 'Why is a man climbing a volcano like an Irishman trying to kiss his sweetheart?'"

"What do I know about kissing, Sam? I'll give it up at once."

"He is trying to get at the mouth of the *crater*."

"Delightful!—for the Irishman, surely, when he succeeds; for the climber, when he looks into the dazzling chasm; and for me, as *de light* is full enough for me to see the point."

During our combined watches we passed through much of the Strait of Messina, missing a view of the city of Messina, owing to the darkness. Morning showed us the charming country about the famous Scylla, as the headland guarding the entrance to the strait on the Italian coast is called.

"This is fine!" said Mr. Perkins. "Now, if we could only see the old monster—Scylla—herself, with her twelve feet, and six mouths, each with a triple row of teeth, and could hear her bark, how nice it would be!"

"Yes, it would; but she is not there, though

the rock is. So let's look for the whirlpool—the Charybdis of the ancients—and see if the old fellow is sucking much water in this morning."

"I do not understand you, Sam."

"What! Don't you remember the myth about Charybdis?"

"No; I only remember that it was thought to be a dangerous place for ships," said Mr. Perkins.

"The myth was, that a monster named Charybdis lived on the Sicily coast, nearly opposite Scylla, under a big fig-tree that grew out of the rock. Three times a day he sucked down the water of the sea, and as often threw it up again. This kept the water in violent agitation about all the time, and produced the powerful whirlpool which the ancients so greatly feared."

We studied the waters carefully, to see what ground there might be for the opinion of the ancients that a dangerous whirlpool was there. We saw nothing of the kind; only a ruffling of the water could we detect, not enough to inconvenience a small sail-boat. However, the Sicilians say that certain winds, blowing strongly, do create a strong current, associated with which is a temporary whirlpool, sufficient to endanger a vessel should she unwarily approach its vortex.

Leaving this interesting locality, we bore away to the west, and were soon at anchor before the city of Palermo, the capital of Sicily. No city which I have seen within the Straits of Gibraltar will compare with this beautiful place. It is of much commercial importance, but out of the usual course of men-of-war. A vessel of war had not been in the Gulf of Palermo for three years previous to our arrival.

The city is an oblong parallelogram, surrounded by walls some four miles in extent, provided with bastions and pierced by twelve gates. The city is traversed by two elegant, broad streets, passing at right angles to each other, and terminating at opposite sides of the city in large gates, beautifully adorned with statues. The place of their intersection, at the center of the city, is called the Piazza. It is octagonal in shape, and bordered by the palaces of the nobility. Marble statues and fountains greatly add to the beauty of the Piazza. One of these large gates, called Porta Felice, opens on the side toward the sea into a magnificent promenade, called the Marina. It is along the line of the old fortifications, and is bounded on one side by the city walls, and on the other side by the sea. The other streets are also wide and regular as a rule. The houses are large, elegant, commodious, flat-roofed, balconied, and provided largely with glass doors in place of windows. The streets are full of well-dressed, intelligent-looking people. But all those who make any claim to respectability in Palermo ride in carriages. To walk is fatal to one's reputation. A single appearance on the streets on foot would debar the pedestrian from good society.

In the center of the Marina is a building used as an orchestra-stand. For four months of the year it is so hot here that night is devoted to the uses commonly peculiar to day. At midnight, therefore, the band strikes up in this building in the Marina. The people flock to this elegant walk, or driveway, in carriages, and ride up and down, chatting and enjoying the music. At two o'clock the music ceases. Then the public gardens are sought for enjoyment. A peculiar thing is that no lights are allowed in these gardens, a custom which our civilization will not tolerate. The citizens ranking highest, nightly frequent these gardens (in fact, the common people are not admitted). Many of the wives and mothers wear masks; for flirtations are the order of the hour, and it is convenient to be, at times, *incognita*.

The coming of the *Lexington* to Palermo was somewhat of an event, and, by order of the viceroy, we officers were admitted to all the public amusements. We were not slow in accepting this politeness. As a result, our stay in this charming city was one of extreme gayety.

A singular custom, peculiar to Palermo, is this: When a child comes to swell the numbers in any household, it is obligatory upon every acquaintance of the family to call and pay his or her respects to the mother. This call of courtesy may not be omitted, for such an omission would be considered a marked disrespect.

The churches of Palermo are over three hundred in number. Many are very fine, especially the cathedral. Some claim that only St. Peter's in Rome surpasses it. Not being a connoisseur in churches, I can neither affirm nor deny this statement. Surely, I have never seen anything to compare with it, either in size or elegance of its rich altars, tombs of porphyry, or pillars of granite and marble. A chest of silver is said to contain the jawbone of St. Peter and an arm of John the Baptist. Seven tombs of finest porphyry are said to contain the remains of a like number of the ancient Norman kings of Sicily.

The Capuchin convent is a most interesting place to visit. Though small, it possesses a beauty rarer than the cathedral.

The burial-places, as also the manner of burial, are peculiar. The place is a deep cellar or excavation—twenty feet perhaps—beneath the entire church. This cellar is divided into apartments by walls, in which are niches of the proper size to receive a human body. Into these upright niches the bodies are stood, clad in their usual clothing, and with the arms tied across the chest. Royal and wealthy personages, however, are placed in handsome chests, elegantly finished, the keys of which are kept by the relatives.

Bodies brought here for sepulture are subjected to a process for preservation by which the skin and muscles are hardened. This takes several days. They are then placed in a small room for about six months, by which time all odor has left the body. Upon the day of our visit, two bodies were undergoing preparation. One—that of a man—had come the day before, the other—a child—had been there three days. The smell declared that the child should be at once removed to the small room.

Saint Rosalie is the tutelary saint of Palermo. The Annual Feast of Saint Rosalie is the event of the year in the city. To our regret, we were too late for it. Who was Rosalie? The legend is, that during a reign of terror from the plague, a monk found the bones of a female on Mount Pelegrino, which, a miracle told him, possessed miraculous powers. He brought them to the city, when the pestilence at once departed. This gave rise to the beatification and saintship of Saint Rosalie. The bones are preserved with the utmost care, and are the most valued possession in the city. A well-executed marble statue resembling the saint is erected on the spot where the bones were found. It possesses, in the belief of the citizens, miraculous powers. It is inclosed in a coat of beaten silver, and six monks are appointed to watch over it.

Palermo lies in a plain of wonderful fertility. Industry has made of this plain a veritable garden. Our rides through it will never be forgotten. Is it a wonder we sailor-boys enjoyed Palermo? Our stay was all too short. But depart we must; and the 3d of September found our anchor at the bow, which was headed for Leghorn.

Only one unpleasant thing struck us at Palermo, but it struck us hard and hot. That was a blast of the famous sirocco wind. I was on shore at the time, enjoying a ride about the city with one of the beauties of Palermo whom I had met. Taking the lady speedily to her home, I repaired forthwith on shipboard, hoping for escape from this enervating wind. The streets of the city were deserted, none remaining abroad unless necessity compelled it. Alas! there was no escape from the blast permitted me for a time on the ship; for there was work to do, and most of the officers were away on excursions. So, on deck I had to stay, to see that the ship was given proper cable, that the awnings were snugly furled, and all made "ship-shape." At last I got below. Acceptable relief it was, though but partial; for the mercury in the thermometer stood at 112°, and there it staid all night. Boreas came to our relief next morning, and superseded the sirocco.

Leghorn is in Tuscany, on the west coast of Italy, pretty well up toward the north of the peninsula.

We laid our course along the Italian coast, at times being but two or three miles distant. Thus we passed close to the mouth of the Tiber. There was Rome—think of it—Rome! It was a feast in which my eyes delighted. The majestic dome of St. Peter's was distinctly visible from the deck, though naught else of the city was. From aloft (Perkins and I went clear up) the view was fine. Yes, there was Rome! We could easily see that, as in old time, she sat upon seven hills. With the glass, the individual buildings could be seen distinctly. Many ruins occupied the suburbs. The country about was low and flat—some of it marshy. The remains of ancient buildings, roadways, and brushwood seemed to cover most of the view. However, evidences of great fertility were visible, and much of the land was cultivated. It was a beautiful picture, in the midst of which passed the Tiber. We could trace its meanderings clear to the mountains.

Ostia is in a ruinous condition, and, were it not at the mouth of the Tiber and the seaport of Rome, would not deserve mention. Its houses of white stone are going to decay; and only two little brigs were in the harbor.

We passed close to the Island of Elba, where Napoleon was imprisoned. We had a fine view of the little island, being becalmed there for several hours. We did not land, however; and, on September 9th, we dropped our anchor in Leghorn Roads, close to the United States ship-of-the-line *Delaware*, which had been there for twenty days.

CHAPTER XV.

LEGHORN—STORY OF LEOPOLD—PISA—DUOMO—BAPTISTERY—LEANING TOWER—CAMPO SANTO.

LEGHORN, the ancient Livornia, is a city of much commercial importance. It is regularly laid out, thickly populated, and adorned with images and statues. Among them are five bronze images of tremendous size. They represent an occurrence resulting in the tragical death of one of the sons of the king of Tuscany. This son, Leopold, was executed by order of his father. This is the story:

Four immense piratical cruisers had long infested Italian seas, to the great detriment of commerce. For a time all efforts to capture them were fruitless. Finally, Leopold, after a desperate battle, succeeded in taking them. Happy, indeed, was he. In his enthusiasm he sailed proudly into port, to carry the glad news, without observing the quarantine regulations.

For this the penalty was death. Would the great victory mitigate the great sin? Paternal love and kingly justice contended. What we have called justice conquered, and Leopold was executed by the father's command. But the father's love and pride in his son caused the erection of these five images. They represent the four pirates crouching in chains beneath the authority of the conquering Leopold. They are situated near the sea, and close to the quarantine ground, as a terrible warning to any who may be tempted to neglect quarantine regulations.

We were to be at Leghorn but a short time, but there was much we wanted to see. So Perkins, two other officers—Lieutenants Viele and Clements—and myself obtained leave from the morning of September 11th to noon on the 13th. We jumped into a boat, and started for shore.

"Where shall we go first?" asked Clements.

"There's lots to see," said Perkins, "and I can see best with a full stomach. So I suggest breakfast."

To breakfast we went. While eating, we decided to go to Pisa. We hired a servant (cicerone it is here), who speedily—for he was a good cicerone—got us a carriage. We were soon off for Pisa, distant fifteen miles. The road, which was a delight—being smooth as a floor—took us through a pleasing country. The roadway was bordered all the distance by rows of grapevines, on which were pendent most luscious fruit. About half-way to Pisa the carriage stopped before a church.

"What's this, Antonio?" I asked, addressing the cicerone.

"Church. See cross on top?"

"Church? It looks more like a heathen temple," said Viele.

"Built for temple—for goddess Diana."

"O! Promoted, was it?"

"Do n't know *promoted;* but Saint Paul and Mary Magdalene been in this church."

"You do n't say so!" said one of us.

Antonio had told the tradition, on account of which the pope has always extended to this church especial privileges. I wanted to believe the tradition, but could not.

Noon found us in Pisa, distinguished alike for its antiquity and beauty. The Arno flows through the city. The quay is said to be one of the finest in Europe. Surely I never saw anything of the kind, which presented at the same time such a magnificent row of buildings, together with wharves, boats, and churches of the most beautiful workmanship. Canals lead in all directions from the river toward Leghorn and other towns. The streets are well paved, and the houses large, stately, and beautiful.

"What do we want to see, Antonio?"

"The cathedral, the baptistery, the Leaning Tower, and the Campo Santo, I expect."

"You expect? You are supposed to know!" said Viele. "So take us to the cathedral."

The cathedral, or Duomo, is a Gothic structure, in the form of a Latin cross, built in the eleventh century. It is remarkable for the richness and variety of its marbles. The eastern front is ornamented with a great many columns, some of Grecian marble. Three modern bronze doors, which attract much attention, are probably of Egyptian, perhaps Grecian, workmanship. The pulpit is ancient, and composed of elegantly carved marble. The dome, supported by seventy-four pillars, is beautifully frescoed, and the whole church is rich in paintings, statuary, and mosaics. From the nave hangs a chandelier, originally fine, but showing the ravages of time.

"Look at that chandelier!" said Clements.

"Ah, yes," said I; "it's very nice."

"Needs cleaning, I think," said Perkins.

"Ignoramuses, both of you! The swinging of that chandelier gave Galileo the idea of the pendulum. Needs cleaning, indeed! Better rub up your ideas!" said the lieutenant.

"We have n't many to rub, Lieutenant; so, please enlighten our ignorance by telling us about the pendulum."

"As a philanthropic act, I will. Galileo was a medical student. One day—when in this church attending service, I suppose—that chandelier got to swinging. It struck the student that it was wonderfully regular in its swing; so he timed it. He did n't have a watch; they were scarce in those days. He timed it by his pulse, which was in his line. Yes, the swing was regular, and put him to thinking. Soon he had developed the theory of the pendulum, and produced an astronomical clock."

The baptistery is a German-Gothic edifice of the twelfth century. It is round, with a dome top, and built of marble. The interior represents an ancient church, supported by immense pillars of Sardinian granite. The pulpit is a hexagon, resting on nine pillars and covered with work in bas-relief.

"Here, my Baptist friend," said Perkins, addressing me, "is proof that the builders of this church believed in immersion."

He referred to the font. It is in the center of the building, elevated on three steps of marble, and is large enough to accommodate a dozen persons at once. There is also provision made, in three smaller fonts, for the immersion of children. The font throughout is ornamented with most exquisite mosaic-work. The height* of the dome to this building is one hundred and seventy-nine feet. The effect of this building upon the observer is most impressive, whether the view be from the exterior or within.

The Campanile, or Leaning Tower, was next visited. It was probably intended originally for a belfry. It has a circular base, with a cylindrical shaft composed of eight stories, and adorned with two hundred and eight columns of granite and marble. The eighth story, which is an open gallery, is reached by a winding stairway. It is a twelfth-century structure. It was originally perpendicular; but the foundation gave way—probably as the result of an earthquake—and it was thrown from an erect position. The declination is enough to carry the top thirteen feet to one side of its original location. The tower is one hundred and ninety feet high, being well named the "Leaning Tower." We all went to the top, and had a fine view of the surrounding country. Just think what that height—one hundred and ninety feet (some say it is only one hundred and eighty)—takes one to! Twelve feet is an aver-

---

*Not given in the journal. Taken from "Europa," written by D. C. Eddy.

age height per story for a residence. This tower, then, is as high as a fifteen-story house. As it is small enough at the base to be a true tower, it is a somewhat remarkable structure. Such lofty edifices are usually made tapering; but this is not; it is as big at the top as at the bottom. Then think that this lofty cylinder is so far "out of plumb" that the top passes thirteen feet beyond the base; and you have a faint idea of what the distortion is, and what it means to go to the top. Go to the lower side, if you can, without a sensation of falling. If you are really courageous, and have a steady head, lean far enough out to see the base. Sailors as we were, it was impossible to approach the balustrade, on the lower side of the top story, without the thought of falling.

"And this," said I, "is where Galileo demonstrated to the Aristotelian philosophers, that bodies of equal specific gravity, though of different weight, would fall to the ground in the same time."

"What's that?" asked Clements.

"Ignoramus!" cried I, glad to get a return joke on Clements. "Better go and rub up your ideas!"

Clements was teased, but he was not posted; so we told him that Galileo had brought the philosophers here, who said a ten-pound cannon-ball would fall to the earth quicker than a one-pound ball of like material, and proved to them their error by dropping one of each weight at the same instant. Of course they struck the ground together; and the Aristotelians had to accept Galileo's theory, which they did with ill grace, and drove him from the town.

"It was a good place for that experiment," said Viele.

"Come see Campo Santo," said Antonio. "Late; get late pretty soon."

The guide was right. We scampered down the winding stair, the nimble Perkins proving that the smallest got there first.

The Campo Santo is a burying-ground—a vast, rectangular inclosure, surrounded by sixty-two light and beautiful columns of white marble. Some of the soil has been brought from Mount Calvary. I suppose they think it better than common earth to be buried in; but it is, so say the residents, dangerous to sleep on; for, should one essay to sleep on this sacred soil, the morning would find him a corpse. I bought in the Campo Santo a number of pictures of these wonderful buildings, which we had this day seen, for the delectation of my many Indiana friends. It had been a wonderful day; and I wanted the friends to live it over with me, as far as possible, when I was again with them.

We took a walk along the quay after dinner, and went into what is called La Madonna della Spina, or Thorn Church. The church is small, and of little note, save that it once contained one of the thorns with which our Savior was crowned; but it was taken when the French, under Napoleon, captured this part of Italy.

We visited the hospital, which is very fine and modern, having been built by the present Grand Duke of Tuscany. It is doing much good for the people, and, with other good works, has greatly endeared him to his subjects.

We visited the Botanical Gardens, which well repaid us, for they are very fine. Antonio was most anxious about us while here, owing to the presence of a certain tree, and our recklessness.

"Kill a man to go sleep under that tree," said Tony, as we had learned to call him.

"No, it won't," said Viele. "I 'm tired, and I will take a nap, to show you there is no danger."

Down he dropped under the tree; but he did n't sleep—not a bit of it! Tony dragged him to his feet in a second.

"Do n't look at it!" cried he. "Make you blind in five minutes!"

Tony believed what he said, and we had to go, to appease the poor fellow.

Back to Leghorn we started, passing the custom-house officers with no trouble; so potent a talisman is the uniform of the United States Navy.

We were riding along quietly, enjoying the view, when Lieutenant Clements said:

"Let's go to Florence to-night!"

"Hurrah for you, Clements!" cried Lieutenant Viele. "You're a trump!"

It was decided to go to Florence.

CHAPTER XVI.

OFF FOR FLORENCE—BANDITTI—"MAKE WAY FOR MY MASTERS!"—PALACE OF THE PITTI—GARDEN OF THE BOBOLI—ROYAL GALLERY—THE GRAND DUKE—SUFFERINGS—PRIME MINISTER HELPS US.

FLORENCE—"City of Flowers"—was nearly seventy miles from Leghorn, right back from the sea, in the very heart of Italy. If we made that voyage we must spread all sails, and see that there was wind to fill them. In other words, we must be diligent. So we urged the driver to greater speed. Arriving at Leghorn, while Tony was getting suitable horses and carriage, we procured from Mr. Appleton, American consul-general of Tuscany, our passports.

We took time to eat a good supper; and off to the east, into the darkness, we rattled, fast as two good horses could take us. The night was pretty black, for there was no moon; but the road was good and white. Hence the postillion could see it plainly, and our progress was rapid.

We aimed to be in Florence at eight o'clock next morning. As it was nine when we left Leghorn, rapid progress was necessary, and we were to change horses every twelve miles. About the middle of the first stage, conversation lagged, and we were getting a little drowsy from the monotonous movement of the carriage, when the sound of horses' feet reached our ears.

"What's that?" asked Perkins.

"Horses," said Clements; "and a lot of 'em, too."

"And coming as though Tam O'Shanter's ghost was after them," said I.

A moment after, they dashed past us, going toward Leghorn, a dozen of them perhaps, each with an armed man upon his back.

"Who are they, Tony?" I asked.

"Mounted patrol. This road bad for banditti. Lots of 'em! Big fellows! Patrol catch eight of 'em the other night. Banditti catch us, if we don't look out!"

"Why didn't you tell us this before we started, you avaricious Italian?" cried Viele.

"Don't know 'avaricious.' Is it bad?"

"Come now, you old sinner—you know *sinner!* Of course it's bad. Confess that you did n't tell for fear we would n't come, and you would miss a fat job!"-

We made him confess, when he said:

"Me not avar—what you call it?"

"Avaricious," we told him.

"Me not avaricious—take good care of you. Look!"

He reached down and took from under the seat a big pistol, a regular "horse-pistol," almost as big as a blunderbuss.

"Do n't be 'fraid. I shoot 'em if they come."

How we did laugh at this artillery, and at Tony's attempt to clear his character of avariciousness.

"Hush, gentlemen, hush! Banditti hear you."

Tony was right. We had done a reckless thing in coming on this road, infested with robbers, in the nighttime; a dangerous road even in the daytime. Fortunately, we were each well armed, and, with Tony and his pistol at our head, could make a strong defense. Thinking of danger sharpened our senses; we were ever on the alert, and if a toad hopped by the roadside, or an apple fell in an adjoining orchard, we were startled. Once a man, roused from slumber beneath a tree by our approach, sprang to his feet. It frightened the horses, which began to run. We thought the brigands were after us sure, and that our postillion was racing to escape from them. We grasped our pistols and threw open the doors of the carriage, determined to give the rascals a warm reception. When the speed of the vehicle became less, we all sprang to the ground, that we might fight at better advantage. Tony and his blunderbuss were the first out, and, had it been necessary, they would have been in the heat of the fight; and they would have done something, too; for, if Tony had missed his mark, the report would have scared the robbers off in a hurry.

Daybreak found us thirty miles from Florence. The night had been tedious, for we could see nothing. The remainder of the ride was a continual delight, being up the vale of the Arno. The view was one of indescribable beauty. Nature has here done much, but art far more. Here reside many of the nobility in mansions of great attractiveness. Such is the situation of the vale that, at times, hundreds of these country-seats were within view.

Eleven hours after leaving Leghorn we approached the western gate to the city of Florence. A long line of carriages—perhaps a hundred—were waiting for entrance. As but one could go in at a time, and as many had passports which required examination, much delay and loss of our limited time seemed probable.

But Tony—our precious Tony—came to the rescue.

Opening the carriage doors, he said: "Sit where you show."

We made as much display of ourselves as posible, when Tony cried in Italian:

"Make way for my masters! Make way! make way!"

Tony's manner and our uniforms did the work. The carriages drove to one side, and we speedily reached the gate. Our papers being all right, we scarcely stopped.

We went to the London Hotel, where we were refreshed with food and a bath, changing our traveling clothes, of course. Then off we started for the sights. There were many of them, more than we could see in a day.

We first went to the Palace of the Pitti. This magnificent structure was built by Luca Pitti. Misfortunes, however, overcame the noted family, and the palace passed from their possession. It is now the residence of the Grand Duke of Tuscany. We were courteously received by the master of ceremonies, and shown over the palace. It surpasses in elegance any of my wildest dreams. The floors of four of the corridors are laid with petrified wood; the rooms are spacious, and furnished with regal magnificence; one table of mosaic-work, representing the city of Leghorn, is valued at $25,000. The galleries are filled with paintings and sculpture from the hands of the finest artists, such as Titian, Raphael, Rubens, Michael Angelo, and others, whom I can not name. In one corridor is the Venus of Canova, thought by many to equal the Venus de Medici.

Upon leaving the palace, we were presented with a ticket of admission to the Duke's Imperial Garden of the Boboli. This was an honor not expected, as only distinguished persons are admitted. Our uniforms did it. I can not describe this garden; but it is worth a trip across the Atlantic to see it. In it are a modern amphitheater and many fine statues, that of Ceres being thirty feet in height. The view from the garden includes all Florence and suburbs, and the vale of the Arno, as far as the eye can reach. A fount between the garden and the palace throws water to the height of one hundred feet, whence it descends as spray and rain in the midst of most pleasing rainbows.

Leaving the garden, we crossed the Arno on Goldsmiths' Bridge, so named from the character of the traffic upon it. The bridge is wide; and shops for the sale of jewelry, etc., are built upon the sides, thus giving it more the appearance of a street than a bridge.

The Royal Gallery, which we next visited, is

in the second story of the Palazzo Vecchio and the Arno. In the first story is a fine library, also the archives of the courts. The gallery comprises twenty-three rooms, arranged about a space much like the Campo Santo in Pisa. This gallery is the finest in Italy, and second only to that of the Louvre in Paris. In the finest room, called the Tribuna—which has a marble floor and a dome inlaid with mother-of-pearl—is the statue known as Venus de Medicis, said to be the most perfect piece of sculpture known.

I did not, upon entering the Tribuna, recognize that this marble was superior to much other about it; for all there possesses great merit. But when pointed out to me, I could appreciate that the ideal of the sculptor was indeed perfect, and that the execution was fully commensurate therewith. To whom this statue owes its existence is, I believe, not known. It is of Parian marble, and was brought from Greece, where it was found broken into several pieces, by the family of the Medici—whence the name—when they were on the throne of Tuscany. It is the image of a nude female.

The cabinet of gems and precious stones is a noble sight; but the man of much cupidity will be happier to stay away. We knew that some of the officers of the *Delaware* were in Florence.

Where should we find them but as close to these gems as they could conveniently get?

We visited the anatomical museum, and then to dinner; for the fashionable dining-hour had arrived. Having eaten, the cloth was removed, and wines were brought on. Fortunately, they were very light, having, probably, not more than two per cent of alcohol; for we were inclined to imbibe more freely than was best. We drank to the health of Leopold, the grand duke; then to the health of the President of the United States.

"Is this right?" said I to myself.

"No, it is not," was my mental response.

"Shipmates," said I, "it is time to quit."

They took the hint, and we arose. Our party now divided, the lieutenants going to see the cathedral and to visit the grave of Michael Angelo, who is buried in one of the churches; but Perkins and I got horses, and took a ride in the Casino. The horses were splendid and elegantly caparisoned, but each horse cost a dollar an hour.

The Casino, or Imperial Promenade, is eighteen miles in circuit and very elegant, having driveways for carriages, other roads for equestrians, and walks for those on foot. It is the favorite resort of the nobility. We rode out six miles, and then started back.

"What's that coming?" said Perkins.

"Don't know," said I. "Hope it is the grand duke."

It was. He was preceded by two outriders on fine horses, and clad in brass armor from heel to crown. His carriage was drawn by six noble horses, with silver-mounted harness, the carriage also being trimmed in silver. He is a fine-looking young man, of perhaps twenty-eight. His wife accompanied him.

" Well, Sam, we've seen enough for one day."

"Yes, indeed, George. We must make for Leghorn at once, for the sun is down."

We reached the hotel without incident, save that, in going through the city gate, my horse got me against the stone pillar. The stone refused to give. So the skin on my shin, for a distance of some six inches, gave freely; so did about a foot of the bottom of one leg of my trousers. The missing cloth made me look very bad, but the missing skin made me feel far worse. My little friend Perkins let me hide behind him in getting into the hotel; but the officers from the *Delaware*, as also the two from our own party, got sight of me, and for a few moments made my life a burden. Glad was I to don my traveling-suit and enter the carriage for return to Leghorn.

It is said misery loves company. If so, I should have been happy; for just at that moment Lieutenant Clements came from the hotel to enter the carriage. He was the picture of despair.

"What's the matter, Clements?" we asked in a breath.

"I paid the hotel bill!" said he.

"How much was it?"

When he told us, we put on the same look he carried. I even forgot that my shin ached, so big was the bill. We showed our passports at the city gate, when we were informed that our papers must be signed by the police officer before we could get out.

"Where will we find the police officer?"

"I don't know. He is out of town."

"When will he be back?"

"Don't know."

"What will we do? Our ship sails tomorrow."

"Don't know. I can't let you out till your papers are signed."

We drove to headquarters to make an appeal to the authorities, but we could find no one to appeal to. Accidentally the prime minister heard of our dilemma. He took our papers, and signed them at once, stamping them with the royal seal. The gatekeeper was nonplused, having never seen such a signature and seal to a trivial passport; but he could not refuse to pass us. So away we went rejoicing, and spent the night watching for banditti, who came not. Morning found us thirty miles from the sea, and so tired we could scarcely endure it; but endure it we must. Poor Tony, however, succumbed when about ten miles from Leghorn, and sank senseless to the floor of the carriage. What should we do? None of us knew; but the postillion did. He was well acquainted. He called on every saint in the Italian calendar, at the same time rubbing Tony's limbs vigorously. Either the rubbing or the saints did Tony good, for he soon came to. Now, I had lots of faith in our postillion. So, while he said mass, and the others helped rub and took care of the team, I went to the roadside and ate grapes. O, but they were good! I brought a lot for the others, though, which much refreshed them, and did Tony good.

We reached Leghorn, with time to spare. So, after getting breakfast, we went to the English cemetery, to visit the grave of Smollett, as also that of several American naval officers. The cemetery is fine indeed, and I believe there is some ground for the claim that it is the best kept in the world.

After doing a little shopping, we went on

board ship, getting there before our leave had entirely expired. We had been gone about fifty-six hours, had traveled one hundred and eighty miles, and visited the cities of Leghorn, Pisa, and Florence, without closing an eye in sleep.

CHAPTER XVII.

An Equinoctial Storm—Yellow Fever—Gayety—Sickness—Homeward Bound—Smallpox—Stormy Passage—America.

THE *Lexington* sailed from Leghorn, bound for Gibraltar, on September 13th. We passed to the north of Corsica—Bonaparte's native island—of which we had a good view. When off Nice, in France, sailing along with all sails set, a squall suddenly struck the ship. Would we go over? Surely it looked so. The deck was at the time in charge of a midshipman of little experience, which added much to the danger. The noble ship rode the squall out safely, only to be subjected within forty-eight hours to a more severe trial. It was the equinoctial storm. The old sailors said it was one of the most severe blows they had ever experienced. Surely, in my year and a half on the water, I had seen nothing to compare with it. Lack of sea-room made it more serious.

It was just after nightfall on the 17th of September. We were standing along to the north of the Island of Majorca, about four miles from shore, with light winds and all sails set. The horizon to the northeast suddenly grew black with clouds, across which the distant lightning played. Soon the blackness had crawled well toward the zenith, and the electrical display became grand, but so vivid as to be also frightful. About the ship it was calm and as still as death. From afar, however, came the subdued mutter, gradually becoming a roar, which foretold the severity of the approaching tempest.

The thunder increased in intensity with a rapidity which gave us some idea of the velocity with which this storm was approaching. We sprang to prepare the ship for the terrible contest soon to be waged. First, we took in the studding sails; next, the royals; then, the topgallant sails; and, with all possible dispatch, we hauled up the courses. By this time the wind was felt, and we reefed the topsails. As it grew stronger, we double-reefed, and finally close-reefed them.

Orders were now given to furl the courses and mizzen-topsail; but before the latter could be taken in, it was shivered to rags, as was also the spanker, so intensely violent was the wind. The thunder and lightning now surpassed what I supposed to be possible. The lightning seemed to be in our very eyeballs, and the thunder was right in our ears. The flashes and reports were simultaneous. The rain descended in torrents, and the sea was white with the spray.

The fore-topsail was now furled, and the weather-clew of the main-topsail hauled up, every stitch of canvas on board being furled, except the lee-clew of the main-topsail, which we were obliged to carry to keep the ship off of a lee-shore.

We were now practically under bare poles; but the wind was so strong the vessel lay over till the lee bow-guns were muzzle under. For half an hour the wind blew so strong that, as the sailors say, it took ten men to hold one man's hair on his head. Then it lessened, and a calm ensued. But there was a heavy swell setting directly on shore, and it was carrying us steadily, though not rapidly, with it. Our danger of stranding on this lee-shore was imminent. Had not a breeze sprung up, we would surely have been beached.

This danger passed, we speedily made the coast of Spain, along which we sailed with much pleasure, as we could see the land very plainly.

We had an especially fine view of Malaga. At one time, while off this coast, we were becalmed near a shoal of blackfish. I studied them with much interest. From a distance such a shoal looks like an island; at nearer view it resembles a lot of logs floating together. Each fish is about ten feet long, and as black as coal. They lie packed together as closely as possible, perfectly motionless, save that they occasionally roll over each other.

We soon hove in sight of the Rock of Gibraltar, from which time we had, till at anchor, a head wind. In beating around Point Europa, therefore, we had both the current, which always flows from the west, and the wind against us. It is not often that a vessel can stem both; but the grand old *Lexington* weathered the cape on a single tack.

This was observed at the fortress, and established a most desirable reputation for the sailing qualities of our ship.

We anchored, on the 24th of September, right at the height of an epidemic of yellow fever. We communicated with the shore by receiving on board the quarantine regulations. The question was, would the person who took the paper take the disease as well? I was the person ordered to receive the paper. Uh! It made the chills creep over me to do it, but I did it. It was duty! It was right! Then I watched myself, for days, for evidences of disease, and in this vigil my shipmates assisted me most assiduously; but the disease came not, and all was well.

Half an hour after receiving the paper, the ship's anchorage was shifted across the bay, near to the city of Algesiras. Consternation seized the inhabitants, and the governor sent us peremptory command to depart.

"We will go when we think proper, and not before," was the answer we gave.

We thought proper to go at once, and the 2d of October found us at Mahon.

On the way we had a little variety. A strange vessel of war began to fire her guns in a most unusual way. Thinking her intent was hostile, we beat to quarters and cleared ship for action. Standing toward her, we showed our colors and fired a gun. She at once showed English colors. We demanded an explanation of her strange conduct, and received the reply that she was scaling her guns. It was H. B. M. brig *Kingfisher*.

We were now on our old familiar cruising-ground, and the next year and a half the *Lexington* spent in the harbors of Mahon, Malta, and Smyrna, or *en route* between them. The winter of 1829 was passed mostly in the harbor of Smyrna. It was a gay winter; a succession of balls and parties.

I worked about equally hard that winter at dancing and studying. I was such an enthusiast in my chosen profession that the latter was quite as much enjoyed as the former. I was determined to stand well in my class, though little was expected from the first appointment from Indiana.

On May 11th we officers gave a grand ball on board the *Lexington*. I was appointed one of the managers. It was a great time, and we did not cease dancing till six o'clock in the morning. I formed, at that ball, some lady acquaintances, which were to me a great enjoyment and advantage. Nothing more greatly promotes a noble manhood than association with intelligent and decorous women. The greatest objection to the navy is, that one is so much deprived of this pleasure.

On the 2d of October we had cucumbers for supper. They were rather a new dish, and usually considered unwholesome. Quite a discussion arose about them. I ate none, but the next morning I was sick. Had I eaten cucumbers, they would surely have had to take the brunt of the abuse for my sickness. It proved to be bilious fever. Unfortunately, the surgeon salivated me very severely. Mr. Mooner, our generous sailing-master, kindly gave me his room, and there I lay till December 1st, learning what it is to be sick on shipboard. December 1st found us at Mahon, where, by the advice of the surgeon, I went ashore. I secured comfortable lodgings, at which I remained till February 22, 1830, when I again joined the *Lexington*.

Glad was I, while sick at Mahon, that I had befriended, in the time of need, the Cochlins. Little Clara was an angel of mercy to me; and dainties prepared by her own or her mother's hands added much to my comfort and hastened my recovery. Mr. Cochlin's reformation had proven lasting.

Upon returning to the *Lexington* in February, I found a new set of officers. Captain Hunter was in command. Almost all of my old shipmates had returned to America, in November, in the *Delaware*. I could have done so had health permitted.

On July 16, 1830, the *Warren* sailed for America. I could have gone on her, but a court-martial, on which I was to serve, prevented. Human nature likes variety and change. I had been eager—so eager!—to take this cruise; now I was desirous—O how desirous!—to see America and my friends again. I had been gone over three years, and that is a long time.

The court-martial was completed, so as to allow us to sail from Mahon for home—think of it!—on the 22d of September.

A Dutch admiral and his ship were in harbor when we left. We passed near his vessel and cheered him. He returned the compliment, and had his band render "Hail Columbia." It was a pleasant courtesy. Our commodore was also there. We cheered and saluted him, which, of course, he returned. We thought these good omens, and were happy. Yet our happiness was not without alloy.

One of the midshipmen of the *Constitution* had recently had smallpox. He was convalescing finely; but he was a passenger for America on our vessel. Now, this is a dread disease anywhere; but on shipboard it is especially so. Isolation of the patient is impossible; and to start out on the broad ocean with a reasonable certainty of the disease appearing on the ship was not a pleasing prospect. We all loved the sea; but we did not want to be buried in it—not for a while, at least. Hence the alloy to our happiness.

In five days we made the harbor of Malaga, in Spain, where we staid eight days to lay in supplies. Fortunate stay! While we were there, one of our midshipmen came down with the smallpox. We sent him on shore to the hospital, and started on our voyage.

It was October 5th when, for the last time in the Mediterranean, we weighed the *Lexington's* anchor.

On the 6th, with a fair wind, we passed Gibraltar in glorious style. Before sundown we were out of sight of land, on the broad Atlantic, happy, indeed, were it not for fear of smallpox. Favoring gales wafted us in a week to the Azores Islands. By this time our fears of smallpox were mostly allayed. Suddenly, "Breakers ahead! On the lee bow, close aboard!" was heard ringing through the ship. It was a narrow escape—very narrow. Had we struck, all hands would have gone to Davy Jones's locker, and I would not have completed the diary of this voyage.

The winds now hauled ahead, and we had a tedious time of it. They blew us in every direction but the right one, and almost wrecked us on the Island of Bermuda. The sea was very rough; and most of the time our pleasant steerage had three or four inches of water in it, which "swashed" about in a most miserable fashion.

We were delayed so long, provisions gave out. Only salt meat and hard bread did we have. Not an ounce of sugar, tea, or coffee was there in the ship. Salt meat and hard bread will prevent starvation; but it is slim living, and some of the company really suffered for food. All of us were fearfully hungry.

Finally a calm came, and we tried to catch a big turtle we saw asleep on the surface of the water. A boat got quite near to him; but he awoke, and down he went. So did our hopes of some soup. But during that calm, we caught a shark and a dolphin. They are fair eating when properly prepared. To us, they were luxuries. When the wind again blew, it was dead ahead. So we felt our way cautiously and slowly toward our blessed America, amid fogs and clouds, which prevented us from taking a meridian altitude to find our whereabouts, and from seeing land when we approached it. We knew the Gulf Stream when we struck it by the warmth of the water; and at last we knew we were near land, by finding bottom with the lead.

About this time we caught another shark and dolphin. They were scarcely on deck ere they were transferred to frying-pans, and the pans had but received the steaks, when the famished men rescued them from their warm berths and devoured them, half-cooked as they were.

We almost went ashore in the night near Cape Henry, and we fired signal guns every hour for a pilot. In the morning we saw land ahead. It was Cape Henry, and at 9 A. M. we got a pilot. At one o'clock we were in Chesapeake Bay. Passing Old Point Comfort—I tell you, it is well named!—and the Rip-raps, we came to anchor, having been gone just three years and a half, to a day. The next day we took the ship to the Norfolk Navy-yard.

The next day, November 21, 1830, I took my baggage and went ashore, bidding adieu to my first love, the *Lexington*.

I passed the time in Norfolk till December 16th most delightfully, having the great happiness to spend many evenings at the hospitable home of Commodore Sinclair.

On the 16th came unlimited leave of absence. I at once started north, taking the steamboat *Pocahontas* for Baltimore. We had a rough passage, and all the passengers were seasick save myself. I laughed heartily at the poor sufferers, but atoned therefor by doing all in my power for them. They did not know that I was an old sea-dog, and watched to see me come down, which, of course, I did not do.

Reached Baltimore at 10 A. M. on Friday. Viewed the city a little, saw some shipmates, among them dear little Perkins, and at 1 P. M. took stage for Washington City.

Chance placed me beside a very pleasant traveling companion. For two hours we enjoyed an uninterrupted conversation. I told him much of my travels, in which he manifested keen interest, and he told me much of the vicinity through which we were passing. I afterwards learned that it was J. Q. Adams, Ex-President of the United States. Another fellow-passenger was Sir William Campbell.

Saturday morning I called on Senator Hendricks, of Indiana. He gave me a cordial welcome, and introduced me to President Jackson; also to many of the heads of departments; likewise to Mr. Speaker Stevenson and many other members of Congress. I took tea with him that evening, where I met many of the dignitaries of the city, among them Colonel Pepper, of Indiana, Mr. Doddridge, and Judge Marks, all members of Congress.

On Sunday I visited the Capitol with Senator Hendricks, and attended divine service in Congress Hall.

CHAPTER XVIII.

Marriage-bells—Examination—Victory!

HOME again! A happy home-coming it was to others as well as myself, as evinced by the fact that a marriage occurred on February 10, 1831, at Waynesville, Warren County, Ohio. The contracting parties were Miss Harriet Ann Goode, and he who is known in this narrative as Samuel Trumbull.

The groom went into this alliance most boldly, not even stopping to ask if it were right. The bride was equally determined, though she was well aware that she would, by so doing, lose her Goode name.

On July 15, 1831, came orders for me to report for duty at the navy-yard at Pensacola, Florida.

The 17th found me *en route*, via the steamboats of the Ohio and Mississippi Rivers. In due time I reported to Commodore Dallas at the yard, where I did duty for about a year, when I was ordered to appear before the Naval Board, soon to assemble in Baltimore, for examination for standing in my class, preliminary, if successful, to promotion. I went at once to Baltimore, stopping a few days with my wife in Madison, Indiana.

The Examining Board consisted of Commodore Jones, Commodore Ridgely, and Captain Ballard. The class was composed of the midshipmen who were appointed in 1826. There were about fifty of us. It was an anxious time, for much depended on the result. Some would fail. Those who passed would be arranged in a list, and numbered according to proficiency and the judgment of the board, and in that order would promotions be made. Much, therefore, depended on this examination. I did not expect to fail; nor did I anticipate passing high. I hoped to be about the middle of the list. I had studied very hard and diligently, and felt justified in entertaining such a hope. Indiana had in me her first representative, and I was almost as anxious to stand well upon my State's account as upon my own.

Ten of the applicants failed; forty-two of us passed, and received warrants as passed midshipmen. To my extreme surprise and my most intense delight, my name headed the list. Indiana was victorious, and the Hoosier boy led his class! Every one was surprised, but no one so much as the Hoosier.

With a happy heart I returned to Madison, where I remained until ordered into active service.

NOTE.—Several persons who obtained distinction as naval commanders in the War of the Rebellion were in this class. Among them, Raphael Semmes, captain of the Confederate cruiser *Alabama*, who stood second in his class; Admirals Dahlgren, Glisson, Rowan, and Briggs.

THE AUTHOR.

CHAPTER XIX.

PLEASING ORDERS—CRYING BABIES—DOCKING THE "DELAWARE"—AGROUND—GAYETY—THE SUICIDE—A FATAL FALL.—VISITORS FROM NEW YORK.

ABOUT the first of May, 1834, I received orders from the Secretary of the Navy to report to Commodore Warrington, at Norfolk Navy-yard, for duty on board the United States ship-of-the-line *Delaware*. With the orders I was pleased, for the *Delaware* was one of the finest frigates afloat. She was pierced for a hundred guns, though she carried but seventy-four. Her full complement of men was a thousand, but eight hundred only were commonly enlisted. Seventy-four guns, however, are a powerful armament, and eight hundred souls are a community in which there is constant variety. To cruise on the *Delaware* was a delight to which we naval officers all aspired.

Then, she was bound for the Mediterranean.

True, I had spent three and a half years in this great sea; but it was pleasant to visit old associations, and Egypt and the Holy Land I had not seen. So the orders were gladly received. I found, however, that leaving home for a protracted stay in a foreign land, with the possibility of never returning, was very different from my first departure from home. I was now leaving a loved and loving wife; and my little boy, Philip, was an idol from which I parted with the keenest regret.

On the 4th of May the steamboat *Portsmouth* came along, bound for Wheeling, Virginia, and upon her I took passage. The river was very low, and we repeatedly ran aground.

"I am glad," thought I, "that on the *Delaware* we will have no such experience as this. She sails in deep water, and does n't run aground."

A stage across the mountains was the style of conveyance from Wheeling. The scenery was fine, but it was a sorry journey. Among the passengers was a termagant, who no doubt aspired to be considered a lady. She had the freedom of tongue peculiar to the most garrulous of her sex, and exercised it all in scolding. She had also a husband with her, of whom she was jealous, and upon him she exercised this freedom of speech. A baby, of the milk-bottle age, completed the family trio. The baby was indeed the son of its mother, as was proven by the crossness of its disposition.

> "The father, quite wise, looked about with both eyes,
> And remarked that the stage was small."

Now, that is not a correct quotation, but it tells accurately the mind of the husband and father. He evacuated the stage, as the wise fox did the hencoop, and took refuge with the driver.

The baby squirmed and kicked and cried, and the woman scolded. We passengers squirmed, and felt like kicking, till, in desperation, I cried:

"Give me the child."

Now, connubial felicity had taught me a little of the art of taking care of children, for I had practiced on my little Philip. Only too gladly did the woman comply. Alas! she washed her hands of the child then and there, though she did deign, betimes, to fill the nursing-bottle for me. Behold me—a dignified officer of the United States navy, crossing the Alleghanies in a jolting stage to join the magnificent frigate *Delaware*—in the capacity of nurse to a cross baby, plying, betimes, the bottle to still its peevish cries! I know I had the sympathy of my fellow-passengers; but I had also to stand the silent smiles which would, from time to time, possess their countenances, though they tried hard to suppress them. To say that I was vexed almost beyond endurance, is using English most mildly.

Fortunately, the stage broke down at Frederick. Thus were we released from the termagant and the baby. At Frederick we took a railroad-car; and in this were three women, with as many crying babies. They were all, however, nothing to the one from which we had escaped; and to these I did not bear the relation of nurse.

We reached Baltimore at eleven o'clock at night. Going to a hotel, I spoke for a room as far as possible from scolding women and crying babies. Alas! there was no escape for me that night. They had made such a hold on my mind that they were with me in my dreams. Nor could I get these thoughts to depart till they were replaced by those of the dear wife whom I had left behind, in whom were exemplified all the amiability and loveliness almost divine of the female character; and of the blooming boy, but four weeks old. To me he was the emblem of innocence; and the knowledge that the precept and example of his pious mother would confirm in him a respect and love for morality and religion, thus perpetuating that innocence, was to me most pleasing.

A board of naval officers was in session as I passed through Baltimore. It reminded me forcibly of a year before, when I was before a similar board in the same city. The board passed thirty-eight out of fifty applicants. Inability to establish satisfactorily a moral character sufficiently high, was the cause of the rejection of most of the unfortunate ones. It is to the friends of the navy a great pride that the portals of entrance to this branch of the service are so carefully guarded. Thus will be secured a corps of gentlemanly and competent officers, who will be a credit to the country, and sustain the honor of the flag on any and all seas.

I spent several days in this, the Monumental City, and met there Captain Henry E. Ballard, who had served on the Examining Board which I passed the year before. To my great delight, I learned that he was to command the *Delaware*.

Arriving at Norfolk, I reported to Commodore Warrington, and learned, to my great regret, that the *Delaware* would not be ready for sea for two months or thereabouts. She was to go into dry-dock, and the dock would not be completed for several weeks. So we must wait. As this had to be, I was glad it was in Norfolk; for it is a most hospitable city. The time passed quickly, and the day was appointed for the docking of this great vessel. Never before had a ship-of-the-line been docked in America. It was a noted event; and an immense crowd witnessed it, being estimated at ten thousand. Commodore Warrington superintended the ceremony. He had six aids, and it was my good fortune to be appointed one of these. It was early in the day—June 17th—but the people were all there; the ladies comfortably placed in the large engine-room, the men on improvised seats erected about the dock. The band, which has been playing the national airs, suddenly ceases; for the great ship is approaching the dock. All eyes are upon her, and absolute stillness prevails. Suddenly, upon the air thunders the report of a cannon, indicating that the bows of the frigate have entered the dock. Slowly but majestically she moves, and soon the roar of the cannon tells that half the ceremony is accomplished. Erelong a third report announces its completion. The *Delaware* is in dock! And America is no longer dependent upon Europe for the repair of her large vessels.

Amid the huzzahs of the multitude, the ponderous gates are closed, and the immense pumps set in motion to empty the dock of water. The guns of the receiving ship *Java* now belch out a national salute, honoring not only this ceremony, but the anniversary of the battle of Bunker Hill as well. We who were favored, now repaired to the home of Commodore Warrington, where an elegant collation was served.

As the water receded from about the *Delaware*, she settled upon the timbers prepared for her reception. Lateral supports were placed about her; and, in two weeks' time, the old copper had been removed from her hull, all defects in woodwork repaired, new copper put on, and the vessel restored to her native element. In two weeks more, the armament was aboard and the vessel ready for sea. On the 15th of July, we officers left our temporary quarters on the *Java* or on shore and repaired on board, when the regular duty of the ship began.

On the 17th, two steamboats came alongside to tow us down the roads. At night we anchored, with two pilots on board, ready to go over the bar at high tide next day.

We made the start according to program, but speedily stuck in the mud on Seal's Point. It sealed us more pointedly than we liked, and I thought of the *Portsmouth* and the bars in the Ohio River. We sent out kedges, and hauled off, only to ground again. We kept this up for two days, and all the time I thought of the *Portsmouth*. On the night of the 19th the tide was very high, and we floated finely. The steamboats soon had us going through the water at three knots an hour; the tide took us two more, making five, very respectable progress. Suddenly we struck an oyster bank with force sufficient to lift the bows two feet out of the water. There we staid, and I still thought of the *Portsmouth*. When the tide fell, the ship had a list to port sufficient to bring her lower deck ports to the water's edge. By the assistance of the steamboats, we ran the larboard bower out astern, and brought the cable in through the lower gun deck stern ports, and at high tide hove her off again, fortunately without injury. It was hard work all this time, and, when done, Captain Ballard expressed most warmly his thanks to the officers and crew for their efficient assistance.

The ship being safely moored in deep water, we spent a happy week; for parties from Norfolk came often to visit us on the ship, and we frequently went to Norfolk. On shipboard and in the city, dancing was the order of the day.

Andrew Jackson, President of the United States, visited us on the 29th. With him were other dignitaries. He was received by the officers in full dress, the whole marine guard, a national salute, and the yards manned.

We sailed for New York on the morning of July 30th.

When we were fairly at sea, " Man overboard!" rang through the ship.

"Throw him a line!" cried the officer of the deck. It was well thrown, but the man refused to take it, and soon sank beneath the waves. He was a deranged seaman, and thus committed suicide. It threw a gloom over the entire crew.

We anchored off Sandy Hook light, early on August 2d, and next morning, with two tugs, attempted to pass the bar. Could we do it? That was the question with us, as also with many on shore, for the New Yorkers wanted it proven that their harbor was available for the largest vessels afloat. We went over the bar with two feet of water to spare, and anchored near the battery.

Scarcely had we anchored when a seaman fell upon the deck from the fore topsail-yard. It was a terrible sight. I never want to see another such. Fortunately he was so stunned that he knew no pain, and soon breathed his last. He was buried in the New York Cemetery.

We were besieged with visitors while in New York harbor; perhaps five hundred a day, mostly the *élite* of the city. We gave them cordial welcome, and showed them all over the ship, though it was hard work, and became very monotonous.

The Common Council of New York City

came one day, and I was directed to bring them on board with one of the ship's boats. They were surely the most timid set I ever saw, especially their president. He asked my name and called me Captain.

"Now, Captain Trumbull," said he, "do you think this boat is safe?"

"O, yes, perfectly."

"Won't it sink?"

"Not the least danger."

"Nor tip over?"

"No, you need not fear."

"But I am very heavy!"

That was so, he was; so I said:

"Yes, sir; but she will carry twice as many as are to go to-day."

"Let me go first then, and get fixed; the light ones can come after."

Before I could prevent, he started, and stepped, like a land-lubber, on the gunwale. Of course the boat tipped. With a cry, he sprang back quicker than I supposed possible with so large a person.

"I told you she would upset!"

"No danger, sir, if you will step in the middle as I direct you."

At last I got him and the others stowed away. They clung to each other and the boat in a most amusing manner. Then, to get them up the side of the vessel was a task; but it was fun, too, and we rather enjoyed it.

While in New York, the gunroom, on the lower gundeck, was fixed up comfortably, and assigned to our mess. The mess is a pleasant one, consisting of six passed midshipman, three assistant surgeons, and two professors, one of mathematics and one of languages. Also the captain's clerk.

CHAPTER XX.

DISTINGUISHED PASSENGERS—A PERILOUS NIGHT—AN ENJOYABLE CALM—CHERBOURG—TO PARIS IN A FRENCH DILIGENCE.

THE *Delaware* was to take as passengers to France, Hon. Edward Livingston, as minister plenipotentiary to France, and his son-in-law, Mr. Barton, secretary of legation. Each of these gentlemen was accompanied by his wife.

On August 12th the vessel dropped down to quarantine ground, and on the 13th she passed farther out toward Sandy Hook. Just as she began to make the latter move, I was ordered to take a boat and crew of ten men, and set a citizen ashore; also to bring aboard any stores there might be on the wharf for the ship. I found, on landing, a quantity of ice for the minister, also a passed midshipman who belonged on the *Delaware*. A young midshipman had come with me on this errand.

Anticipating a long pull ere the ship was reached, I got a bucket of fresh water and some bread, butter, cheese, herring, and a bottle of wine.

The sequel proved that it was well I did so. A breeze from the northwest took the ship rapidly down the bay, and she soon disappeared through the Narrows. We followed as rapidly as possible, expecting to see her when we rounded the fort.

We left the landing at sunset, and passed the fort at dark, but no ship was to be seen. What should we do? I advised with the other officers, and we decided to pull for Sandy Hook light, twelve miles farther out, believing the ship would anchor near there. It would be a long pull, and a hard one; for the wind had kicked up a rough sea. We prepared for the ordeal by eating the "grub" I had brought. It took us till midnight to make the light; but no ship was to be seen, nor was there any light which could come from her.

Our men were completely exhausted with the hard pull of six hours; we determined, therefore, to land, if such a thing could be done. With this intention, we pulled for the shore close under the light. We were so blinded by its glare, that ere we knew it, we were entering a surf which would have swamped our boat in an instant, and drowned us all.

"Put the helm hard up!" I cried. "Pull men, for your lives!"

All knew the danger as well as I. They put their whole force upon the oars, and after a terrible struggle, we gained again the open sea.

Another council of war decided that we pull back to Staten Island, twelve miles away. Easier said than done. We tried it; but, when once fairly clear of the land, the wind, which was blowing a gale, with the tide, which was against us, carried us out to sea in spite of our efforts. We officers took the oars, and endeavored, by example, to inspirit the crew, but in vain.

Our situation was desperate. The sea was so heavy it made a complete breach over the boat, the men were utterly fagged out, and we officers not much better off. I put the officers to bailing and directed the men to lie on their oars for a little rest. In a moment they were unconscious, and sank, oblivious to danger, into the bottom of the boat. To rouse them was impossible. All we officers could do was to keep the boat in the best position to ride the waves, and to bail the water out as best we were able. Thus, till three o'clock, we drifted farther and farther out to sea. At three the tide changed. The men had now had some sleep, and, by hard work, we got them again at the oars. With the tide to help us, we held our own. I knew that in the morning the steamer *Hercules* was to come out to the ship. Half an hour after daylight we were gladdened by the sight of her. But we were far to the leeward of her course. Hope gave the men strength, and they pulled to windward with a will. In the meantime, I fastened a white frock to a boat-hook, and, Robinson Crusoe like, waved it as high as I could. Fortunately it was seen, and soon we were on the deck of the steamer. The men dropped on the deck like dead men, so great was their exhaustion. Never before did I have to exert my authority to get seamen to drink a glass of grog. The officers, too, were used up, and were soon asleep on the sofas. I kept moving, and, with the aid of a cup of hot coffee, the drowsiness soon left me. At eight o'clock we were on shipboard; at nine the *Hercules* towed us across the bar. At four P. M. Mr. Livingston and party came aboard, and we departed at once for Cherbourg, in France.

The weather proved favorable, and we had a delightful voyage. We were becalmed in midocean for three or four days. This time was improved by target practice. A cask was placed about a mile off, and at this we fired with a cannon. It was fine sport, and everybody enjoyed it. We came very close to it almost every shot, but no one hit it. The professor of languages, who was in our mess, was a little, near-sighted man, and a great favorite with everybody. Captain Ballard proposed that Professor Hopkins try a shot. The idea was thought a rich joke, and we all had a laugh at it.

"Can he hit the water?" was the way we put the query.

"I would love dearly to try, Captain, if you will give the gun the right altitude for me. I believe I can aim it all right," said Hopkins.

"That's fair, Professor," said the captain, adjusting the gun.

Then Professor Hopkins adjusted his spectacles, having previously wiped them, and aimed the gun. It was well done; for the ball flew straight to the mark. It struck the water a time or two, and, on the ricochet, knocked the cask to atoms. I believe everybody was pleased, though it teased the graduates in gunnery to be beaten. The professor was much elated, but he declared it was a chance shot.

Many fish gathered about the ship during this calm, attracted probably by the broken victuals thrown overboard. We got out our hooks and lines and went fishing. There were a shark and several dolphins. The seamen were bound to have the shark. They threw him several pieces of pork to whet his appetite, each of which he took in out of the wet in fine style, turning on his back and coming up under them, as is usual with these monsters. Then one was thrown which concealed a shark-hook. He took hold of it bravely; and it as bravely took hold of him. Then for a few minutes there was fun. The water about him was churned into foam; but he couldn't get away. There were some old whalers among the crew. They produced a harpoon, and, after several unsuccessful throws, lodged it firmly in the fish's carcass. With the two lines he was drawn on deck, still very active. So we gave him a wide berth. Several dolphins were also taken. Altogether it was an enjoyable calm.

In running up the British Channel we had an exciting race with a large English frigate. Each ship spread every possible stitch of canvas, but neither was the victor.

The Island of Guernsey was made on the 11th. The morning of the 12th an English pilot boarded us and conducted us safely to the harbor of Cherbourg, where we dropped anchor at 4 P. M. The town of Cherbourg amounts to little; but the naval arsenal is of much importance to France. The harbor is strongly fortified, and is made by a breakwater which has cost a mint of money. The docks are immense, and will take the largest ships in the world; but they are not so convenient as the big one at Norfolk; neither have they the lateral supports for vessels when on the stocks.

A steamer, with a ship in tow, had just arrived from Egypt. They carried one of Cleopatra's Needles—a present from the pasha to the king of France—and were bound for Havre. It—the Needle—is in three pieces, and is to adorn the capital in Paris. Three days after arrival, a party was formed to visit Paris—two hundred and fifty miles distant. Fortunately, I was one of them. There were fourteen of us— Captain Ballard, six from the wardroom, three from the gunroom, and four from the steerage. Those from the gunroom were Professor Hopkins, Passed Midshipman Thoms, and myself. We three had become intimate, and were glad to be together.

The purser gave us exchange on Paris, and the consul and prefecture of police fixed up our passports—those necessary evils in European travel—and we left the ship Sunday evening, to be ready to take the diligence at four o'clock, Monday morning. A French diligence waits for no one, nor does it call for any one. You must go to it, and be in your place ahead of time; for when the moment for starting comes, off it goes. So we got up at half-past three, and left our hotel through a pouring rain to go to the diligence-office.

"Paris!" said Thoms. "Never mind the weather; we're going to Paris!"

The captain expected his party to be introduced to the king, and directed us all to take our full uniforms, though we traveled in citizens' dress. Our baggage had preceded us, and was already packed when we reached the diligence.

A French diligence is a unique affair. It has four apartments. The most desirable and highest priced is the *coupé*. It is far forward, and seats three people. Next back of it in location, and next below it in price, is the *interior*, which has six seats. Back of this still, and yet cheaper, is the *rotunda*, having from four to six seatings. Over all these—on deck, we sailors would say—is the *imperial;* fare same as in rotunda. It has no seats. One must sit on the deck, *à la* Turk, or any other way that he can dispose of his legs. The driver or postillion sits up forward, and with him the conductor. The latter combines the duties of guard and manager. He wears a badge of office, keeps the waybill, collects fares, and is a general director.

I knew a little French. So I asked the conductor where we three went, telling him our names. He answered, "In the interior."

"What does he say, Trumbull?"

"He says in the hold—amidships."

In we all climbed, making, with some civilians, a full load.

Off we went in a few minutes, the four horses in a full gallop, which gait they kept most of the time. The number of horses used varies from four to twelve, owing to the nature of the road and the load. Six was the most frequent number. The vehicles are well named "diligences;" for they start on time and keep going, making about one hundred and fifty miles in twenty-four hours. Taking the roads, good or bad, that is fair progress.

They frequently drive the horses three abreast. When they first did that thing, Thoms was looking at the procedure out of one of the windows.

"Trumbull," said he, "look here! They are rigging a yardarm abaft the aft horses."

Sure enough, they were. They had spliced the doubletree so that a third horse could be hitched along the right side. The diligence was very comfortable, and we rather liked it.

The old dukedom of Normandy, through which our course first lay, is a pastoral country. It is a vast, level meadow, covered with herds of cattle, with their herders caring for them. Butter and cheese are the principal products.

"Look at the ditches, running everywhere!" said Mr. Thoms. "Funny, isn't it?"

"Not when you understand it," said the professor, who knew much that others did not. "They use those in place of fences."

Sure enough, not a fence was to be seen, and every farm and field had a ditch around it.

Every ten or twelve miles there was a post erected, on which was a full-length image of our Savior on the cross.

At St. Loo, perhaps forty-five miles from Cherbourg, we breakfasted. We were hungry, and the meal was so good, we tarried too long. Hopkins left the table before Thoms and me. When he reached the door, he saw the diligence had started. He called back:

"She's weighed anchor and sailed, boys!"

Sure enough, she had, with the wind in her favor. We gave chase, overhauled, and boarded her, by which time we were out of wind, though the diligence still made progress.

"Well," said I, as soon as I could speak, "time, tide, and a French diligence wait for no man!"

At Caen, which we reached at seven that evening, we changed to another diligence—that is, all but four of us did. Thoms and I were of the four. We could not get seats; and the best we could do at six next morning was to anchor on deck—that is, take the imperial. As the day looked fine, that was well enough; but soon it began to rain, and it kept it up. The leather, supposed to cover us, leaked badly, and we got very wet. To mend matters, I grew very sick— so sick, I almost wished I was on shipboard again, even though I should miss Paris.

"Too bad, Trumbull!" said Thoms. "Your breakfast did n't suit you."

"That's it! I'm wondering what it was. These French dishes are fearfully and wonderfully made. I found temptation and distress in the dish of meat."

Toward night I succeeded in exchanging for a seat in the interior, and did much better. We were passing through a pleasing country, with here and there a chateau of the feudal times. They are usually three-fourths of a mile back from the road, with a triple row of beech-trees, extending from the chateau to the highway, on each side the driveway.

By daylight next morning we were in St. Germain, where the king, Louis Philippe, has a royal palace.

St. Germain is on an eminence, overlooking the valley of the Seine. The view is a charming one, and the ride of twenty miles down the winding road will never be forgotten.

Midway between St. Germain and Paris is

Malmaison, erected by Napoleon, and presented to Josephine at the time of his divorce from her. Its style is truly royal, and splendid pleasure-grounds surround it. Here, after his marriage to Marie Louise of Austria, he used to visit Josephine, whom he passionately loved; but whom he had basely put aside for reasons purely ambitious and political, thus foully blotting an escutcheon than which the world has not produced one otherwise more brilliant.

About seven o'clock on the morning of September 18, 1833, it was my great happiness to enter the gates of Paris. It was a moment of supreme enjoyment. Soon we passed the triumphal arch erected to Napoleon.

"We're here, Trumbull! we're here!" said Mr. Thoms.

"Yes; and I feel as though this magnificent arch was for my especial happiness," said I.

Soon we crossed the Seine, and stopped at the Bureau des Messageries, where our baggage was overhauled, weighed, etc.; then, to the Hotel de Montmorency, where the rest of our party were stopping. It was full, only part of our company being there. We went, therefore, to the Hotel des Princes, where we staid while in Paris. It is in Rue Richelieu, a fine house, near the Boulevards, being close to the center of the city.

CHAPTER XXI.

Paris — Cemetery of Père-la-Chaise — Ney — Jardin des Plantes — Versailles — St. Denis — Royal Gallery of the Louvre — Fish-Market — Notre Dame — Pantheon — Disappointment.

THE day of our arrival at Paris was spent in resting. The next day, Thursday, Thoms, Hopkins, and I took a carriage to see the sights.

"Where shall we go first?" I asked.

"To the cemetery of Père-la-Chaise," said Professor Hopkins.

"The cemetery!" exclaimed Thoms; "that is the last place to go to, I thought, and you make it first. But I am with you, so drive on."

The cemetery of Père-la-Chaise is named for the confessor of Louis XIV. It is north of the city, about one hundred acres in extent, and surrounded by walls. At the date of our visit it was the common burying-place of Paris. It is modern, having been used for sepulture only since 1804. Many distinguished people are here buried. The monument which attracts most attention is that of Abelard and Heloise; but for it we did not care a great deal. When we came to a plain, simple grave, marked only by a rough stone on which was the word NEY, we cared much.

"I consider it an honor to stand at the grave of Marshal Ney," said Professor Hopkins, removing his hat—an example we all followed.

"Napoleon pronounced him 'the bravest of the brave,' yet his grave is almost unmarked."

"It was unmarked till one of his old soldiers scratched his name on that stone with the point of his sword," said I. "You can scarcely read it; but I would rather see that name scratched there by the hand of a loving comrade than the chiseling of the finest artist on the purest marble."

"So would I!" said Thoms. "And just think what those comrades had to do!"

"What do you mean, Thoms?"

"When he was condemned to be shot, this man—the bravest of the brave—stood erect and composedly said: 'My comrades, fire on me.' They did so, and he fell with twelve bullets in his heart."

We next visited the Jardin des Plantes, called

also the Musée de Histoire Naturelle. It was founded in 1626 by Louis XIII. The celebrated naturalist, Buffon, devoted himself, with persevering zeal, to the interests of this garden. So dear was it to the French populace, that, during the Revolution, it was respected, and no injury done it. All kinds of animals and plants are here collected. There are, first, a botanical garden, with spacious hothouses and greenhouses; second, several galleries for the scientific arrangement and display of specimens from the animal, vegetable, and mineral kingdoms; third, a gallery of anatomy; fourth, a gallery of botany; fifth, a menagerie of living animals; sixth, a cabinet of natural history; seventh, an amphitheater, with laboratories for public lectures on every branch of science connected with natural history. This museum is the richest in the world, and so extensive that I will not attempt a description. It took us till dark to go through it and give it the most cursory examination.

Very tired were we when we reached the hotel that evening.

"Now for supper, boys, and then to bed," said Professor Hopkins.

"To bed!" cried Thoms. "Not by a long time! We will rest ourselves by going to the Académie de Musique Royale to see Madame

Taglioni dance. Go to bed when you can go nowhere else!"

Of course we went with Mr. Thoms; for the whole city of Paris was raving over the wonderful dancing of Taglioni. Europe had never before seen such a dancer as this Italian lady, who has recently wedded a peer of France.

The next day we went, by diligence, to Versailles, and spent a most enjoyable day. But Versailles would take a volume for description. As such descriptive volumes are abundant, I will not try to describe the sights of that day in this meager journal.

Saturday morning we went to St. Denis, six miles north of Paris. We had our first experience with a cabriolet—a kind of a carriage, much used by the poorer classes, as it is cheap. We liked the economy; but the forward wheel on the larboard side struck a breaker in the shape of a kit of mackerel, which fell from a cart just as we were passing. The wheel was wrecked, and we sailors were stranded on the roadway. We completed the journey, perhaps a mile, on foot, Thoms declaring that it was "a pretty kettle of fish" that made walking necessary.

The town of St. Denis owes its celebrity to the fact that its church was the chosen burial-place of the French kings from the earliest date of French royalty. Saint Denis was martyred and buried where the church now stands, about the year A. D. 250. The superstructure has been several times torn down, that it might be rebuilt larger and finer. The present edifice is pure Gothic in style, in the shape of a Latin cross, three hundred and ninety feet long by one hundred wide. No other church in France has ever been so rich in relics as this; but the year 1793 saw their dispersion. The Oriflamme—that celebrated banner, for ages the palladium of French nationality—was long kept in this building.

Napoleon found this church much out of repair, and, in 1806, began its restoration, having the vault of the Bourbons cleared out that those of his own dynasty might there have sepulture. The high altar of the church was made for his marriage with Maria Louisa. It is of veined black marble; and the royal monogram, of gold.

Many of the tombs are very fine, being adorned with statuary representing the departed monarchs—some in an erect posture; others in a recumbent one.

The latter part of the day we spent in the Royal Gallery of the Louvre. When examining our passports for entrance, our autographs were taken, as were also statements of our native country and the hotel at which we were stopping. I am not foolish enough to attempt a description of this, the finest gallery in the world. It occupies the whole space from the Louvre to the Tuileries, being a fourth of a mile long, and is filled with the finest paintings in the world. Those which pleased me most were the "Shipwreck of the Menelaus" and a scene in the Deluge.

That evening we rested again by going to the opera, where Madame Taglioni was dancing.

Sunday we went where all good people go; viz., to church; selecting the Church of Notre Dame. In trying to find it without a guide and on foot, we wandered into the fish-market, where we had an awful time. These piscatorial venders seemed to think with the poet Tusser:

"All's fish they get
That cometh to net."

They were bound to sell to us; for why should we come there, if not to buy? Purely in self-defense, we bought a few fish to quiet their clamor. Then we hunted our way out of this labyrinth, and gave the fish to a beggar. We reached the church in time for mass.

The Church of Notre Dame is on the Island La Cité, in the River Seine, where the first settlement was made. 'Way down the ages, a heathen temple stood where the church now is.

THE PANTHEON, PARIS.

It gave place to a Christian edifice, which, in 365 A. D., was dedicated to Saint Stephen. The present structure was commenced in 1010. It has been often rebuilt, enlarged, and improved. The present church is in the form of a Latin cross; length four hundred and fifteen feet, width one hundred and fifty. The front is remarkable for its fine statuary. The bell is quite an institution. It was hung in 1682. Multiply that date by twenty, and you have very nearly the weight of the bell and clapper—the exact figures being 32,000 and 976, which state the respective weights in pounds. Both the church and bell are immense; and the elegance of the interior is in accord therewith.

For a *buono mano*, one of the brothers showed us about the noble building, when mass had been said. The choir was most competent; among the singers being many artists from the Italian, French, and comic operas. There is a high and elegant altar, before which Bonaparte was crowned. I stepped forward to occupy for a moment the exact spot where the coronation took place; but the old monk put me back in short order, much to the amusement of my associates.

We visited the Pantheon that afternoon. Originally the Church of St. Genevieve, it is now considered a monument to the memory of those who fell on the 28th, 29th, and 30th of July, 1830, their names being engraved on tablets. Among many others, Voltaire and Rousseau are here buried. The dome of this building is the finest in France. The frescoing, which covers a space of three thousand two hundred and fifty-six square feet, cost nearly $20,000. We went to the top of the dome, getting a fine view of the city.

Paris is so immense—there is so much to see, which can not be described in a meager journal like this—that I concluded not to try to follow our every movement. Suffice it to say that we staid four more days, and saw all that could be crowded into that time. So many books descriptive of Paris are extant that I will refer to them, in future, for reference.

Our immediate party—Thoms, Hopkins, and myself—had one grievous disappointment ere leaving the city. We expected to see the king—Louis Philippe—and had brought our "Sunday clothes" for that purpose. About noon on Wednesday we learned that the king had requested Captain Ballard, and the officers in the city with him, to call the ensuing day at the Palace of the Tuileries, when he would be happy to see them.

We at once hunted up Captain Ballard, who said that he thought it would be well for us from the gunroom to decline being presented to the king, as it was then too late to send our names in to the minister of the marine before his office would close. He had sent in the names of the wardroom officers early in the day, and why he should have treated us with such incivility as to leave our names off the list he did not attempt to explain. It was an arbitrary move of Captain Ballard, to which we had to submit. The only comfort we got was the knowledge that he saw what he had done in the true light, and was abundantly sorry for his discourtesy. Keenly disappointed and grieved, we engaged seats in the coupé, and started next day for Cherbourg to join the ship.

Captain Ballard and party called, according to program, at the Palace of the Tuileries, and met Louis Philippe, who invited them to dine with him the next day at his palace at St. Cloud, which they did.

La Fayette also invited them to visit him at La Grange, which also they did. Thus were we deprived, by an arbitrary decision, of this second pleasure, which any American would enjoy far more than the first.

So badly did the captain's party, as well as ours, feel about this matter that these visits were a tabooed topic, and never talked about on the ship.

CHAPTER XXII.

AGAIN AT MAHON— CHANGES — A TRAGEDY — A RASCALLY TRICK WHICH TAKES US TO NAPLES — DIVINE SERVICE IN A GRAND CHURCH.

THE *Delaware* sailed from Cherbourg on the 10th of October, 1833, and with no special incident, save a gale of great severity and fifty-six hours' duration in the Bay of Biscay, and a brief stay at Gibraltar, arrived at Mahon on November 2d.

Upon that day I was put in charge of the main gundeck, an arduous position, which kept me occupied from early morning till eight o'clock at night.

The ship was moored alongside the naval arsenal, refitted, and overhauled throughout. We remained here all winter, with little variety, save such as we could get from balls and parties, and writing letters home when a chance to send them occurred. During the winter I twice got letters from home—most gratifying; for letters are the greatest boon to the sailor on a strange sea.

On the 12th of February, Commodore Patterson hoisted his broad pennant on the *Delaware*, thus making her the flagship. There came with him his wife, three grown daughters, and two sons—one of the latter being a midshipman, the other serving as captain's clerk. They were quite an acquisition; but to accommodate them, we had to shift the quarters of most of the officers of the vessel. The shifting we did not enjoy.

Much change occurred at the coming of the commodore, other than this. Captain Ballard left us for the frigate *United States*, which had been the flag-ship, Captain John B. Nicholson coming to us. Many exchanges among the subordinate officers also took place. I was to have gone to the frigate *United States;* but, at my personal request, Commodore Patterson suppressed my orders to the *United States*, and retained me on the flagship.

"Good!" thought I. "That means a tour through Egypt and Palestine."

I learned, while in Mahon, that my old friends, the Cochlins, had returned to England.

Not till the 6th of May did we get away from Port Mahon, and not till the 13th did we reach our port of destination—Toulon—so strong and so constant were the head winds.

In the harbor of Toulon we found the United States ship *Constellation*, and we learned from her officers of a terrible accident—or, rather, blunder—which had occurred with the *United States* frigate but a few days before, and which bid fair to rupture the pleasant relations existing between the American and French navies.

The *United States* had occasion to fire a salute of seventeen guns, and the gunner was directed to draw the shot from eighteen, leaving one gun for reserve, in case any should miss fire. After the salute was fired, occasion arose for another salute of twenty-one guns, and the gunner was ordered to prepare for it, using the eighteen just emptied and three additional. He failed to remove the balls from the last three guns, and they went whizzing through the French shipping. One shot struck a frigate in the fore-chains, just abaft the spare sheet, piercing her bulwarks and passing through her iron galley. It at last brought up against the pommelion of a gun, where it burst, the pieces killing three men, and seriously wounding two others.

Naturally, great excitement and rage among the Frenchmen followed this terrible tragedy, and with the utmost difficulty did the French officers prevent their crews from firing on the *United States.*

The matter was happily adjusted in a short time, but not till it had been carried to the Chamber of Deputies in Paris, and a purse of a thousand dollars made up by the crews of the *Constellation* and *United States* for the relief of the families of the deceased sailors. This purse the French Admiral declined to receive, but it was conveyed to the families by private hands. The *United States* had just sailed upon our arrival.

Many of us visited Marseilles while the ship lay at Toulon. It was my good fortune to spend an evening while at Marseilles, at the house of Mr. Fitch, our navy agent. Commodore Patterson and family were visiting there. I greatly enjoyed going one evening with them to the opera.

On May 21st I received a leave of absence for three months, sent me by the department at Washington, at the request of Senator Hendricks. I could use it or not, as I wished. Going to the Commodore, I said:

"I have just received this, Commodore." He examined it, and asked:

"What do you want to do, Mr. Trumbull?"

"I would like, sir, to remain with the *Delaware* till after the visit to Egypt and Jerusalem, and then go home on the *Constellation*, if she does not sail before that."

"She will not sail, Mr. Trumbull, till after we fall in with her again in September. So you can stay with us till then."

"Thank you, sir!" said I, taking my departure with my cup of happiness full.

On the 3d of June we sailed for Marseilles, having as guests on board Mr. Fitch, wife, and daughter.

On the evening of the 7th, Mr. Fitch gave a grand ball for our entertainment; some three hundred invitations. We counted on a fine time; but alas! when the time came, the wind was blowing a gale, and it was an utter impossibility for a boat to leave the ship. Some of the officers were on shore. They went, and, with eighty guests, had a good time; but it was a great disappointment to all.

A couple of days later we weighed for Leghorn. We had favoring winds, and a race with a whole fleet of French men-of-war and merchantmen; but the *Delaware* felt her oats, and sustained the honor of her flag by running right through them, and leaving them all behind. Some of the men-of-war died hard; but we ran them down the horizon, just the same.

Forty-eight hours put us at anchor in Leghorn Roads. A party for Florence was made up. As I had been there a few years before, I did not join it. Moreover, I hoped to go to Rome, but was disappointed, as the ship would not touch again in Italy.

I spent the 13th of June in Leghorn. Professor Hopkins was with me. We visited the English burying-ground; but I was a little blue that day, owing to disappointment at not going to Rome.

"Trumbull," said Hopkins, "the best thing for the blues is to take a bath and put on a clean shirt."

"The bath is well enough, but don't you dare insinuate that my linen is soiled. It was fresh this morning; but I do need some new clothes. Let's have a bath."

We each took one—warm—and I must say it was the finest bath, and in the most elegant bathhouse, I ever enjoyed. Then for the clothes.

Clothing is very cheap. I got a complete undress uniform. The coat cost $11; fine black pantaloons, $6; black silk vest, $2; in all, $19 for a suit which in the United States would have cost $40 if not $50.

On Wednesday, June 18th, we got away from Leghorn. A happy company indeed were we; for we were to visit Egypt and the Pyramids, Jerusalem, Damascus, Rhodes and Cyprus, Smyrna and Greece. The weather was all that was possible for enjoyment, even beneath Italian skies. We coasted down between Elba and the main land through the Piambino Channel. It was delightful, though our progress was slow, for the *Shark* was in company with us. She is a slow sailer, and we had to shorten sail to keep from running away from her. We had hoped to see Rome from the vessel; but this slow progress put us opposite the city after nightfall, and we were disappointed.

We had not expected to touch again in Italy; but, to our surprise, we discovered that the supply of fresh water was very low. One of the cooks so reported to the quartermaster. I happened to be in conversation with him at the moment. He was surprised; for a full supply had been taken at Leghorn.

"Do you know, Mr. Trumbull," said he "that there is mischief afloat?"

"Why do you think so?" I asked.

"Some one who was determined to stop at Naples has let that water go to waste to compel the vessel to stop for more. It is a rascally trick; but we will have to stop."

I suspect the quartermaster was right.

We approached the Bay of Naples at night. Never was mariner guided by an older or more brilliant light from a more magnificent lighthouse than were we. It was nothing less than

Vesuvius, in an active eruption. It was forty miles away; and daylight found us still outside the harbor. Having gotten within six or seven miles of the entrance of the mole, we were becalmed. It was Sabbath morning. Never was the holy day passed amid more pleasant surroundings. The Bay of Naples is one of nature's masterpieces, and art has done much to intensify the beauty of the scenery. The calm was a delight, and we luxuriated in our surroundings.

It is but a short step from communion with nature to communion with nature's God; and when the hour for divine service on the quarter-deck arrived, an appreciative audience assembled. Our enjoyment of the service was the more, for we had—what is uncommon on a man-of-war—both instrumental and vocal music. The chaplain has had for several weeks a choir in training. This was their first appearance in public. They had made good progress, and their singing was a great addition to the service. The fact that Saint Paul had been in the glorious church—the Bay of Naples—in which we were worshiping, added much to the interest; for near Baiæ, just on our left, was the place called Puteoli—modern Puzzuoli—where the apostle landed on his way to Rome. (Acts xxviii, 13.)

The calm continued till Monday morning. The moon was at its full, and that calm Sabbath night was one of the most entrancing I have ever seen. Luna's mild yet brilliant light, associated with the frequent flashes from Vesuvius, illuminated a scene of beauty never to be effaced from memory.

It would take three days to lay in a supply of water. Were we sorry some rascal tapped the supply? This diary shall not be marred with a confession. We would surely see Naples. Would we be able to visit Vesuvius? Only the violence of the eruption would prevent. The lava could be seen at night, running down the side toward Portici. It was half-way to the base, and might stop us, should we attempt to ascend the mountain.

CHAPTER XXIII.

NAPLES—TOMB OF VIRGIL,—GROTTO OF POSILIPPO—GROTTO DEL CANE—LAKE AVERNUS LAZZARONI—ASCENT OF VESUVIUS—AN ERUPTION.

ABOUT eleven o'clock, Monday, the breeze came. At half-past one, our ship, as also the *Shark*, came to anchor in the bay already mentioned near Naples.

The *Constellation* was there, making arrangements to take a couple of statues to America. They were to be placed in the Capitol at Washington.

No sooner had we anchored than guides for Vesuvius swarmed about the vessel. A party of five of us engaged one, and at four o'clock we went on shore to see the sights.

"Where shall we go first?" asked Mr. Thoms. (As usual, Thoms, Professor Hopkins, and I were together. Two lieutenants completed the company.)

"There is no question," said the linguist, "as to the biggest thing here; and we will go there first."

"Of course," said I, "Vesuvius is the biggest thing; but we are to go there at night."

"Vesuvius!" said the scholar, with a sneer. "I mean the tomb of Virgil."

"We are reproved," said Thoms, taking off his hat most submissively. "To the tomb it is."

We took a carriage, and drove down the Corso, the great promenade of Naples. It borders the city on the south, facing the water, and carried us to the west. The tomb is in a romantic spot, upon an acclivity, embowered in shrubbery, and almost inaccessible. Professor Hopkins was much impressed at standing by the resting-place of the dust of this most illustrious poet. He uncovered; and, out of regard for him, we all did likewise. The professor also indulged in some very apt quotations from the poets. To them we listened attentively; but Thoms thought less of Virgil than did Hopkins. He said:

"Professor, I am not surprised at the poetry. Virgil once stirred the muse in me till I mused out an original couplet."

"I would love to hear it. Can you not give it to us?" asked the professor.

"Think I can. Here it is:

'*Arma virumque cano;*
I hardly think I'm sane, O!
I can not sing the horrid thing.
Get licked, or try again, O!'"

"Thoms," cried the professor, "is nothing sacred with you? You are an inveterate iconoclast."

"And you, my dear friend, must always go to a grave the first thing. It was so at Paris; it is so here; and I verily believe, when we get to Egypt, you will think the Pyramids paramount to all else."

Near the tomb is the Grotto of Posilippo. When, why, and by whom this so-called grotto was excavated, is not known, though it is supposed to be of Roman origin. It is a tunnel a fourth of a mile long through a ridge of rock; width twenty-two feet; height varying from forty to ninety; intensely dark, save as a line of lanterns dispels the gloom. Near the farther end is the village of Puzzuoli, or Puteoli—Saint Paul's landing-place—which we had seen the day before from the ship.

The "Grotto del Cane" is also near here. As every one knows, it is a small cave, the entrance to which is higher than the floor. In this cave is generated carbonic-acid gas, which, being heavier than the air, collects on the floor until it reaches the height of the entrance; then the excess flows over the doorsill and down the valley. A man can walk in here with impunity; for his mouth and nose will be above the level of the gas; but the mouth of a dog will not, and the gas will soon kill him. So it will a man, if he lies down. We all walked in, but—strange to say—neither of us would lie down. We wanted to prove that the name was correct, *Grotto del Cane;* but where was the canine? There are many ways to make a living; and here were boys with dogs to hire, in case we should want partly to test the destructiveness of the invisible gas, or to sell, if we wanted a proof absolute. We hired.

> "He who fights and runs away,
> May live to fight another day;"

and I suppose that dog was ready for business when the next party came. Breathing the gas is not painful; for it produces stupor very quickly. In a minute the dog was, for all practical purposes, dead; but the fresh air revived him speedily, and he was ready "for other worlds to conquer," apparently as well as ever. Here also is the famous Lake Avernus of the mythology; and the natives point out the River Styx. They do not point out the original Charon; but they have improvised a trade in his memory, and, for an obolus in the shape of a modern coin, will ferry you across on their backs. We did not cross. The lake is a dreary place, in the crater of an extinct volcano.

About a mile from the lake are the ruins of ancient Baiæ. Here flourished Julius Cæsar, Domitian, Nero, and others. This was the scene of luxury, but, alas! of licentiousness as well.

We returned by the same route, took an extra turn on the Corso, ate supper, went to the theater, and, at midnight, were ready to start for Vesuvius.

In every city in Europe which I had yet seen, there were many poor and miserable people; many of them were beggars. In Naples this class was numerous, though they all did not seem miserable. Many of them were as careless and happy as gypsies. Lieutenant Barker, of our party, had been here before, and was well informed. When we came out of the theater, I said:

"Lieutenant, who are all these people sleeping in the streets?"

"They are called the Lazzaroni."

"Why do n't they go home?"

"They have no home. They live in the streets; eat, sleep, cook, and beg in the streets. They seldom work, and, as you have seen, are a merry set, without a care. There are about thirty thousand in Naples."

At midnight we entered a carriage, being provided with food from the ship, and with some old clothes which Lieutenant Barker told us to bring. The carriage-ride took us to Portici. It was a delightful moonlight trip, though the last of it was very disagreeable from the ashes which fell about and upon us, as we were to leeward of the mountain. At Portici we left the carriage, put on our old clothes, and mounted mules. It was a new style of navigation for us sailors; but we all got off, under convoy of the cicerone, save Barker. He cried out:

"I guess I'm aground, boys. She won't budge."

"Port your helm!" we cried.

"No use! She brings her head about, but the stern stands fast."

"Starboard with it! May be you can work her off."

"The ears ought to do for mainsails," said Thoms.

"Yes; but I think it is a *spanker* she needs," said Barker.

So thought the cicerone. He found a board, with which he raised enough wind to loose her from her moorings. She started with a lurch, and then plunged forward, bows under. Her cargo was badly shifted, and we feared it wou'd go overboard, but it did not; and soon her helmsman brought her up with a round turn, a ter which she behaved beautifully.

We were to go two and a half miles by mule power, which would take us up to an altitude of twenty-five hundred feet. Our route lay over fields of old lava, some of comparatively recent deposit; some of centuries ago, and now covered with soil, in which flourished vineyards and orchards.

About daybreak we reached the Hermitage, where the Franciscan monks endeavor to promote the comfort and welfare of tourists. They furnish provisions, *lachrymas Christi*, and prayers, each for a consideration.

"We have enough provisions," said Hopkins; "how about the 'tears of Christ?'"

Lieutenant Jones, who was a quiet man, said:

"That's a sacred subject, and it's sacrilege for us to make light of it, and especially for these monks to offer, or pretend to offer, such a thing for sale."

"That's so," said I; "and I am sure we are sadly in need of prayers, but I don't like the kind you pay a fixed price for."

Therefore we did not stop at the Hermitage.

Arriving at what is called, very properly, the cone, we disembarked, and proceeded on foot. The sides of the cone are quite steep, and composed of loose ashes and cinders; the footing is insecure, and the ascent very laborious. We had to climb up twelve hundred feet, and it took us an hour. Immediately upon our right was a stream of molten lava, fresh from the crater. Its progress was slow; for as it cools, the outside hardens into a crust, and dams back the fluid center. The fluid steadily accumulates, however, till its weight is sufficient to burst the crust; then it rushes rapidly for some distance, and this process is repeated.

We met about a score of people coming swiftly down the cone.

"Go back! go back!" they cried. "It is getting worse, and you will all be killed!"

We believed it was perhaps getting worse—but go back? Not for an instant did we think of it. We had heard the explosions in the suburbs of Naples, eight miles away. As we progressed they had increased, till now they were enough to scare any but the stoutest hearts. We had not come to Italy for our health, and our hearts were stout. Up, therefore, we went, and soon stood upon the rim of the outer crater. Dante's "Inferno" does not describe it. Surely, I can not. The heat was so great as to be painful. The earth, which we had felt to quake ere we left the carriage miles away, fairly rocked beneath our feet. The noise of the explosions equaled—ay, surpassed—that of parks of the heaviest artillery. We had come prepared to witness a mighty display of nature's omnipotence. Our anticipations dwindled in comparison with the reality, for imagination can not attain such heights as the verity demanded. We stood upon the verge of an ocean of flame. Far below was the seething, boiling caldron, the heat of which was sufficient to reduce to a molten mass the rock-ribbed hills. Countless masses of glowing lava were constantly shot from this boiling caldron, which resembled vast skyrockets in their ascent, but unlike them in that they descended while still glowing white with heat. Nearly all of them fell within the rim of the inner crater, and rejoined the seething fluid mass, only to be ejected again. Many, however, lit upon the edge of the inner crater, which they rapidly converted into a cone by accretion. Already had this eruption added hundreds of feet to the height of the cone. Grand as was this sight, it was every few moments eclipsed by an explosion of far greater intensity, which carried the flames far above the mountain-top, and illuminated the land and sea for leagues—ay, scores of leagues. To the verge of this fiery abyss had we audacious men dared to climb. Conversation was impossible. There we stood, like minions of the very fire-fiend.

Observing a mass of molten lava fall near and just below me, on the inside of the rim upon which we stood, I determined, if possible, to make upon it the imprint of a dollar; that imprint, when made, I hoped to detach from the greater part of the mass, and preserve as a souvenir of the visit. Cautiously I made the descent. The air was stifling, and the heat beneath my feet almost more than I could endure. Fully appreciating my perilous situation, I stooped and placed a silver dollar upon the glowing mass. It was softer than I had supposed, and my dollar sank deep therein. So sank my spirits, for dollars were scarce with me, and I must not lose my precious coin. To rescue it was now my sole aim. I succeeded, and had a souvenir to carry with me from Vesuvius. But it was in the shape of a burnt hand, and not an imprint of the Goddess of Liberty.

One explosion of great severity expended its force in an oblique direction. Apparently it was aimed at us. Molten masses fell all about us. Small pieces struck us repeatedly. One of considerable size, large enough to have done injury, brushed Mr. Thoms's clothes, and a monster piece, of some twenty pounds weight, bid fair to light fairly upon my head; fortunately, it had within itself some of the explosive principle

It split in two, one piece falling upon either side of me.

The outer crater of Vesuvius is said commonly to be three miles in circumference. In my opinion, it is much less than that. Of the size of the inner crater we could form no adequate opinion, owing to the turbulence of the scene.

Had our visit been at a time when the fires were dormant, we could with safety have descended some two thousand feet within the bowels of the mountain. Grand as that would have been, we rejoiced greatly that our visit had been when the fires were fiercely raging.

Lieutenant Barker told us of his first visit to this celebrated volcano. It was at a time of quiescence. Far down into the yawning chasm they climbed, and walked out upon the cooled surface of a lava-bed, which was molten beneath. The heat was painful to the feet. To show how hot was the lava beneath them, the guide thrust his staff through the crust. It was speedily ignited, and brought to the surface brightly burning.

Previous to the eruption of 1631, the space between the outer and inner craters was a wilderness covered with forest-trees and abounding with game. Farther back, previous to the year 79, when Pompeii and Herculaneum were destroyed, this mountain was not known to be volcanic. What was then the crater of an extinct volcano, was a lake, and about its borders the rebel Spartacus had his stronghold. How great have been the changes!

An hour at the crater satisfied us and we descended. We came down the cone rapidly—for our steps in the loose and yielding cinders were almost equal to those of the wearer of the seven-leagued boots; sailed back in fine style on our mules to Portici, cleaned the grime from our hands and faces, resumed our better clothing, and at nine o'clock were in the carriage *en route* for Pompeii—distant nine miles—over the dustiest road I ever traveled.

CHAPTER XXIV.

POMPEII AND HERCULANEUM—MUSEO BORBONICO—STATUES OF PEACE AND WAR.

POMPEII and Herculaneum, as everybody knows, are buried cities. They were nestled, in their prosperity, at the base of Mount Vesuvius.

This mountain was not then known to be volcanic. On the 24th of August, A. D. 79, it declared itself to be so. Dense smoke, the harbinger of a terrible convulsion of nature, issued from the summit. Spartacus's old stronghold was filled with a mixture of mud and molten lava, which rapidly rose in height till the pressure broke away the western side of the mountain, and emptied itself down the declivity. The city of Herculaneum lay in its path. The fiery flood completely covered it and filled every space about it. Having cooled, this mass of lava held the city in its embrace so closely that its very existence was forgotten, and for seventeen centuries it knew not a place in history. The same fiery ordeal wiped from the knowledge of men the city of Pompeii, though in a way quite different. Vast quantities of ashes were belched from Vesuvius. A strong wind from the north carried them over the city. So abundant were they that the city was entombed beneath them. So suddenly came the lava upon one city and the ashes upon the other, that escape for many was impossible. In Pompeii, probably this fatality was hastened and intensified by the sulphurous fumes which came with the ashes.

The elder Pliny, the Roman admiral, was near with his fleet of ships. He hastened to the rescue, but only to swell the mortality by the death of himself and his sailors. Some think he died of the poisonous fumes; others, that the ashes fell upon his vessels in such quantity as to sink them, thus drowning the occupants.

Many persons in Pompeii had not time to leave the work in which they were engaged. They were found, after eighteen centuries, just as they had fallen. Our guide was a good one, and told us much. As we entered the city he said:

"This the Appian Way; it is one of the

chief streets. And here is the amphiteater, which has passages under the ground for the wild beasts to come through from their cages."

"Who discovered the remains of the city?" one of us asked.

"I don't know. You know the ashes are only twenty or thirty feet deep, after settling for centuries, and the tops of some of the towers and the highest part of Diomede's house stuck out, and probably some one dug about them to see what they were, and so found the city."

"Who was Diomede?"

"A rich man, who lived in a big house with three stories."

The streets of Pompeii are narrow, the widest but thirty feet, and paved with lava-stone, in which are to be seen the ruts worn by carriages. The houses are also of lava, mostly one-story, and in those of greater height the most important apartments are in the lower story. The roofs were flat, and the great weight of the ashes broke most of them in. Diomede's elegant villa was on the Appian Way, in the suburbs. It was spacious. The frescoes on the walls could still be seen, and revealed much as to the depraved taste of the household. Everything movable had been taken away. Before removal, they told the spectator much of the customs of the first century. It was a sad tale, revealing the utter licentiousness and depravity of the times. Diomede's house was one of the finest, and his family among the aristocracy. In an apartment supposed to belong to his daughter were found articles of jewelry, intrinsically of great value, yet of such immodest and sensual import that a description of them is not permissible. A skeleton, supposed to be that of Diomede himself, was found at the back door of the house. Upon the remains of the finger was a valuable gold ring, and within the clutch of the skeleton hand was a bunch of keys. Undoubtedly he was trying to escape. Near him was the person of a servant, the opinion being based upon the fact that a burden of silver plate and money was being carried. In a corridor beneath this house the skeletons of seventeen people were found. They had undoubtedly fled thither for refuge. Of course we saw none of these things, but the guide told us of them.

The Temple of Isis is of much interest. It is not large as compared with other ruins of heathen temples, and everything portable has disappeared, being now in the museum in Naples. The remains of a priest were found here, as he was officiating at the altar; of another, as he sat at table eating. A third was trying to escape from an apartment by cutting through a wall with a hatchet.

SCENE IN POMPEII.

We remained two hours in Pompeii, and then returned to Portici. The city of Portici is built upon the volcanic tufa which overlies the ancient Herculaneum. In 1708, workmen, in digging a well, brought up some very fine mosaics. This led to investigation, but from the slow habits of the Italians, nothing was done till 1738, when the Government took hold of the matter. The well had entered the precincts of the theater. This building was excavated, bringing to light some elegant statuary, mosaics, and frescoes. They were of finer workmanship than those found at Pompeii, but of no greater excellence from a moral point. The excavations are more limited than at the other city, owing to the hardness of the tufa, and a fear that the overlying city of Portici might be endangered by extensive undermining. From seventy to one hundred and twenty feet of this tufa covers Herculaneum, being in seven distinct strata, the result of a like number of overflows of lava.

Several buildings besides the theater have been excavated, but the ruins are not wholly uncovered as at Pompeii. We descend to them as one would into a mine. Provided with torches, we made the descent, and investigated the theater. It was large enough to have accommodated ten thousand people. We were impressed to see how completely the molten mass of lava had filled every corner and crevice. It had carried everything movable before it. At one place a human being had been forced to the wall, and held there. Chemical action had, of course, occurred in the body. It discolored the wall, and there before us was the outline of the form and countenance of this sufferer. It was not a pleasing sight. The place was sepulchral, dark, and gloomy; the walls were damp and cold. We therefore made a short stay.

"How strange it is," said I, to my associates, "that these people will live here in Portici, when at any moment Vesuvius may overthrow them as it did Herculaneum!"

"Yes," said Mr. Thoms, "it is strange; and I am told that there are probably other towns—at least, villas—beneath these strata of lava about Vesuvius; for in digging wells and foundations, evidences of hidden architecture are found. But where do we go next, Barker?"

"To the Museo Borbonico, as the museum of Naples is called."

We found the museum fine indeed, and of especial interest as the repository of all the articles taken from the buried cities—elegant statuary, mosaics, frescoes, and the like; but of far more interest to us were the common articles in daily use, such as cooking utensils, inkstands, pens, musical instruments, bridle-bits, spinning-wheels, locks, keys, skimmers, grates, andirons, mirrors, combs, tongs, curling-tongs, etc. They were odd, but their use was evident.

"What an insight these give us," said Lieutenant Barker, "into the daily life of the people of the first century!"

"Yes, indeed," said I; "and what a commentary upon the profligacy and licentiousness of the age are these nude statues, and the immoral themes represented in the paintings and mosaics! And to think of the best women in the community wearing such indelicate jewelry as we have seen here!"

"Why, Trumbull, you have n't seen the half! There is a room in this building where the worst things are kept. Only special persons are allowed to enter, for the exhibition is too revolting for the eyes even of the Italian populace!"

"Why, I thought an Italian could stand anything!" said I.

"It is fearful to what a degree of depravity the Romans sank at the time they were upon the pinnacle of political and intellectual power!" said the reticent Lieutenant Jones.

"That they could have done so," said the scholarly Professor Hopkins, "would seem a paradox. Yet this base sensuality entered into their very religious worship. Doubtless, when the Roman Empire became Christian, the worst of the statuary and paintings were destroyed. The same was true in Greece; for in all her glory of refinement, sensuality reigned supreme. Works of art, possessing great merit, were found where we have been to-day; but the people were debased and sensual in the extreme. The Golden Age of the Roman Empire, marked with full intellectual development and refinement, was accompanied by brutal force, instead of moral suasion; with the most impure and debasing sensuality, in place of chastened virtue. We admire the beauty of their classics, but blush at their practices."

"That means," said I, "that developing the intellect does not, of necessity, benefit the heart."

"Exactly. These people were as bad as those of Sodom and Gomorrah. They deserved a like punishment, and they got it."

From the museum we went to see the two statues intended for the Capitol at Washington. They were very fine, representing Peace and War. We all hope to see them in position when next we go to Washington. In the evening we visited the king's palace; and toward midnight strolled down the Corso, eating oysters at a number of shops as we passed.

We were tired, but it seemed as though we could not leave the lovely moonlight of the Bay of Naples to go between decks. But the eternal begging of the detestable mendicants helped us to a decision and a departure; and at two o'clock A. M. we were on board, tired, but well repaid for our labors.

CHAPTER XXV.

Stromboli — Scylla and Charybdis again — Burial at Sea — Egypt — Alexandria.

JUNE 28th found us trying to get out of the Bay of Naples. It took all day, as the winds were light and dead ahead. The next day, Sunday, it was better; and we got well to sea. Divine service of a most interesting and enjoyable kind was held, the choir again adding much.

At night we sailed amid the light of another of nature's light-houses—the volcano of Stromboli.

Monday we sighted Sicily; and evening found us at the entrance to the Straits of Messina, where are Scylla and Charybdis, which the ancient navigators so much dreaded. My friend Thoms had never been here before. He said:

"Do you think the captain will venture to enter the strait at night?"

"Why not?" asked I.

"O, the whirlpool, you know."

"I've been through there, Thoms, and I could go again in a ship's boat; but the wind is so light we can scarcely go anywhere."

Partly from necessity, therefore, and partly out of the bad reputation of these waters, we stood off till morning. The little *Shark*, however, our consort on this cruise, went ahead, with a mail-bag for Messina. The big ship flinching from the danger, and the little one facing it, greatly amused Professor Hopkins. He came in the forecastle, quoting Shakespeare:

"Wrens make game where eagles fear to perch."

The quotation was apt. Next morning a fine wind from the north took us through the strait at a nine-knot rate. Scylla was there on our left. We did not strike it, but we ran right through what should have been Charybdis. No whirlpool, and but little agitation of the water.

The *Shark* joined us opposite the city of Messina; but, alas! she had no mail for us.

The Fourth of July found us off the coast of Greece. It is *the* day of the year to an American; and we made it a gala-day, with much conviviality at the mess-table, and an evening with the ladies. We passed close under the southwest of Candia—the ancient Crete—and near to Calabosa, where we of the *Lexington* had the warm time with the Greek pirates in 1827. It was terribly hot on shipboard, and the snow-capped mountains of Candia looked most inviting; but we did not stop to play snowball, for Egypt was before us.

While off Candia, the shrill call of the boatswain sounded through the ship, followed by the hoarse voices of his mates, summoning "All hands to bury the dead; ahoy!"

The officers were informed, as usual, when all hands are called and assembled on the quarter-deck, headed by the commodore, and the chaplain in his gown. The crew collected about the larboard gangway. A seaman had died in the night, and we were assembled to pay the last sad rites to his memory. It was a melancholy and impressive scene, being the first burial at sea I had ever witnessed. The corpse was placed on a board near the gangway, and sewed up in a hammock, with a forty-two pound shot at the feet. At the commencement of the service, every head was uncovered, and silence such as is only heard on a quiet sea ensued, broken only by the voice of the minister and the gentle murmur of the waters as the ship slowly forced a passage through them.

When the chaplain said, "We therefore commit his body to the deep," the board was shoved from the bulwark, and the corpse at once disappeared, leaving nothing to mark the spot save, for a few moments, some air-bubbles. I shall never forget the horrible sound of the plunge of the body into the sea, and the rattling of the plank against the bulwarks, which closed this last act of kindness sadly rendered by his shipmates.

How vividly descriptive are Byron's words in his address to the sea:

"When, for a moment, like a drop of rain,
    He sinks into thy depths, with bubbling groan,
Without a grave, unknelled, uncoffined, and unknown!"

I was inclined to muse over this incident and the quotation, but was ruthlessly called to duty; for the boatswain forthwith piped down, and in a few moments the poor man was forgotten alike by officers and men. Forgotten? Perhaps the man was, but the incident never!

The evenings of this cruise were most delightful. We spent them on the poop-deck, in company with the ladies of the commodore's family. Our talk was mostly of Egypt.

"What do you expect most from, Mr Thoms?" asked one of the ladies.

"Why, let's see. The Pyramids are a big thing, but I expect more from ophthalmia, I think."

"Ophthalmia! Do you mean sore eyes?"

"Yes, ma'am. They say every third person in Egypt has lost an eye."

"We land at Alexandria, do we not, Mr. Trumbull?" asked Miss Patterson.

"We do, though we will have to anchor the *Delaware* some five or six miles out, owing to shallow water. You know the Nile has brought so much alluvial soil that it has filled the sea up all about its mouths."

"And the famous Alexandrian library. Too bad that was burned, is n't it?"

"Yes, indeed!" said I. "Do you remember what the conquering general said about it, the finest library in the known world?"

"I do not. What was it?"

"That if the books agreed with the Koran, they were unnecessary, and should be burned; if they did not so agree, they ought surely to be destroyed. That logic worked both ways, and the library went to the flames."

Such are samples of our talk as we neared the shores of Egypt. We went under peculiarly favorable auspices. The special object of our visit to Mehemet Ali's dominions was to establish more favorable commercial relations between Egypt and the United States. To aid in this, the *Delaware*, one of the largest and finest men-of-war afloat, was made the flagship, and she served the purpose well.

We were to visit Egypt as the special guests of the Government. All honors would be shown us, and all facilities extended to make our stay pleasant and instructive.

The pasha, unfortunately, was absent, being in Syria, where he had gone to quell an insurrection. We knew that Egypt was in a condition of misery, ignorance, and superstition, but we approached her shores with a feeling of reverence and respect for what she once had been. We respected the great antiquity of her monuments, and we remembered that here were cradled the arts and sciences. Moses, whom God had chosen as his great lawgiver, was prepared for his mission by being " learned in all the wisdom of the Egyptians." Solomon, whose wisdom was conceded to be superlative, was said to have "excelled all the wisdom of Egypt." No stronger description could be framed, for no more powerful ideal existed. Hither the sages of Greece and Rome repaired, as to the fountain-head of literature and learning.

It also was the scene of much of the most interesting history recorded in the Scriptures. Here Joseph was a slave and a ruler; here his brethren sought and found food, but also slavery, and thence they were miraculously rescued. We approached it with gladness and solemnity.

We saw land on July 13th. I had expected to see first the shafts of Pompey's Pillar and Cleopatra's Needle. In this I was disappointed. We saw nothing till within fifteen miles of land, and then we made the sandhills to the west of the city. Arriving within six miles of shore, we anchored.

Three days after, a party of us, some thirty in number, headed by the commodore and his family, went on shore to make the tour of Egypt. With us were our servants from the ship, for we were to provide and dress our own food.

The *Shark* took us into the harbor, and soon our feet pressed the historic soil of Egypt.

"Look there, Thoms," said I, the minute we landed. "There is your ophthalmia." I pointed as I spoke to a number of Arab children, who wore nothing save an air of distress, and a loose skin over their emaciated bodies. A little to one side were their parents, lying alongside their miserable mud hovels, in the hot sun, eating some very poor melons, which at this season constitute their chief food. They were half naked, and as miserable specimens as I ever saw. Thus did we see the abject condition of the natives the moment we landed, and the sad sight was before us during our entire stay in Egypt.

Modern Alexandria is a walled city of considerable commercial importance, and the location of the pasha's shipyard. The inhabitants are Egyptians (of Arab descent), Christians and Jews. The natives live in little huts, some six or eight feet high, and ten or twelve feet on a side, built from the ruins of the old city. Their part of town is most repulsive. The Franks, as persons from the west of Europe are called, have good homes upon wide, airy streets, much like those in European cities. It is west and north of the ancient city, between it and the sea.

The ancient Alexandria was once second only to Rome. It was named for, and was the pride of, him who wept that there was only one world to conquer. It was the center of literature and refinement. But this successor of Tyre and seat of the Ptolemies is now a mass of ruins. The blighting hand of Islamism has laid its desolating grasp upon this ancient metropolis and cradle of the sciences. At the time of its capture by the Saracens, the Arabian general addressed the Caliph Omar as follows:

"I have taken the great city of the West. It contains four thousand palaces, four thousand baths, four hundred theaters, twelve thousand shops for the sale of vegetables, and forty thousand tributary Jews."

To-day, what of these remain? Only Pompey's Pillar and Cleopatra's Needle are standing.

Pompey's Pillar is a misnomer. The shaft was not erected because Pompey was buried at Alexandria, as many suppose. It was erected in honor of the Emperor Diocletian and his conquest of Alexandria, in 296 A. D. It is a well-executed shaft of syenite granite, seventy-three feet in length.

It stands upon an inverted pyramid, which inscriptions thereupon declare to have been used centuries before in another monument. A Corinthian capital of ten feet surmounts it, upon which once stood a statue. The height to-day is about one hundred feet.

Cleopatra's Needle is a quadrangular obelisk, or spire, sixty-five feet in length, eight feet at the base, and covered with hieroglyphics. A similar shaft lies prostrate near by. They were, probably, the portals of some public building.

The ruins thereabout are extensive, but so covered with dirt and *débris* that they appear as mounds of earth. In these mounds may be seen broken shafts, columns, and pieces of statuary, as also much broken pottery, which attest the former opulence of the city.

Her glory is departed. The world-renowned Alexandrian library is no more. The Pharos, celebrated as a lighthouse, and one of the seven wonders of the world, no longer exists. Even the Island of Pharos, upon which it stood, may not be found in its insular capacity; for it is now a peninsula, and an important part of the pasha's shipyard.

> "Thy foes had girt thee with their dread array,
>   O stately Alexandria! Yet the sound
> Of mirth and music, at the close of day,
>   Swelled from thy splendid fabrics, far around
> O'er camp and wave. . . .
>
> Wake, Alexandria! Through thy streets the tread
>   Of steps unseen is hurrying, and the note
> Of pipe and lyre and trumpet, wild and dread,
>   Is heard upon the midnight air to float."

CHAPTER XXVI.

OFF FOR CAIRO *via* CANAL. THE NILE — THE DESOLATION OF EGYPT.

THE first of our journey to Cairo was to be by canal, and Mr. Gliddon, the American consul resident at Alexandria, had provided boats for us. Just how they were procured we did not know, but we learned the process the next day.

The best boat, as we all thought, was assigned to the commodore and his party. The lieutenants had one and the chaplain and an assistant surgeon another, the last being rather small. The surgeon was a dignified and pompous person, and could have appropriated a boat all by himself. We reefers had the last pick, but, the sequel proved, the best boat of the lot. As we were embarking, Thoms said:

"I do n't know about this, Trumbull! I 'm

a little afraid of the water. I've crossed the ocean only three times."

"Well, Thoms," said I, "the country is level and you may walk. But I will stay by the boat."

Things did look a little funny, and Thoms's ridicule seemed just. We kept up appearances, however, and showed our colors. The commodore's broad pennant was hoisted, not at the masthead, as the rigging did not favor that location, but at the yard end. From the mainbrace of each vessel proudly floated the Stars and Stripes.

Our crew consisted of eight or ten ragged Arabs. They seemed willing to work, however, and by sunset we were off on the raging canal.

"This beats all, Trumbull," said Thoms, "sailing on a canal!"

"Yes, just look at the commodore! Isn't it comical?"

"Indeed it is," he replied; "but nothing to compare with the doctor. Just see the dignity he is trying to assume among those dirty Arabs."

"A word as to this canal, Thoms; do you know about it?"

"Not much. Tell me."

"The present ruler, Mehemet Ali, had it built to connect Alexandria with the Nile. It is forty-eight miles long, ninety feet wide, and fifteen feet deep."

"Who told you all this?"

"The chaplain. You know he has been here before. This low salt-water swamp on the right, with which it connects at this end, is dignified with the name of Lake Mareotis. On the left, you see, are well-cultivated lands. As the country is level and the soil light, the canal was easy to build. How long do you think it took?"

"O, perhaps a year or two."

"It was done in six weeks; and to do it, two hundred and fifty thousand men, women, and children were compelled to leave home, and, at the point of the lash, do this work. Thirty thousand—about one in eight—died of disease and overwork ere the six weeks had passed. And then their bodies were thrown into the embankment to help along the work."

"Trumbull, you do n't mean that!"

"Indeed I do. The chaplain says they care nothing for the lives of the common herd here in Egypt."

"But, I understand, the pasha is energetic and public-spirited, and doing much for the country."

"He is—such things as render him more secure in authority and power; but he does absolutely nothing to help the masses."

At dusk we ate supper—the first in Egypt—coffee, bread, cold ham, and watermelon. The last are abundant and good. At this time of the year, the Arabs almost live on them.

An officer of the pasha, called a *cavasse*, accompanied our expedition, to afford protection and assistance. He had authority to call any one at a moment's notice; and he must obey.

Our boat had outsailed the others. The chaplain and doctor had abandoned theirs, and took passage with the commodore, whose boat was some better, though not much.

Most of the time the wind was favorable, and our progress all that we expected. At times, the curves in the canal would render the wind of little help, if, perchance, not a hindrance. Then the Arabs would jump in the water, swim ashore, and tow the boat by a line from the masthead. By sunrise we reached a settlement composed of mud hovels. They were teeming with human beings, who poured out of them in large numbers, to see who were coming, and to beg. This town, which is upon both sides of the canal, is called Atfeh. It is upon that branch of the Nile which forms the western side of the Delta.

We saw, with surprise, that at the end of the canal, which we had now reached, there was no lock or any similar contrivance.

"How does the water get into the canal?" we asked, and learned that when the Nile rises, it fills the canal, and that lasts till the next year."

While waiting for the commodore's boat, we visited the town. Destitution and misery were on every hand. The huts are of brick, made with earth and straw and dried in the sun. They are without floors, and swarm with vermin, as do most of the dwellings of the Egyptians. We bought some fruit for breakfast, and at six o'clock were standing upon the bank of one of the branches of the Nile. Yes, the Nile!—that wonderful river that cradled upon its bosom the prophet Moses. Among such rushes as these his little ark was nestled! Thus was I soliloquizing when Thoms, the iconoclast, asked:

"Trumbull, why was Pharaoh's daughter like a Wall Street money-lender?"

"I am sure I don't know. Why was it?"

"Because she drew a prophet from the rushes on the banks."

"O you sinner! to obtrude that old conundrum upon one at such a time and place!"

"Surely you can find no fault with the time; and, as this is only the Rosetta branch of the Nile, you would better reserve your ecstasies till we reach water from which Pharaoh's son probably drew the little girl."

"Thoms, what are you talking about?"

"About the little girl Moses, whom the king's son had the raising of."

"Why, you are crazy! Moses was a boy."

"You will admit that Moses was a sensible person; will you not?"

"Yes, of course."

"Well, Moses preferred to be called the daughter of Pharaoh's son, and would not wish to be so called unless a just regard for sex would justify it. My words are true. Moses was the (daughter of Pharaoh)'s son, as writing the expression *daughter of Pharaoh* in parenthesis will show you.

"I see your sophistry, young man. (Daughter of Pharaoh)'s son is different from daughter of Pharaoh's son. One makes the child a boy, and the other a girl."

When the commodore came, he gave us a great scare. His boat was so miserable, he thought seriously of going back to the ship; but our horoscope—I guess that is what one should call it in Egypt—proved favorable, and we went on.

We now learned the process of obtaining boats and crews. The cavasse pressed them into service. His power was feared, and instant, if not willing, compliance followed.

"Are the poor men not to be paid?" asked one of the ladies.

"Yes, they will be paid; but the cavasse will name the price, and it will be about half what they have been asking."

The entire populace was about us by this time, and all were begging. The women brought the children, which sat, perfectly naked, astride the mother's shoulders, with their hands clutched into her matted hair to prevent their falling. Those not accommodated upon the shoulders walked beside her. The cavasse carries a long staff, or baton, a token of authority. Its mystic power soon effected the transfer of our baggage, and we set sail on the Nile.

"Get the chaplain to come on our boat, Trumbull. He'll tell us a lot we don't know," said Thoms.

I invited him, and he came gladly, for our chaplain likes young people.

The wind was favorable, and we were soon going at eight knots an hour. Favorable winds may be counted on in ascending the Nile. It is the result of the intense heat over the land. The air is warmed and rarefied by the hot sands, and rises; the cool air from the Mediterranean to the north rushes in to supply its place. Thus is produced a typical sea-breeze, which blows from daylight to midnight, and of which commerce takes advantage.

"Chaplain," said Mr. Thoms, "tell us something about the Nile."

"What I know is at your service. You know that it rises far to the south of this, but just where is not now known; but it will be ere many decades. We are most interested in the Lower Nile. You know of the Delta, that it has several mouths, the chief being the Rosetta and Damietta branches, and that we are now on the former. For fifteen hundred miles the Nile receives not a single confluent. It is the means of communication throughout Egypt, and at the same time the creator of the country; for without the Nile, Egypt would be a sandy waste. With it, it is wonderfully productive. You know the Nile overflows every year. It begins to rise in June, and is at its height in September. It is about half-way up its banks now, as you know."

"How much does it rise?" I asked.

"That varies. Far to the south the rise is about forty feet; near the mouths it is only about four feet, as the water runs out speedily to the sea. In the vicinity of Cairo it is about twenty-five feet."

"Does it never fail?" asked Mr. Thoms.

"It never fails. I think the record covers three thousand years, and without a failure."

"Why such wonderful regularity?"

"It is owing to the perfect certainty of the rainfall in Central Africa. That is as constant as the change of the seasons."

"But does not the height of the rise vary?"

"It does vary, and on that depend the crops and the prosperity of Egypt for the year. The wonderful thing is, that it varies so little. Year after year it will vary but a few inches. If it falls short a foot or so, there is a scarcity in crops; if it is as much in excess, sickness ensues—notably the plague and murrain."

"What is murrain?" Mr. Thoms asked.

"A disease very fatal to cattle. In September this whole country, for a width on an average of a dozen miles, will be a lake. The villages are on the highest ground to be found, and are protected with dikes. They then are islands, and look very odd. If the Nile should not rise, there would be a terrible famine. If there should be a shortage in the rise for a few successive years—as in Joseph's time—famine would ensue. So you see, young gentlemen, how important to Egypt is the overflow of the Nile. And did you know that this rise of the waters first directed the ancient Egyptians to the study of astronomy, in which they became very proficient?"

"No, sir. How was that?"

"The Egyptians were the first nation to pay especial attention to the cultivation of the soil, and of course they wanted to know when to prepare for seedtime; in other words, when to expect the rise of the Nile. They noticed that when the star Sirius rose with the sun, the rise began. By this, therefore, they judged as to its nearness in time. Having the hint, they studied the other stars, and became the ablest astronomers among the ancients."

"How long does the river stay at its highest point?" asked one of us.

"About twelve days; and in that time it deposits on the land about a fourth of an inch of the richest nutriment, and that keeps the land in a productive condition. In fact, it will raise two crops a year, and some of it three."

"But only one is commonly raised, I understand," said Mr. Thoms. "Why is that?"

"Mainly the indolence of the fellahs, as Egyptian farmers are called. One crop takes little work, as the overflow leaves the ground in fine condition. But the second crop needs irrigation. That means work. Pools of irrigation water are left in various places among the plantations after the river falls. This water is lifted from the pools by Persian wheels and sweeps, (like our well-sweeps), and distributed about the land in ditches. Cattle, horses, mules, camels, and buffaloes are used to work these wheels, but, as the men have to work too, this second crop is usually not raised. One will keep soul and body together, and that is enough for an Egyptian.

"Again, if a surplus is raised, it will probably be seized by the Government, and taken as a tax. The pasha—like those who ruled before him—claims most of the land, and demands, as a tax, from one and a half to two and a half dollars per acre each year. The tax-gatherers take as much more. Every province has to pay a fixed sum. If one fellah is short, his deficiency is made up from his neighbor's granary."

"I should think they would hide their crops."

"They do try to. But the tax-gatherers are not indolent. They watch the farmers as closely as the fish-eagle does the osprey, and, at the right moment, pounce upon them. If the crop has been hidden, the terrible bastinado speedily compels the fellah to reveal its location."

"What a mistake such a course is!" said I. "It keeps the people ground down, and the country desolate."

"It does indeed!"

Going to his baggage, the chaplain got a Bible, and, handing it to me, said: "Read the sixth and seventh verses of the thirtieth chapter of Ezekiel."

Taking the book, I read:

"Thus saith the Lord: They also that uphold Egypt shall fall; and the pride of her power shall come down: from the tower of Syene shall they fall in it by the sword, saith the Lord

God. And they shall be desolate in the midst of the countries that are desolate, and her cities shall be in the midst of the cities that are wasted."

"Now, gentlemen," said the chaplain, "if that prophecy has not been fulfilled I do not read rightly the signs about me. Think of the wasted cities of Egypt! As yet you have seen but Alexandria. You know well from the ruins her former greatness, and you have seen her fallen condition. The desolation—the utter desolation—of the people, you have seen."

"To our sorrow, we have; but what," asked Thoms, "is the tower of Syene?"

"Syene was a city far in the south of Egypt, and that expression means from one end of the land to the other."

"I see; but do they ever sell these Egyptians as slaves?"

"Not exactly; though the pasha at times transfers villages, when the fellahs go with the soil, as do the serfs of Russia."

At this point in our talk, the wind became light, and we went ashore for a walk. The land here was well cultivated, and we saw corn and cotton growing, and evidences that wheat, rice, barley, sugar-cane, the indigo-plant, fruits, and melons were among the products. This was on the Delta; the other side of the stream was a waste of sand, with only a grove of palm-trees to relieve the dreary landscape.

"Do you know how they raise rice?" asked the chaplain.

"I do not," we answered.

"They sow it in the water just before the water falls. There is then little current, and it sinks in the mud, where it speedily takes root. 'Cast thy bread upon the waters, and thou shalt find it after many days,' is a figure drawn from this procedure."

CHAPTER XXVII.

An Egyptian Landscape—Alma Dancers—A Nocturnal Songstress—Milk, Whisky, and Chickens—A Sad Sight—The Nile Proper—Goshen—The Pyramids—Bulak—Warm Reception—Cairo—A Mad Doctor.

THE scenery upon the Delta was truly Oriental, and, from a distance, very pleasing. Immediately around us were the waters of the historic Nile, teeming with fish, as was shown by their often leaping therefrom. Near the banks were cattle at times, and buffaloes very often, standing in the water with only their heads and backs visible.

The water is the only refuge they have from the flies. At times a buffalo would be seen swimming across the river, with an Arab woman perched upon the back. Occasionally a crocodile would be observed basking in the sun upon the shore. The villages, which are numerous, are surrounded with groves of palm-trees.

251

Approaching them, at times, are seen camels and other quadrupeds of burden. The villages look well from a distance, but, invariably, close acquaintance dispels the pleasing delusion; for they are all filled with wretched and miserable people, and alive with vermin.

"Look there, Trumbull! What are those things on the bank?" at one time exclaimed Thoms.

"I don't know. Ask the chaplain."

But the chaplain did not know. An interpreter who was with us, did, however.

"Ichneumons," said he. "They hunt crocodiles' eggs."

They found them, too, as we could see.

"Let's land, and try to get a shot at them," said I.

"No! they sacred!" said the interpreter.

But we would not take "no" for an answer. Landing, we slipped up—or, rather, tried to—close to them; but they took to their heels, and, in a moment, were gone. We fired our pistols at them; but they are active creatures—a little larger than a cat—and soon were out of sight.

"My usual luck," said Thoms.

"Yes," said I; "but it is something to say we have hunted them."

There were many boats upon this Rosetta branch of the Nile, mostly engaged in commerce.

Occasionally we met a boat with a press-gang and their unfortunate victims—the latter chained together by the necks—on their way to some work which the pasha was having done, or, perhaps, to his navy.

It was again our fortune to have the best boat; that is, the speediest. We rigged up some awnings which kept off the intensely hot sun, and, with the breeze from the sea, made us quite comfortable. We often stopped to wait for the commodore and party, when we would visit the villages, and, for a trifle, buy such fruit and melons as we wanted.

We visited the city of Fouah. Size made no difference in the community. They were beggars, living in filth and distress.

The moon being near the full, the nights were beautiful. At one village we saw an immense pile of watermelons, and went ashore to get some.

"Ah!" said the chaplain, "here are some Alma dancers. Let's give them a few piastres, and set them in motion."

They were soon going; but, after the novelty passed away, they afforded little amusement. We were in shape for a lark. So one of our party produced a flute, and another a guitar, and we had a dance on the grass. Think of it—dancing on the Delta of the Nile! The

Arabs stood as though entranced; then they tried to imitate our movements. But we might as well have tried to copy theirs; and they brought up on their beam-ends. They applauded us, however; and that we liked, for we were considered as contesting for honors with the Alma dancers.

"That beats all!" said the good chaplain. "Officers in the United States navy vying in a dancing contest with a lot of miserable Arabs, for the approbation of their still more miserable associates!"

"We are out for adventure, Chaplain, and 'all is fish that comes to our net,'" was our reply.

"A couple of you show them a little fencing," said the chaplain. No sooner said than done. In an instant, two of us had crossed swords and were hard at it. The Arabs took it in earnest, and every heel among them tried to see how quickly it could help its owner out of danger. We were masters of the field, and returned to the boat, making the air resound with the noise of our hilarity. Just then the commodore's boat arrived.

"O dear!" said one of the ladies, "you are having all the fun."

"It is a little jolly!" replied our worthy preacher.

At midnight we had to lie up, owing to failure of the wind. The first night, an Arab woman came down to the river bank, and, sitting down, sang a song for us, descriptive of the want of herself and her children, and praising the beauties and merits of the latter. It was her way of begging. The song was an attempt at improvisation. It impressed me deeply, and I will never forget our nocturnal songstress of the Nile.

The second night, an old Arab man brought us a present of milk. We were pleased, and gave him, in return, a bottle of gin.

"Now, boys, that's too bad! He will be drunk in an hour," said the chaplain.

The man was much pleased, and showed us his gratitude by bringing us a score of chickens. The chaplain was right, as usual; and ere morning the man was dead drunk.

As we neared the head of the Delta we saw some seven thousand Arabs—men, women, and children—at work, carrying dirt in baskets. Turkish masters were over them with the cruel lash, which they used most freely, age and sex obtaining no favor. It was a hard thing to see. They were making a kind of dam for the pasha, by which he hoped to water the Delta at *low Nile*, as it is called.

About four o'clock P. M. of the third day we

passed the Damietta branch, and were on the Nile proper. There, on our left, was the land of Goshen! The iconoclast was not near, and I gave my thought full sway. There dwelt, for four centuries, the chosen people of God! There they suffered a grievous bondage! Thence were they miraculously released, and the passover instituted! These had been with me favorite themes of Bible study, and I was deeply impressed. The chaplain saw it, and joined me, saying:

"That is a scene long to be remembered, Mr. Trumbull."

"Yes, indeed! I am much interested."

"Do you know why it was called the land of Goshen?"

"No, sir."

"From an Arabic word—*gush*—meaning *heart*. The heart is very precious to the animal; so was this land to Egypt. Hence the name. Do you know why the Israelites were located in Goshen?"

"I think I do. It was a grazing country, and they were a pastoral people—their business being to raise flocks and herds. Thus it was an excellent place for them, and Joseph wanted to do the best possible for them; and it was nearest the land from which they came, being in the north of Egypt, and east of the Delta of the Nile."

"Good, Mr. Trumbull! Do you think of any other reason?"

"No, sir, I do not."

"Did the Egyptians like shepherds?"

"No, sir; they considered them an abomination."

"Do you know why?"

"No, sir."

"Because Egypt had been overpowered, generations before, by the Cushites—descendants of Ham by Cush, his oldest son—and ruled by them for two hundred and sixty years. They reduced the Egyptians to bondage. These Cushites were a pastoral people, coming probably from about the Persian Gulf. Their kings were known as 'the Shepherd Kings,' and reigned during the fifteenth and sixteenth dynasties. So hated were they that all shepherds became an abomination to the Egyptians. Now, that was probably another reason why Joseph had his family stop in Goshen, rather than conduct them farther into the country, and excite the animosity of the populace against them."

Our conversation was interrupted by a cry of delight from some of the party:

"There are the Pyramids! There they are! The Pyramids! the Pyramids!"

Of course we could see nothing else for a time. They looked very small from such a distance; but they were the goal for which we were journeying, and we were glad.

That evening we had some of the old Arabian's chickens for supper. Our crew asked permission to dress them for us, which we willingly granted, though a little surprised at the request. We had tried to get them to eat some of the food prepared by our cook—such as beef, fish, etc.; but their superstition was so great they would touch nothing cooked by a Christian. In dressing the fowls they reserved for themselves the offal and heads, from which they made soup. In this they dipped their coarse black bread.

"Disgusting!" thought I; "but only another proof of the truth of prophecy, which declared that the Egyptian should fall from his high estate."

We reached Bulak, the port of Cairo—where we were to leave the boats—at eleven o'clock at night. Upon going ashore in the morning we found abundant preparation for our reception. There were the pasha's master of horse; four cavasses; thirty fine Arabian horses from the pasha's private stable, elegantly caparisoned, and each accompanied by a groom; and the pasha's private carriage for the ladies. It was a magnificent vehicle from London, adorned with gold and silver, lace and velvet, and drawn by four splendid gray horses. Extra servants and runners were in attendance, to care for the baggage.

The American vice-consul, Mr. Geo. Gliddon, was also there to welcome us, and to invite us to make his house headquarters during our stay. Our reception was almost regal. We expected much, but the reality greatly exceeded our anticipations. Never before had the pasha's carriage been occupied unless he himself were of the party. That we should mount his Arabians was a concession scarcely less to be expected.

Our cavalcade, when formed, was indeed imposing. First went the cavasses, with their batons. They cleared a passage speedily, and, when necessary, thrust a camel through a doorway into the shop of some affrighted merchant. Then came the master of horse, escorting the gorgeous carriage. After the carriage, on a magnificent steed, white as milk, rode Commodore Patterson. We officers, in full uniform, were next, and, with our magnificent mounts and brilliant trappings, were by no means an insignificant part of the procession. In all we were forty horses and one hundred souls.

We were the cynosure of all eyes, especially the carriage; for never had the people seen it except the pasha were within. Thus we passed through Bulak, and out onto a plain of some two miles width, separating Cairo from the river. About eleven o'clock we arrived at the consulate in Grand Cairo. It is a large, spacious building, well adapted for our use and comfort.

Speedily converting our entire party into one large mess, we were at home in Cairo, and all well pleased with our surroundings. All? No, not all. After having been anchored half an hour, we heard a familiar voice from without. Its owner was evidently as mad as a hornet, and berating everybody and every thing—especially all things Egyptian—in most unmeasured terms. We knew the voice instantly, and the commodore said:

"Why, what's wrong with the doctor?"

He appeared to tell his own story.

"What's the trouble, Doctor?" we asked.

"Trouble enough! I'm disgusted with Cairo and Egypt and all there is in them, and I'm glad the curse of God is upon the country."

"Careful, Doctor! Careful! That is strong language. Tell us what's the matter," said the commodore.

"Why, I'm no horseman, and I did not like to stride one of those fiery Arabians, so I chose a donkey. But the thing would n't go, and soon I was back among the servants. They could not understand a word a Christian could speak, and there I was. You were all soon out of sight, and even the servants went on, for my driver left me to take care of myself. And then the beggars took absolute control, and plagued the life out of me. If the driver had n't come back I would have been there yet. Trouble enough! And I 'm done with Egypt!"

It was very, very funny. Had it been any one else, only sympathy would have been aroused; but this man was so pompous we could see only the comical side of his trouble, and we laughed till we cried. It was hot and dusty; his rage and effort to get the donkey along had covered him with sweat. Every grain of dust stuck, and he was about the color of the Arabs who had surrounded him.

CHAPTER XXVIII.

GRAND CAIRO — TOILETS — TOMBS OF THE CALIPHS — THE CITADEL. — THE MAMELUKES — TOMBS OF THE MAMELUKES — THE GOVERNOR'S RECEPTION — MUST I SMOKE? — THE HAREM — VIEW FROM THE CITADEL — ON, AND PROPHECIES ABOUT IT — JOSEPH'S WELL.

GRAND Cairo, the capital of Egypt, is a city of the tenth century. Population, at our visit, something over three hundred thousand, consisting mostly of Arabs; but there are a number of Jews and Christians. The last are a low type, not much above the Arabs. Each class has a separate part of the city, and communication between different parts is regulated by gates across the streets, and a gatekeeper, who opens the gate when any one wishes to pass.

The houses are mostly two or three stories, the lowest story having no windows; the upper stories are latticed, and project past the lower.

The first stories of the best houses are built of stone, brought from the quarries of Mokattam, near by, or from the Pyramids. The walls which surround the city are built largely by stone from the Pyramids. Most of the houses are constructed of sun-dried brick, plastered with mud. The roofs of the houses are flat, and provided with what is called a moolguff. It is a kind of a shed, built in the roof, open to the north, and so constructed as to catch the sea-breeze, and divert it down through the rooms of the house. It adds much to the comfort of the dwellings, and secures good ventilation.

The streets are narrow and dusty. Owing to the projection of the upper stories, they are also dark, and, as dogs and stock are the only scavengers, very, very filthy.

Ladies of the higher class seldom appear in the street; then they are usually riding in the saddle, and always closely veiled, only the eyes being exposed. The veil extends nearly to the feet. A cloak of silk, looking like a black shroud, covers the person. Socks of yellow Morocco leather and Turkish slippers, complete the outer toilet. The lower order of females wear a tunic, or gown, of blue cotton, a lengthy veil of black crape, the head being covered by a piece of cotton, and the feet bare.

The men wear the turban, full gown of blue cotton or brown woolen bound to the waist by a girdle, full trousers, and, at times, slippers; at other times, the feet are bare. Long beards are also worn.

The children are scantily clad, and almost universally are diminutive, sickly, and sore-eyed.

The Tombs of the Caliphs afford the best specimens of architecture about Cairo. We visited them the afternoon of our arrival, using the pasha's horses and carriage. In fact, these horses were at our service during our stay. Mr. Gliddon, the vice-consul, was our guide in all our rambles about Cairo; and a better one could not possibly have been obtained. His sole aim was our pleasure.

The tombs are without the city, in the edge of the desert. They were built by Saladin the Great. They constitute an immense rectangular building, with a minaret at each corner. Within are an immense court and a mosque. In fact, minarets and mosques abound everywhere about Cairo.

Monday, the 21st, after an early breakfast, we went to the citadel. It is south of the city, upon Mount Mokattam, the summit of which it crowns. We approached the citadel through a wide passage, cut from the solid rock, and closed at the end toward the city by massive gates. It was in this passage that the terrible slaughter of the Mamelukes occurred in 1811. A word as to these Mamelukes. They were originally Turks and Circassians, brought as slaves to Egypt to serve in the army. Of more natural ability than their masters, they gradually grew in influence, as in numbers, till, in 1254, they made one of their number sultan. This Mameluke dynasty ruled wisely, for their own good and for the prosperity of Egypt, till the time of Selim I, of Turkey, who, in 1517, overpowered them and added Egypt to the Ottoman Empire. However, Selim had to continue twenty-four Mameluke beys as governors of provinces. Again they became influential; and when the present pasha, Mehemet Ali, was striving for authority, these Mamelukes were his chief opponents.

"And right in this passage where we now are he got rid of them by foully murdering them," said the chaplain. "Under the guise of an invitation to the citadel to witness the ceremony of making his son a pasha, Mehemet had the gates of this passage closed on four hundred and seventy of the leading Mamelukes. While he coolly looked on from a hidden window, complacently smoking his pipe, these men were fired on by the Albanians upon the walls, and every one killed. Escape was impossible; and all, save one, for whom death was desired by this monster, were brutally murdered. That one was a little tardy, and did not reach the gates ere they were closed."

"He is a monster!" said I; "and if this was not such a fine horse, and so very convenient, and so very cheap, I would refuse to ride him."

"Curb your indignation for policy's sake, Mr. Trumbull, and ride on," said the chaplain. "The Mameluke who escaped did so by leaping his horse from the wall, forty feet high, killing the animal but saving his own life. Mehemet followed the surviving Mamelukes till he effected their extermination. I will tell you more of him when convenient, if you would like it."

"Indeed I would," was my reply.

The tombs of the Mamelukes are near the citadel. They are odd affairs, and look more like summer-houses than depositories for the dead. They have several apartments, and are often nicely carpeted.

"What are the carpets for?" asked Mr. Thoms.

"To make it pleasant for these people when they rise from the dead," said I. "You know, the Egyptians believe in the immortality of the soul and the resurrection of the body. They think pleasant surroundings when they rise will help them along, and they arrange the graves accordingly."

"Just as the Indians bury bows and arrows

and tomahawks—sometimes a pony, too—to help the braves along in the happy hunting-grounds," suggested Mr. Thoms.

"Exactly!" said I. "And these Egyptians believe that, as long as decomposition can be kept from their bodies, their souls will hover about the bodies. That, they greatly desire; and hence they have studied and learned the art of preserving the bodies for an indefinite period, as the thousands of mummies show us. The ancient Egyptians were the first to teach the immortality of the soul. Their belief, which was quite complicated, included, also, the transmigration of the soul, after it had left the human body, through the bodies of various animals. This transmigration was continued for a period of three thousand years; and the good passed through the long ages of time much more easily than did the wicked. Toward the last—if I understand it—the body was to be again possessed and animated by the soul; and the more perfectly the body was preserved, the better for both soul and body through eternity. Hence the intense desire of the Egyptians to preserve the body, and the perfection to which they brought the process of embalming, as shown by the mummies."

"Do you know the process?"

"Only partially," said I. "No one knows it

all to-day; for the process died with the persons of some of these mummies. But they evacuated all the cavities of the body—such as the cranial cavity, the thorax, and abdomen—because their contents were very susceptible to decomposition. These cavities were, after being emptied of their natural contents, filled with spices and other preservatives. Then the limbs and body were wrapped in bandages, called mummy-cloths, containing preservatives."

"How did they empty the cranium? I do n't see how they could," said Mr. Thoms.

"Through the nostrils. There is a thin layer of bone between the nostrils and the brain, full of holes like a sieve. The nerve of smell, the olfactory nerve, passes through these holes from the brain to the nose. It is easy to break through that layer of bone. Through the passage thus formed the brain was removed."

"Where did you learn all that, Trumbull?"

"O, I read a little medicine when I was a boy."

"Well, it seems to me that a body without brain, lungs, heart, stomach, and bowels, would not be worth preserving."

"True. But the ancients thought otherwise. Hence the mummies."

"Here, gentlemen," said Mr. Gliddon, "is the mausoleum of the present pasha. In it are the remains of Deftudah Pasha (if I remember the name). He was immensely rich, and a modern Hazael. Some think Mehemet feared him and desired his removal. Be that as it may, the man suddenly died after drinking a cup of coffee with the pasha, and all his riches became Mehemet's."

"Why, what a monster Mehemet Ali must be!" was the comment of us all; but we kept it to ourselves, for we wanted no fight with him, and his horses were very fine.

"Two of the pasha's sons, his wife, and nephew," continued Mr. Gliddon, "are also buried here. You see their tombs are well cared for, carpeted and neat, all but the nephew's. That is unfinished, as you see."

"Why is that?" we asked.

"He was a cruel monster, and no one cares to finish his tomb. Once he was sent to correct some rebels who had murdered the governor of the province—a heinous crime, indeed—but his severity was more than commensurate with the offense; for he collected ten thousand together, and burned them to death."

"The hideous monster!" we cried. "He deserves no tomb! Tartarus will be none too hot for him!"

"And once," continued Mr. Gliddon, "his groom forgot to have a horse shod, as directed.

'I'll teach you to forget my commands!' he cried in anger. 'Here, take this man,' he said to the attendants, 'and have him shod.' It was done, and in a day or two death kindly came to the sufferer's relief. His favorite companion was a fierce lion, which he had cowed into submission by his own fiercer spirit. He is gone, and he has practically no tomb, which, to the Egyptian, is one of the most terrible calamities possible."

Having arrived at the citadel, the governor, in the absence of the pasha, received us in state within the walls of the palace. Having done the formal part required, the governor descended to the level of social converse in a pleasing way. For half an hour he chatted in French with the commodore, while pipes mounted with diamonds, and coffee, were passed around.

Thoms sought occasion to whisper to me:

"Sorry you don't smoke, Trumbull. Pretty fine pipes, and first-rate tobacco."

"I suppose," said I, "that politeness requires me to light a pipe; but I never did such a thing before, and I will draw lightly."

"Go easy, boy, and it won't make you sick."

I scarcely smoked at all, though pipes were offered so often within the next few days, and such elegant ones, that, had I wished, I could easily have learned to smoke. To me, smoking did not seem right, and I would not do it.

The governor offered us every assistance in his power to make our visit enjoyable, and the ladies were invited to visit the harem of the pasha. It was an innovation upon the customs of all time; for never before had a Christian female been admitted within its precincts.

While they were gone, we strolled through the elegant apartments of the seraglio, and visited the Royal Academy, where the pasha has several hundred youths in training for the army and navy.

Upon their return, the ladies told us that they were received at the gate by male attendants, from whence, to the palace, they were escorted by gayly-dressed girls, dancing, and playing on instruments of music. The sultana there received them, and conducted them to the saloon.

"O, it was fine!" said one of the ladies. "You should see the dresses! They were decidedly Oriental, and the head-dresses just sparkled with diamonds."

"And there were a hundred attendants," said another of the ladies, "and, like the rest of the daughters of Eve, they were full of curiosity, especially about our clothes; and when the ladies' backs were turned, they investigated our toilets in the most unceremonious manner. It was not pleasant; but—poor things!—they never see anybody or anything."

Justice to the citadel demands a word relative to the fine view it commands of the country around. To the north, and almost below, is the city of Grand Cairo, with its many mosques and minarets, bordered by the tombs of the caliphs and Mamelukes. Farther north, some five miles, is a grove of palm-trees, which marks the former location of the city of On—called also by the Greeks, Heliopolis; and by the Hebrews, Beth-shemesh. Herodotus says Heliopolis was the center of learning and science among the Egyptians. Here Joseph "went in and out before Pharaoh." Here he married the daughter of the priest of On. Here Moses was taught in "all the wisdom and learning of the Egyptians." But On knew not the one true God, and was given to idolatry, even above other cities about it. These very names—On, Heliopolis, and Beth-shemesh, in the Egyptian, Greek, and Hebrew respectively—signify the "City of the Sun," and show that the worship of the sun was the nucleus of their religion. So wholly was it possessed by idolatry that the Hebrews gave it another name, as a nickname; it was Aven, or Beth-aven, meaning "the house of vanity"—that is, idolatry.

The prophet Jeremiah said (xliii, 13): "He shall break also the images of Beth-shemesh, that is in the land of Egypt; and the houses of the gods of the Egyptians shall he burn with fire."

Ezekiel said (xxx, 17): "The young men of Aven and of Pi-beseth shall fall by the sword: and these cities shall go into captivity."

These prophecies have surely been fulfilled, the instrument probably being Nebuchadnezzar.

Only one thing remains in an erect position to mark this former center of learning in the great land of Egypt. It is a column of red granite, seventy feet high, covered with hieroglyphics. It is considered the most ancient work of this kind, in a perfect state of preservation, which the world can produce. We could faintly discern the top of the column as it protruded above the palm-trees.

These facts about On, which the chaplain gave me, added much to my interest in the view.

Farther to the north spreads the land of Goshen; still beautiful in its productiveness, but probably greatly below its former condition.

To the west of Goshen was the Damietta branch of the Nile; then the Delta itself, with the other branches; and beyond that the desert.

To the west of us the conspicuous features

were the Pyramids, and ruins of Memphis, Bulak, and Old Cairo, and the Nile, amid green banks, bordered by palm and other trees; beyond, the desert.

When the ladies returned from the harem, we all went to see Joseph's well, as they call it, though it was probably built by Saladin. Perhaps Saladin being called also Joseph, may explain the name. The well, which was built to supply the citadel in case of a siege, is dug from the solid rock. Its depth is four hundred and twenty-six feet. The shaft, which is square, is thirty feet on a side for half that depth; then it is twelve feet on a side for the remainder. We went down to where the well narrows by a winding, filthy passage; but we did n't stay long. The water is raised by horse-power, and is brackish.

From here we returned to the consulate, the ladies going by the lions' dens; we gentlemen, by the manufactories of small arms, cannon-foundry, etc. The pasha is very proud of them, and it was to please him that the commodore wished us to go. They are all run by steam. That motive-power is a wonder to the people here, as ten years ago they knew nothing of it. We were not much interested, however, and were glad to get home; for by that dear name we called the consulate.

CHAPTER XXIX.

MEHEMET ALI—PALACE OF IBRAHIM—A WISE DOG—THE SLAVE MARKET—A SYRIAN HOME—DINNER AT THE HAREM.

AFTER supper that evening we were serenaded by a band of Egyptian musicians. The music had no charm, save its novelty; and that soon wore away. So I said to Thoms:

"The chaplain promised to tell me something about the pasha when he had a good chance. Let's ask for it now."

"All right; I would like to hear it."

The chaplain was willing, and said:

"Mehemet Ali is surely one of the most singular men of the age. He was born in 1769, in Albania. He is eminently a self-made man. In early life he was a tobacconist; later, a tax-gatherer; and finally, a soldier. In 1798 or 1799 he entered Egypt with a contingent of three hundred Albanian troops, to assist the English against the French, who were invading Egypt under Napoleon. Military ability of no common order soon showed itself, and he rose rapidly. Deep and well-laid schemes aided him, and he became commander of all the Albanians in Egypt. In 1806 he was recognized by the Porte as viceroy of Egypt and pasha of three tails."

"What kind of a thing is that?" asked Mr. Thoms.

"You should know that; so I will tell you. The badge of a pasha is a horse's tail. It floats from a staff surmounted with a gilt ball. There are three grades of pashas. The lowest can display but one tail; the second is allotted two, while the highest may attach three to his standard. Now, this high authority brought him in conflict with the Mamelukes, who had long been the practical rulers of Egypt. How this struggle ended in the massacre of the Mamelukes in 1811, we have been to-day reminded. The Porte now became alarmed at Mehemet's growing power, and, with a hope to break it, gave him command of an expedition into Arabia, against a religious sect called the Wahabis. Mehemet's son Ibrahim aided him. Victory was theirs in Arabia, and thus the pasha was made more formidable than ever in Egypt. Next he captured Kordofan, and opened up a most nefarious trade in black slaves from the interior of Africa.

His next move was to reorganize his army and navy after European models; but he got a severe check when the combined naval force of England, France, and Russia annihilated the fleets of Turkey and Egypt in the Bay of Navarino. In 1832, with Ibrahim's help, but without any justification, he subdued Syria, and added it to his dominions.

"And he is there now, is he not, trying to keep the Syrians under subjection?" I asked.

"He is. He is an able, energetic ruler; but he does nothing save that which will increase his power. The people are ground down by taxation, and kept in ignorance. The few schools are only for his friends, who, through education, will increase his authority. The people are forced into the army and navy. The wheels in the factories he has established turn only in his own interests. Farming is neglected; for he grasps the surplus above what is necessary to sustain life. The population has dwindled nearly one-half since his reign began; and the desert is rapidly encroaching upon the arable land, from want of cultivation. But Mehemet is firmly fixed; and thus is fulfilled the prophecy, 'There shall be no more a prince of the land of Egypt' (Ezekiel xxx, 13); 'And I will make the land waste, and all that is therein, by the hand of strangers' (Ezekiel xxx, 12); 'It [Egypt] shall be the basest of kingdoms; neither shall it exalt itself any more above the nations; for I will diminish them, that they shall no more rule over the nations' (Ezekiel xxix, 15). Now, young gentlemen, if those prophecies are not being fulfilled, I do not rightly read the signs of the times. An utter stranger is on the throne of Egypt, and there is no prince of Egypt. These strangers are desolating the land, and it is becoming waste. Surely, *surely*, Egypt is the basest of nations, not only in the character of her people, but in the low position she occupies among nations—she who was once the most exalted."

Much impressed with the chaplain's words, we retired to rest.

The next day, Tuesday, we spent mostly out of the city. First, out of compliment to the pasha, we visited his cotton-factory and calico print-works. They were three miles out, but the ride with our splendid mounts was a delight. Returning, we examined the shot-tower. All these industries respond to the magic influence of steam.

The feature of the day was a visit to the palace of Ibrahim Pasha, the son of the ruler. His palace is said to be the most elegant of Oriental palaces in existence. It is situated on the Nile, two miles above Bulak. It is indeed magnificent; and my pen will not attempt a description farther than to say that it has an immense saloon in an upper story, quite different from anything common to modern architecture.

We were treated with the greatest politeness and consideration, coffee, pipes, and sherbet being given us. Ibrahim's garden is a most elaborate and elegant one. It has been my privilege to see some fine horticultural work, but this surpasses any display I have yet seen.

It occupies an island in the Nile, opposite the palace. Four years ago it was a desert. Ibrahim sent to the Horticultural Society of London a request that a gentleman familiar with landscape gardening enter his employ. Mr. Trail thus came to Egypt in the service of the pasha. He has literally made this desert to blossom.

A ride of a quarter of a mile brought us to the landing. Leaving there our horses in care of the grooms, we crossed to the island on the pasha's boat, with his royal colors—the Crescent and Star—floating over us.

How I wish I could describe that garden! But it is impossible. I will only say that so rapid is the growth of vegetation that trees two and a half feet in circumference are to be seen.

After spending a few hours most enjoyably

in this elysium, we returned home. We gentlemen examined, on the way, the horses in the pasha's stables. Well did it repay us. They were noble specimens of the purest strains of the Arabian breed. Being passionately fond of fine horses, it was even harder to leave the stables than the garden.

After supper I strolled a short distance from the consulate. Suddenly I heard Mr. Thoms call me:

"Come here, Trumbull; come here!"

"What is it?" I asked.

"You could n't guess in a year. It is a dog-show."

Sure enough! There the dog was, entertaining our entire company. His chief accomplishment was the ability to say "papa" and "mamma" plain enough to be understood. He could also spell common Italian words by selecting—or indicating—the letters in the alphabet.

The next day, Wednesday, we devoted to rest. Sight-seeing is hard work, and we had worked hard at it. Thoms and I took a walk about the city, however. The bazaars of Cairo are very fine, and we made some purchases as mementos of our visit.

"Thoms," said I, "there is one thing I want to see."

"What's that?"

"The slave-market."

"O!" groaned Mr. Thoms; "my taste would not take me there; but I'll go with you."

We found it readily. Never will I forget the misery of that scene! Grief and despair were the especial emotions of the human chattels, as shown by the countenances. Cunning, cruelty, and greed of gain were written on the faces of the dealers. The physiognomies of such slaves as had surrendered themselves to hopelessness were an interesting study. We knew not their language, but their hopes and fears were open to our comprehension. Here was a comely girl, whose "points" were being discussed by two prospective buyers. That she, knowing slavery was her doom, hoped that the milder man would buy her, was evident at a glance.

"Look at that girl, Trumbull," said Thoms, "hoping that Frank will buy her. It is an awful state from which sale as a slave—no matter to whom—can be a thing wished for!"

"You are right. Look at that big black fellow whom that sinister-faced Arab just slapped. I tell you there is blood in that slave's eye, and, if the Arab buys him, and a good chance comes, the slave will kill him."

"I believe you. But let's get out of this. We have seen enough."

"O, Mr. Trumbull," said one of the ladies, "will you go with us after dinner to call at the house of a Syrian merchant? We want to go. Father is very tired, and you are the only married man in the company except the doctor and chaplain, and they are not here, so we thought we would ask you."

"I am glad you did. What a fortunate thing is matrimony! If single, I would miss the pleasure of this call. I am very desirous to see the interior of one of these homes."

"So are we. We will go, if you please, about two o'clock."

It was a pleasant call, and gave us quite an insight into the daily life of these people. The lady of the house entertained us with much ease and courtesy. She was richly attired, with a profusion of jewels and precious stones in her headdress. She wore clogs, which kept her feet fully six inches from the floor.

When we returned to the consulate, the ladies found an invitation from the proper source for them to dine the following day with the ladies of the pasha's harem. Of course they accepted. Mr. Gliddon said to them:

"I am pleased beyond expression, but even more surprised, at this invitation; for it is a thing without a precedent. Your invitation to call, the other day, astonished me beyond measure; but a request to dine is almost astounding."

So thought we all.

"O, Mr. Trumbull," said one of the ladies, "great as is matrimony, it can not this time procure you an invitation! I'm sorry, but you can not go."

"Yet it is a potent influence, and I rejoice that I am a Benedict."

The next morning we all went a second time to the citadel—the ladies to accept the invitation to dine at the harem; we gentlemen to pay our further respects to the governor. As before, the pipes and wine were presented and accepted, and the governor was profuse in offers of assistance to make our visit enjoyable. Our stay was a little protracted, and it took my best efforts to handle the pipe enough for politeness and not to get sick. I escaped, however; but never did I come so near smoking as then.

After getting home to the consulate, the ladies told us of their dinner-party.

"We were received," said one of the ladies, "the same as before, and the curiosity of the attendants was also the same. The entertainment consisted of performances by dancing-girls, which were very pretty."

"What were pretty," asked the chaplain—"the performances, or the girls?"

"That a man of your cloth should ask such a question! Knowing the cloth, I answer, both; and, had you been there, either would have occupied your attention fully."

The chaplain was teased by that reply, and the laugh we all had at him. The speaker resumed:

"The dinner consisted of thirty-six courses; and they aimed to serve it up in true American style, with knives and forks. Only one dish was placed before us at a course, and that was put upon a small table, a foot square. Necessarily each person had a separate table. The food embraced mutton, fish, and rice in various forms; fried nuts and lemons; bonny-clabber, melons, and fruits."

"Were they good?" one of us asked.

"Tastes vary. I should say everything was very good and nice, though, personally, the fried nuts and lemons were not pleasing; and, you know, some people do not like mutton. The funny thing was to see these ladies try to use knives and forks. I was possessed to laugh, but of course did not. It was an art they had not yet mastered; and, remembering that 'fingers were made before forks,' they finally resorted to the primitive style."

"But you liked the visit?" we asked.

"Liked it? We were delighted! It was

kindly conceived, and handsomely executed amid Oriental splendor, especially in the way of rich garments and rare jewels, which we ladies so much admire. Of course they could not entirely succeed in sustaining the American style; but they tried to, out of compliment to us; and we say, 'May happiness be the portion of the ladies of the harem!' And to think that we, *we*, are the *only* Christian women to whom this honor has ever been extended!"

"You will roll that as a sweet morsel under your tongues, I suppose?" said the commodore.

"Ay, father, and we will keep it rolling! Trust us for that!"

The next day was to be the acme of our stay in Egypt, for we were to visit the Pyramids. The start was to be at three o'clock in the morning; and, ere return, we would visit the ruins of Memphis. Two days would be required; and, that we might be ready and rested, we all retired early.

CHAPTER XXX.

OFF FOR THE PYRAMIDS—DONKEYS AND SOUR GRAPES—SITE OF THE BATTLE OF THE PYRAMIDS—DESCRIPTION—ASCENT—VIEW FROM THE TOP—REMARKS—A FOOLISH RACE.

WE were ready on time the next morning, and, thanks to Mr. Gliddon's care, everything was ready for us. This was not a trip suitable for the pasha's carriage—the only carriage, by the way, that we saw in Egypt—and the ladies had to take the saddle. All told, there were seventy in our company; and, in addition to the pasha's thirty horses, there were camels, mules, and donkeys.

"How are you going, Trumbull?" asked my chum, Mr. Thoms.

"I am intending to ride a donkey."

"You are a donkey for doing it, when you can have one of these fine Arabian horses just as well."

"I like the horses; but just think of visiting Egypt and not riding a donkey!"

"Then why not mount a camel?"

"I tried one yesterday, and I do n't like the motion."

By this time the company were mounted, the ladies having chosen donkeys as their saddle animals. Thoms, seeing this, came to me, and whispered:

"I see it, Trumbull! I see it!"

"See what?" I asked.

"Where 's your home in Indiana! Madison, is n't it?"

"Yes, but what are you driving at?"

"I am going to write to your wife! You chose a donkey just because the ladies did. You are not such a donkey as I thought. But you are a deep schemer. You have been gallanting the ladies all over Egypt, and yesterday you and they were grief-stricken because you could not dine at the harem with them. You, the married man! Your wife shall know about this!"

"Once there was a fox saw some grapes hanging—"

"No, it 's not sour grapes, either!" cried Thoms.

"The trouble with the fox was he could n't get the grapes. His taste was all right, and he knew a good thing when he saw it. Some foxes have good taste and get the grapes, too."

"O, Trumbull, you are incorrigible! Little did I know what I was undertaking in attempting to look out for you!"

Our passes, permitting us to leave the city, were made out to allow seventy shoes to go out the gates. Seventy shoes meant thirty-five persons, and how would the matter be arranged? We all went through without delay, however; for shoes was the password or countersign. So the pass was good for seventy.

Our route lay up the east bank of the Nile, past Ibrahim's palace, to old Cairo, where we crossed the river in rather small boats. It took till nearly seven o'clock to get us all over, but it landed us on historic ground; viz., the battle-ground where Napoleon fought the famous battle of the Pyramids. Upon the plain before us had ten thousand Mameluke horsemen—the finest cavalry in the world—performed those wonderful evolutions, and shown that irrepressible bravery, which caused Napoleon to exclaim: "Could I have united the Mameluke horse to the French infantry, I should have reckoned myself master of the world."

But there was no time for reminiscence; we must away to the Pyramids. Soon we were in motion and riding at will. It is a perfect level from our landing-place to the Pyramids, and some of the horsemen fairly flew over the plain, notably Thoms, who could ride as though he were a centaur. The camels, too, were urged to a pace far in excess of what I supposed possible. And the donkeys! I learned a thing that day about donkeys and donkey-drivers. Every donkey has a driver—a fleet-footed Arab—who runs behind or beside the animal. Now the offer of a liberal *buono mano* wakened up my driver, and he wakened up the donkey. He had a stick armed with an iron point, with which he prodded the animal as occasion required. It was more potent than a whip, and secured excellent results. But when the driver meant business he bit the donkey's tail. The little quadruped knew what that meant, and the way he flew over that old battle-ground would have been a credit to a Mameluke. Had not the dri er, though a very Asahel in speed, held tightly to the donkey's tail, he could never have kept near that animal. But he clung tightly, and by an occasional bite, kept us a-flying. It was fun for everybody, but rough on the donkey. However, we soon let him cool down, and take a gait more after the custom of his kind. This eight-mile ride was a most delightful one, and will ever be remembered.

The Pyramids from a distance appear insignificant; but, as we drew near, the falsity of our first impressions became evident. The things kept growing, and, when we stood at their base, it was a spontaneous act to uncover the head, for we felt as Napoleon said to his soldiers, "Forty centuries are looking down upon you;" also that the ancient monuments, which so spoke and linked us with the unknown past, were deserving of the greatest respect and veneration we moderns could pay them.

In size they transcended our expectation, and impressed us most forcibly. Cheops, the largest, extends its broad base along the rock foundation till each of its square dimensions has consummated a distance of seven hundred and sixty-four feet, and claimed from the sands an area of nearly thirteen acres. It ascends at an angle of fifty-one degrees and fifty minutes till it has attained an altitude of four hundred and eighty feet and nine inches; the distance along the inclined surface being over six hundred feet. That is, it used to be, before the casing was removed. The casing was of marble, and thirty feet thick. It was put on in immense blocks arranged in layers, each one extending a smaller distance toward the outer boundary of the base than the one subjacent; the amount of the lower layer left exposed being such as to preserve constantly the angle above named. When completed, the external surface of the vast pile presented a succession of plain surfaces, alternately perpendicular and horizontal. In other words, each side was an immense marble stairway, of triangular shape, terminating, with the other sides, in a common apex.

It was not left thus by the original builders, however. They removed enough of the uncovered portion of each layer of marble to convert the two plain surfaces already named into one, inclined at the angle also previously named. They began this work of removal at the top, and worked downward. How do we know? First, they would have been simpletons to have done otherwise, as the "stairs" gave them a splendid footing while at labor. Second, we know it from the hieroglyphics representing the work being done. And, by the way, the second item is what tells us that the stones composing the external course of each layer were put on as rectangular prisms, and not triangular or trapezoidal ones. Thus did the pyramids, when completed, have a beautiful, smooth, plain, triangular surface for each face.

But it was not allowed so to remain. These monster pyramids were too convenient a quarry for the builders of the walls of Grand Cairo to leave unutilized. The Vandals stole the stone to build a wall, with which to protect themselves from other Vandals. A layer thirty feet thick over this vast structure is no insignificant amount; and abundantly did it assist the builders. Just think! There are over twenty-seven million cubic feet of stone in it; and it would build a wall, thirty feet high and ten feet thick, over seventeen miles long. That was more than the walls of Cairo required. Where has the rest gone? Into the better class of buildings in the city. Then there are eight other pyramids in this group, called the Pyramids of Gizeh; and their casing is also mostly gone. Not all, however; for on one at least, near the summit, considerable remains.

The second largest pyramid was cased in red granite; the next, in black granite. So the Vandals had quite a variety with which to build.

How did we find these structures at our visit? "Beautiful for situation," being placed upon a ridge of limestone, running north and south some hundred feet above the surrounding country, along the eastern border of the great Libyan Desert, and three miles west of the River Nile—conveniently situated; for the stone composing the bulk of the structure was quarried from this ridge in the immediate vicinity.

So vast did we find them, that the eye could not miss from their magnitude the outer covering. In size, great Cheops seemed adequate for all demands. In fact, as we stood at the middle of his north base-line and looked up, he was overpowering, almost, in his immensity. But the finish—the casing—was gone, leaving the limestone layers with the stair-steps arrangement, already described as originally pertaining to the marble casing.

Of course, the first thing to do was to go to the top. So thought we all; and so thought a swarm of Bedouin Arabs who fastened upon us like bees, determined to be our assistants in the climb. We were helpless in their clutches, when, fortunately for us, they got to fighting among themselves. Mr. Gliddon, the consul, endeavored to quiet them; but his authority was *nil*. So he laid the whip keenly across their naked shoulders. When he began that summary procedure, Thoms whispered to me:

"There will be trouble, Trumbull. We must be ready to help."

We therefore grasped our pistols, and I noticed the other officers did the same. The Arabs, however, took the lash meekly, and became orderly.

It is no joke to climb one of these pyramids. Knowing that, we selected Arabs to assist us, and began the ascent. The layers of stone are from three to five feet thick; and these, therefore, were the heights of the steps. Without the Arabs it would have been laborious; but they are nimble, strong, and used to it. They would mount a layer in advance, and pull us up. Twenty minutes we were in ascending. That is considered good time, though it has been made by travelers in twelve.

Part of the apex is gone, leaving a space upon which to stand, some thirty feet square. The altitude we had attained was indeed imposing; and impressed us, if possible, even more with the stupendousness of this ancient work than did the view from the base. The thought that we were at the summit of the highest structure in the world was gratifying. That one of the seven wonders of the world was beneath our feet, impressed us pleasantly.

Mr. Gliddon said:

"The view from here is one that I am sure you will always carry in memory."

"Indeed it is sublime!" said the commodore.

"We are nearly six hundred feet above the plain, and that gives a broad expanse of landscape."

"It does. How distinctly we can see the Delta, with the two branches of the Nile and the beautiful plantations between them; and the land of Goshen, east of the river, with the great city of Grand Cairo, surmounted by the citadel, perched aloft on the hills of Mokattam!"

"And, father," said one of the ladies, "just see that beautiful garden of Ibrahim Pasha on the island, and his elegant palace on the east bank!"

"Yes, it is fine, daughter. And how far we can trace the meanderings of the Nile toward the south! I suppose those ruins, a few miles up the river on the west side, mark the location of Memphis?"

"Yes, that is the site of Old Memphis. It is utterly deserted, and only ruins remain. It is a wonderful instance of the fulfillment of Scripture prophecy."

"What was the prediction?" asked the commodore.

"Jeremiah said: 'Behold, they are this day a desolation, and no man dwelleth therein.' (Jeremiah xliv, 2.) Again, he said: 'Noph shall be waste and desolate, without an inhabitant.' (Jer. xlvi, 19.) But it will be time to talk of Memphis when we get there."

"I infer, Mr. Gliddon," said one of the ladies, "that 'Noph' is another name for Memphis?"

"It is so called in the Hebrew. We were, I think, talking of the view. To the west is the vast Libyan Desert, an ocean of sand. Now, all about us are tombs. They are located in every direction, for we are in a vast necropolis—a veritable city of the dead; and on the top of the chief monument in this vast charnel-house we are coolly considering the greatness of the departed millions."

"How much stone is there in this pyramid, Mr. Gliddon?" asked a lady.

"It has been computed at eighty-nine millions of tons. We can speak the words, but we can form no conception of their meaning."

"How large are some of the stones?"

"Thirty-five feet long, and from five to eight feet in the other dimensions."

"Is it possible! How in the world did they handle them?"

"That question can not be answered. It is a mystery; but probably they were lifted by vast machines, for round holes are found which look as though they were made to place something in to lift by. But that is only conjecture. Their surfaces are, at times, so perfectly smooth and uniform that it is probable they were brought into shape by friction—the stone itself having been rubbed upon some prepared surface until the desired perfection was obtained. So closely were many of these immense stones adjusted that to-day, after four thousand years, it is impossible to pass the thinnest knife-blade between them. Now, the easiest way to explain all this is to suppose the existence of machinery of which we know nothing."

"How long," said one of the ladies, "it must have taken to build it!"

"Yes, indeed. It is estimated that one hundred thousand men were occupied in the work for thirty years. I doubt the estimate, especially the time; for Cheops ruled over fifty years. Now, these old rulers used to spend all their reign in building their own mausoleums. The work of enlarging continued through life, and the casing was put on after death. The work was usually commenced by excavating first the sepulchral chamber out of the living rock, with a shaft to approach it of suitable incline and size to make the placing of the stone sarcophagus easy. Over and about this chamber and shaft the work was constantly extended till the death of the monarch ensued. Then the interment occurred, and the pile was hermetically sealed with the casing."

"What is the age of this pyramid?" asked one of us.

"Chronologists differ on that point. Wilkinson says 2123 B. C. was the time of Cheops's reign. Others place it at a more remote period; some as far back as 3229 B. C. But even by Wilkinson they antedate Abraham by one hundred and twenty-seven years. It is only two hundred and twenty-six years after the Flood."

After an hour pleasantly spent on the pyramid, we prepared for the descent.

"Trumbull," said Mr. Thoms, "I can beat you down!"

"Rather heavy incline for a race, and we may be as dead as Cheops by the time we reach the bottom; but, young man, you can't beat me."

Away we went! From layer to layer we jumped, with more courage than discretion, and in two minutes were standing on the sand at the base. It was a reckless, foolish race; but those adjectives describe some people. It was a close race—in fact, a draw.

CHAPTER XXXI.

Interior of the Pyramid—Hard Work—Dinner in a Tomb—Also a Nap—The Sphinx—A Taste of Desert Travel—Tomb of Psammetichus—We Purchase Human Flesh and Bone—Site of Memphis—Menes's Great Work.

"THESE pyramids are placed in exact accord with the cardinal points of the compass," said Mr. Gliddon, as we were getting ready to enter Cheops; "so absolutely exact that many believe these structures were for some astronomical purpose."

"But they were built for tombs, were they not?" asked the chaplain.

"They were surely so used, and the bulk of opinion is that they were built for that purpose. Of that you shall soon judge. Now take off all superfluous clothing, and leave it here; for we have a hot job before us."

The entrances to these piles are all from the

north; that of Cheops is at the sixteenth layer from the ground. The passage, which descends at an angle of twenty-six degrees, is four feet in both height and width.

With jackets off, we bowed our heads, and entered; doing the proper thing, of course, in assisting the ladies. Two of us officers were assigned to each fair one, while the supernumeraries carried the lights. The lights seemed only to make the darkness visible; but it was impossible to go astray, and we groped our way to the bottom of the passage—a distance of some seventy feet.

Hot? The word does not tell it. And dusty! An impalpable powder—the accumulation of centuries—covers the floor of this passage nearly six inches deep. The moment our feet disturbed it, it arose in clouds which made breathing very disagreeable. But clouds could not stop us; so we kept on.

At the end of this passage we encountered a perpendicular ascent of fifteen feet, up which we climbed with some difficulty. Thence our course led us along a passage of similar width to the first, but much higher—perhaps fifteen feet—with a deep groove in the center. This passage led upward, instead of downward, but at the same angle with the horizon; viz., twenty-six degrees. It is about three hundred feet long, and, with the help of a short horizontal passage, brought us—all covered with sweat and dust, and gasping for breath—into the *sanctum sanctorum*. This was a room thirty-four feet and three inches in length by seventeen feet and one inch in breadth, with a ceiling nineteen feet and one inch from the floor. In this chamber was the granite sarcophagus of King Cheops; but, alas! his remains could no longer be designated by that word. They were gone; and the place that for centuries knew them shall know them no longer forever.

"'Dust thou art, and unto dust shalt thou return,'" said the chaplain, "was the fiat of the Almighty; and man can not annul it."

This was the chamber of death, and we should have entered it with all reverence. Did we? Far from it! We pounced upon that sarcophagus like a flock of wolves on a sheep, determined each to have a piece to carry away as a trophy. The sarcophagus was a battle-scarred veteran. Every vulnerable point had been assailed and carried away by former visitors. There the hoary warrior lay, secure in his very wounds. Not a memento could we force from him. However, other travelers had been there with steel more worthy of this prostrate monster than ours proved to be. Chippings, significant of their success, lay about the floor. We changed our tactics, and hunted them. Finding them, we were obliged to be content.

I had just secured a fairly good piece, when "Where's that married man?" rang throughout the vault.

"That means me," said I, mentally; then aloud, "Ay, ay! here I am."

One of the young ladies, overcome by the stifling heat, had fainted; and, being the only young married man, I was delegated to carry the lady out.

"Another instance, Trumbull," whispered Thoms, "of the felicity of the married state."

My tormentor referred to the fact that this young lady was not one of the ethereal, fairy-like creatures, but a good, substantial American girl, with plenty of bone and muscle. The good chaplain and the dignified doctor, being old married men, assisted me. We got the lady out, but it was "a long pull, a strong pull, and a pull all together." Never did I work harder. Next time I go into a pyramid with the ladies, I will see that more of the escorts are Benedicts.

There were many ancient tombs near the entrance to Cheops. Having all come from the pyramid, we entered one of the most perfect of these, crawling over the sand half-closing the entrance, and spread our carpet on the sandy floor for dinner. Down we all sat, *à la* Turk, to a very good meal.

Knowing that we would be thirsty, I had providently brought from Cairo a large bottle of water, to be used at dinner-time. It had been lots of trouble to carry, and had excited many inquiries as to what it was.

"It is for dinner," was my only reply.

Now, every one was on the alert to see what I had brought. The wrappings I had placed about it had become quite wet. "Strange," thought I, "that a bottle should sweat so much in such a dry climate!" thinking, of course, of the truth that the sweating of the average bottle or pitcher is not a transudation through the ware, but a condensation of the moisture from the air. Alas! this *was* a transudation, and not a drop of water remained in the vessel!

Many of these Egyptian water-bottles are made of porous ware, in order that the water may transude, and, by evaporation from the surface thus dampened, keep the remaining water cool. I had chosen, thoughtlessly, one of these bottles, and all I had left was the bottle itself and the ridicule of the company.

"This is a married man," said Thoms. "He knows how to provide!"

As I threatened to throw the bottle at him, he desisted, and we ate our dinners.

"Isn't this nice," said one of the ladies—"picnicking in Egypt?"

"Very fine!" said the iconoclast. "In the very graves of some of the defunct Egyptians!"

"O, you bad man, to refer to such a thing!"

"But it is so," said Mr. Thoms. "Look at the hieroglyphics! There's one that represents Charon ferrying a passenger across the Styx. Yes, it is gay and cheerful picnicking in the very abode of the dead. I suppose some of the very dust of these deceased Egyptians is mixed with the sand which makes our table!"

"Mr. Thoms, be still!" cried one of the ladies, "and let us eat our dinner in peace; and, if you please, give me a drink of water."

"There is plenty of water, if Mr. Trumbull did fail to bring any; but, alas! there is nothing to drink from, for we haven't a cup in this sepulchral outfit," said Mr. Thoms.

"Perhaps," said I, "you will kindly forgive my failure to provide a drink, if I will furnish a cup from which to drink what another has provided."

While saying this, I handed to the lady a draught of water in an old skull, which I had a moment before pushed from the sand with my foot. Decay had so wasted a portion of this bone as to leave the rest in available shape for drinking purposes. A shriek of horror was the response to my willing offer, followed by the cry:

"Take it away, you naughty man!"

"It is quite clean," said I, "for the sands have scoured it for ages; and the water from it is sweet and good. I will drink first to show you."

My example, however, was not enough at first to remove the prejudice of many of the company. Some drank gladly from the ghastly cup, thinking the horrible procedure a good joke. Thirst is a potent persuader, especially when the tropical heat of Sahara's sands adds force to its intensity, and most of those who shrank from the cadaveric cup at first were persuaded to join us in our potations.

So we ate, drank, laughed, and joked in this ancient sepulcher; and thanked the ancient master himself—probably one of the nobility—for his generous hospitality, which, though it may not have come from the heart, surely did come from the head!

Being excessively tired from the arduous labors of the day, I sought an inner apartment of the tomb, and for an hour enjoyed a most refreshing siesta upon the ever-present sand. I was dreaming of home, when Thoms called:

"'Awake, thou that sleepest!' This is no place to sleep! Wake up! We are going to Memphis."

I was out in a minute from this old tomb, said to be as old as the Pyramids themselves.

We inspected the celebrated Sphinx. As everybody knows, it has the body of a lion, with the face, neck, and breast of a man. It is in a crouching position, and cut from the living rock. It is a hundred and thirty feet long, thirty feet across the breast; and the paws project fifty feet from the body. It was quite perfect, all save the nose.

"Where is its nose?" we asked.

"No one knows," said Mr. Gliddon. "It is said the Mamelukes took it for a target, and have shot it away with their rifle-balls. Wilkinson says the Sphinx dates back to 1446 B. C."

By four o'clock, the intense heat of the day being passed, we got under way. We received, that afternoon, a taste of what desert travel means; for we accomplished a journey of eighteen miles across Sahara's sands. Hot, thirsty, and tired, we reached our camping-place at nine o'clock. Imagine our delight at learning that, by the order of the governor of Cairo, a pasha's tent was there pitched for our comfort. It stood upon the desert, and made our bivouac truly Oriental. After a much-needed and most excellent supper, we spread our blankets on the sand, and were soon in the arms of Morpheus.

Next day we visited the tomb of Psammetichus, one of the Shepherd Kings. It is a vast excavation in the rocky hillside. The walls within are covered with hieroglyphics; and in it are pits, some two or three hundred feet deep. Their object I did not learn. In the excavations about here were millions of mummy birds, neatly wrapped up in mummy-cloth, and sealed up in a crock or jar. While here, an Arab brought to us the half of a human mummy.

"Eight cents. Mummy!" said he, in English scarcely intelligible.

"All right!" said Thoms. "At that price, I'll take a finger."

For the first, and—I suspect—the last time in our lives, we bought human flesh and bone. Giving the man his money, we broke the mummy to pieces; and each of the party took a piece. Each? No! Some would n't touch it with a pole.

A morning ride of two miles brought us to the site of Memphis. It would not do to write that word *sight;* for there was little to be seen.

"For a long time, even a knowledge of the very location of Memphis—the *Noph* of Scripture—was lost. Only the association of ideas makes a visit to this spot interesting. It is pleasing to stand where the very first scenes of definite history were enacted. Noph and No— the latter being the Bible name of ancient

Thebes—are about contemporaneous, though the relics of this place point to a greater antiquity than do those of Thebes. Menes was the founder of Memphis. In the very incipiency of his reign he began a work of inestimable benefit to Egypt; that was, changing the course of the River Nile. Before his time, much of the water of the river passed farther to the west, and was lost in the sands of the great desert, the insatiable thirst of which even this great river could not quench. The rest of the water reached the Delta in such a way as to render it a worthless swamp. The great overflow of the Nile did Lower Egypt little good; for the voracious Libyan Desert greedily drank it. Menes began and, I think, completed an immense dike some twelve miles south of here, which diverted the stream into its present channel, and made the Nile the blessing to Egypt and the Levant which we have all seen it to be. The very spot where we now stand—the site of the great city of Memphis—was once a swamp. Menes's dike reclaimed it; and it became the metropolis of the world, and the center of learning and science."

So spoke Mr. Gliddon.

"When did Menes live?" one of us asked.

"He was the first king of the first Egyptian dynasty. The date is uncertain—in round numbers, four thousand years ago."

"Was it such a great city?"

"Yes, it was. Its walls were nineteen miles around. It was the center of religion. Here was kept—in a temple erected to his honor—the sacred bull, Apis, one of the chief Egyptian deities. Here was a magnificent temple to Isis. But the grand buildings were too many to name. Yes, it was a great capital city; but in naught else was it so great as in its burial-place, its necropolis, a glimpse—only a glimpse—of which you have had yesterday and to-day. Now all is gone; and for what the Bible predicted about Noph, I turn you over to the chaplain."

The site of this former city is now a desolate plain, relieved by nothing, save mounds of rubbish and an occasional acacia or palm-tree. A lake, across which the screaming waterfowl were flying, made it additionally dreary. Only one thing is visible which indicates its former grandeur save some broken columns and pillars; namely, a statue of Memnon, which lies prostrate in the sand. We measured its arm. It was fifteen feet in length. Not a thing stood erect at Old Memphis. What these mounds would reveal if uncovered, is a question some traveler will answer by excavating them.

The chaplain gave us a talk about the prophecies regarding Noph.

CHAPTER XXXII.

A Bible Lesson at the Birthplace of History—Floating Down the Nile — Egyptian Darkness and a Surly Arab Boatman — Stopped at the Gates of Cairo—Noise Opens Them—A Party to Mr. Gliddon—Farewell to Egypt.

"THIS is not sacred ground," said the chaplain, "but it is historic; and, as Mr. Gliddon has told you, right here we may say that history had its birth. Now I propose that we have a Bible lesson on the site of old Memphis. What say you?"

"That will be splendid!" "We would like that!" and similar expressions, were our answers.

So we seated ourselves about the prostrate statue of Memnon, some on the sand, and some on the available parts of the very image.

"I wish you all had Bibles. As you have not, I will ask Lieutenant Corbin to read the nineteenth chapter of Isaiah," said the chaplain.

The lieutentant read, and without any explanation the chapter had a more intensified meaning than ever before. The chaplain asked:

"Commodore, the first verse opens with the expression, 'The burden of Egypt.' Do your surroundings show you what that burden is?"

"Very plainly. It means the loss of national independence, and the abject condition of the people."

"Yes, sir. Once at the acme of national greatness, now they grovel in subjection. The people once living in luxury now are a community of miserable beggars. The first curse mentioned in this chapter is aimed at the idols. Why do you ladies think that was?"

"Because they were their idols; that is, the things they thought most of."

"That's right, and you might add that their worship was so intimately connected with the Government that to weaken one was to weaken the other. The next is to predict the internal broils among the Egyptians themselves. This prediction was made about 714 B. C., when Egypt was under subjection to Ethiopia. About 700 B. C. came Sennacherib, king of Assyria, to the West. He practically conquered Egypt, and then marched against Hezekiah, king of Judah, whom he laid under tribute. But Hezekiah revolted several times, and Egypt was restless. One night, when the Assyrians were confronting the army of Hezekiah, one hundred and eighty-five thousand of the Assyrians died."

"How was that?" we asked.

"It was in answer to an appeal of Hezekiah that the prophet Isaiah pray for them. The prophet comforted them, and promised that the Lord would 'send a blast upon him,' the enemy. (2 Kings xix, 7.) The blast came speedily; but in what shape we know not, for the Scriptures merely attribute it to the angel of the Lord. (2 Kings xix, 35.) Sennacherib fled in dismay, thus leaving the West without a master. A scene of anarchy now ensued in Egypt, fulfilling the prophecy of the second verse, that the Egyptians should be 'set against the Egyptians.' It resulted in a division of Egypt into twelve portions, each under a separate prince. Psammetichus, whose tomb we this morning visited, wrested the power from them, and again united Egypt. In the fourth verse is a prediction that 'a cruel lord' (lords would be a better translation) should oppress Egypt. The conquest of the country by Nebuchadnezzar was referred to, and the year 605 B. C. saw its realization. In 525 B. C. came the invasion of Egypt by Cambyses, who also was referred to. Memphis made a terrible resistance to Cambyses, and, as a result, says Herodotus, was terribly punished. The thirteenth verse says 'the princes of Noph are deceived.' They thought themselves all powerful, but were deceiving themselves in so thinking, and Egypt should be so reduced that there would be no work 'which the head or tail, branch or rush, may do,' as the fifteenth verse has it. But from the miseries described in this chapter the twentieth verse promises a savior, a promise made because the true God would be called upon in five cities of the land (eighteenth verse). That savior came in the person of Alexander the Great, in 331 B. C. Though a conqueror, he was a mild one, compared with the Babylonians and the Persians, and to the Egyptians was indeed a savior. He did much for the country and the people. Alexandria he founded, marking out its boundaries with his own hand, and this he made his capital—a rough blow for Memphis.

" The story goes that Alexander was wonderfully pleased to learn, when in Palestine, of the vision of Daniel (see Daniel, eighth chapter), which undoubtedly referred to him, and predicted his success and greatness. As a result, he was very kind to the Jews, and invited them to Alexandria. This kindness the Ptolemies indorsed and extended through their reign. At one time there were one million Jews in Egypt, and they enjoyed full civil and religious liberty. The prophet foresaw this day, and declared in the twenty-first verse that 'the Lord shall be known in Egypt, and the Egyptians shall know the Lord in that day.' It is a wonderful chapter, and has had a wonderful fulfillment."

"Indeed it has," said one of the ladies. "Must the lesson close? Can you not take another chapter?"

"If you like, I will."

Handing me the Bible, the chaplain said:

"Mr. Trumbull, please read the first nineteen verses of the thirtieth chapter of Ezekiel."

After I had read, he said:

"Allow me to preface what I want to say with the statement, that the city called *No* is ancient Thebes. *Noph*, as you are aware, is Memphis; and *Aven* is the famous Heliopolis, five miles north of Cairo. Ezekiel uttered these maledictions against Egypt and her cities in the year 572 B. C. They refer to much the same occurrences as we have just been studying, and we will not itemize them again. Mr. Trumbull, please read the thirteenth verse again."

"Thus saith the Lord God: I will also destroy their idols, and I will cause their images to cease out of Noph; and there shall be no more a prince of the land of Egypt; and I will put a fear in the land of Egypt."

"Our eyes tell us that these idols and images are gone from Noph, and that she has had the distresses spoken of. She being the great center of idol-worship, that means much. *No* is also in ruins—'her multitude' has been cut off; and at *Aven*, or Heliopolis, only one shaft is standing to mark the site of the former center of learning. But it is of the clause which says 'there shall be no more a prince of the house of Egypt' that I want to speak. At the time this was spoken, the Babylonians controlled Egypt. In 525 B. C., the Persians under Cambyses became the masters. In 331 B. C., Alexander became to Egypt a savior; but he was a Macedonian; and the Ptolemies—a succession of Macedonians, alternating at times with the Romans — ruled Egypt till 625 A. D., when the Saracens captured Alexandria, and assumed control of Egypt. In 1250 A. D. the Mamelukes—originally, Circassian slaves—gained authority; but in 1517 Selim of Turkey wrested it from them, and annexed it to the Ottoman Empire. The Mamelukes would not stay down, and they divided the authority with the Sublime Porte till the time of Mehemet Ali. He annihilated the Mamelukes, and compelled the Porte to recognize him and agree that his posterity should inherit Egypt. Thus is this prophecy fulfilled. No prince has been known in Egypt for nearly twenty-five centuries. She has been, and still is, in the hands of strangers, who are making the land waste."

"Thank you, Chaplain; that is better than a sermon," was the thought of all, as the minister ceased speaking.

"I'm hungry," said Thoms. "Have we any thing to eat?"

"There is always plenty to eat in the desert," said a lady.

"That's news. I thought it was a good place to starve."

"You can always eat the sand w'ich is [sandwiches] there."

"That is excellent, Miss Patterson; but it is dry food," said Mr. Thoms.

"It has the authority of the poet. You know the poet said:

'The traveler in the desert wild
  Should ne'er let want confound 'im;
For he can eat, at any time,
  The sand w'ich is around 'im.'"

"Good again! but pretty dry."
"A sandwich isn't dry. Listen:

'It would seem strange that he should find
  Such palatable fare,
Did we not know the sons of Ham
  Were bred and mustered there.'"

"Very apt, my dear," said the commodore. "There is just enough sauce about that to give us a good appetite."

Dinner was ready by this time. We did it ample justice; and then the return to Cairo was in order. First we rode to the Nile, two miles to the east. Then we dismounted, and embarked on the consul's boat, which he ordered from Cairo for our comfort, sending the animals down to old Cairo to meet us at sunset.

We were to float down the Nile a distance of thirty miles. Very poetical and historic, but it was not a good day to float. A strong headwind was blowing, and we could not make a mile an hour. So Thoms and I took a small boat and an Arab boatman, and started down the river to order the animals back. We overtook them after a long pull, and started them on the back track. Being responsible for the boat, we stayed in it, and undertook to go up the river. Now that we wanted a good wind, it lulled; and night, dark as Egypt, overtook us. We feared to land; for robbers abound. Where we were we did not know; and the Arab became rebellious. Only an uplifted oar would move him.

"I like Egypt," said Thoms, "and I like the Nile; but I do not like Egyptian darkness on the Nile, with only a rascally Arab to guide us. Now, what are we going to do?"

"I say, get to shore, and risk the robbers. Thoms, is that a light on the west bank?"

"It's a light, but on what bank it is I don't know."

"The wind is from the north, and that is west. Let's pull for the light."

"All right. Just knock that Arab with that spare oar if he does n't pull."

Thoms was steering, and soon we made a landing. To our joy the light was at the head of the cavalcade of our friends. Leaving the boat with the Arab, to steal or return as he saw fit, we mounted our animals, and joined the procession. It was midnight. At two o'clock we reached the gates of Cairo. There we stopped. Evidently there was something wrong with our passes. An altercation between our cavasses and the gatekeepers, in which there was much vituperation, ensued. Neither side would yield.

"Boys," said I "noise is the thing to do it! Let's show them the caliber of Yankee lungs!"

So we all joined in, and pandemonium reigned; but we conquered, and got in, having, however, to pass between two rows of bristling bayonets in the hands of angry men. It was not pleasant. Other guards tried to stop us; but with the cavasses at our head, we swept to the consulate on a full gallop.

It was three o'clock Sunday morning. We were excessively tired; but a splendid dinner, which had been waiting about eight hours, was ready for us. We all ate heartily, and hastened to bed.

Sunday we spent in rest. Monday we gave a party to Mr. Gliddon at one of the pasha's palaces, on the banks of the Nile, six miles below Cairo. The palace is in a fine park, or garden, of one hundred and fifty acres. It was placed at our disposal for this entertainment.

Some Spanish ladies, whose father was in the employ of the pasha, graced, with the ladies of our party, the occasion. Wine flowed freely. Music, both instrumental and vocal, enlivened the hours, and, with dancing, filled the day. Mr. Gliddon had been most kind to us. We wanted to give him a fine party, and we did it; for this was no common affair. The palace was gorgeous, and the garden was equal to anything I saw in Paris. Only the garden of Ibrahim surpassed it.

With the coming of evening we turned our backs on the vicinity of Cairo, and started on the return journey to Alexandria and the ship. Mr. Gliddon and Mr. Trail, of the London Horticultural Society, accompanied us to the head of the Delta. With much reluctance we bade them farewell.

The courtesy of the pasha's Government did not leave us when we departed from Cairo; for upon arrival at Alexandria, we found one of the pasha's kiosks fitted up for our use.

The pasha has returned from Syria, and is soon to visit us on board the *Delaware*. To prepare for him a reception appropriate to his position and commensurate with his great courtesy to us while his guests, we repaired on board the ship.

Alas! the pasha came not. In place came the sad news of illness, so severe as to prohibit his coming to us. Thus we failed to see Mehemet Ali, one of the prominent men of the day, whose power was such that he made even the Sublime Porte tremble on his throne. Thus we missed the opportunity to express personally our gratitude to the ruler of Egypt for his great kindness to us while visitors within his dominions.

CHAPTER XXXIII.

Jaffa—Off for Jerusalem—Robbers—Ramleh—Plain of Sharon—Valley of Elah—The City of the Great King.

ON the morning of the 10th of August we weighed anchor, and bade farewell to Egypt, bound for Palestine; the port we desired to make being Jaffa, the ancient Joppa of the Scriptures. We had enjoyed Egypt, owing largely to the favors the Government extended to us. The same advantage would be ours in the Holy Land; for the firman of Mehemet Ali to the governor of the province assured us that courtesy.

"How are your eyes, Thoms?" I asked, after we were well to sea.

"My eyes? They are all right. Why?"

"O, the ophthalmia? You thought it would be the biggest thing in Egypt. What do you now think is?"

"The Pyramids and their antiquity, I think, impressed me most. How was it with you?"

"Well, I believe the fulfillment of prophecy has given me the most to think about," said I.

"Then you will enjoy Palestine."

"I expect to."

On the 12th we were on the lookout for land. We were not disappointed, for on that morning a low and whitish coast rose above the horizon. Back of it was a range of hills, and here and there, as we saw with our glasses, were small villages. Though not an especially attractive view, I gazed at it with an interest most peculiar and thrilling.

It was the Holy Land; the home of the Savior; the place where was first planted the truth of the Christian religion! I longed to land and press its sacred soil. Though not a professed Christian, I could vie with the most earnest Crusader in reverence for these sacred places.

The rays of the rising sun were reflected from a mass of white houses which we knew to be our destination, Jaffa. As we approached, we saw it to be a walled city, situated on a hill. There is no harbor, so we came to anchor three miles out. Should we land? That was the question; for rumors that the plague was prevalent were rife.

The commodore sent the *Shark* in for information as to the rumors. She brought off the American consul, who gave us such conflicting reports that we were as much in doubt as ever.

Then Lieutenant Barker was sent to an Egyptian admiral, whose vessel was near. The admiral said: "Go on, for the disease has abated."

The next day we moved a mile nearer the shore. A courier, just from Jerusalem, brought the good news that the disease had been in subjection for nearly a month. A party, with the commodore and family at its head, was made up at once for Jerusalem. How I did want to go, but no use; those of us who had done Egypt with the commodore had to stay with the ship, while the others took a turn. We were promised a second party; so we lived in hope.

The next day Thoms and I visited Jaffa. The houses come well down to the sea, and are compactly built; but it is a miserable hole, and took away much of the veneration with which I had thought first to press the soil of Palestine. The population consists of some three thousand Arabs, who live in misery and filth. The streets are narrow and dirty. Thoms asked:

"Was n't it Joppa where Peter raised Dorcas from the dead?"

"It was."

"Too bad! It was a shame to call her back to such a miserable place."

"But she was a philanthropist, and worked for the poor."

"I forgot that. I suppose she could not have had a better place. Now, I like Peter for declining to eat anything in the big sheet he saw in the vision."

"Why so?"

"Because it was in Joppa. I would not eat anything in this miserable town."

"You are irreverent, Thoms. I was going to treat you to melons, but you would not eat them."

"O yes, I will! I will draw the line at melons."

We went out east of town a mile or so, where it is very pleasant. There are beautiful gardens, with palm, pomegranate, citron, and lemon trees, interspersed with arbors and fountains. The contrast with the town was marked.

"Now for the melons, Trumbull. This is fine!" said Mr. Thoms.

"These melons are fine, too," said I, when we had tried them; "as good almost as Indiana melons."

The surroundings were so pleasant, we spent the day among the gardens, cutting a number of walking-sticks as mementos of our visit. So passed the first day in Palestine.

Napoleon took Jaffa by storm, and found, among the prisoners taken, many soldiers whom he had a few days before captured at El Arish, and released on parole. They had violated their parole, and were again captured while in arms against him. What should he do with them? Keep them prisoners? Impossible; for his own soldiers were at the starvation point from a scarcity of provisions. Release them again on parole, to fight once more against him? It was not like Napoleon to do that. He ordered that four thousand of them be shot, and that order was obeyed. Their bones were formed into a pyramid, which is still to be seen.

"That is a dark blot on the reputation of Napoleon," said I.

"Yes, it is; but there are some extenuating circumstances, though perhaps not justifying ones."

"What are they?"

"He was fighting with Turks, who never take prisoners, but kill all in the ranks against them."

"Then why did Napoleon not do that? It was awful to capture them, and then order, in cold blood, their execution," said I.

"That was what Napoleon thought, and he

sorrowfully asked his officers why they had brought those miserable people to him. 'Because you directed us to stop, if possible, the bloodshed.' 'Yes,' he replied, 'of the women and children, but not of these men who had been paroled for a year.'"

"Was it not here," I asked, "that, after the capture of the city was assured, Napoleon sent a flag of truce, with a demand for surrender, that the carnage and pillage might be avoided, when the Turkish general took the unfortunate messenger, and cut off his head?"

"Yes, and stuck it on a pole, and showed it to the French as an answer to the flag of truce. They deserved harsh treatment; and as they would have joined the Turkish forces at once to fight Napoleon at Acre, and as the French soldiers censured their commander for proposing to feed these people from the scanty store of provisions, I am not greatly surprised that he ordered their death."

Only six weeks before our arrival, Jaffa had been the scene of warfare. All Syria, as we learned in Egypt, had been in insurrection, and the rebels had surrounded Jaffa. As the governor was in sympathy with them, they would surely have captured the place had not Mehemet Ali arrived to prevent.

Though the insurrection is quelled, the country is infested with bands of armed men, who make prey of any defenseless parties they may meet. In short, they are robbers temporarily, and this fact makes a tour of the Holy Land dangerous at this time. But we are going to Jerusalem—provided we get leave—if we have to fight all the robbers in Palestine.

About eight o'clock on the morning of August 21st, a runner came into Jaffa with word that the commodore and party would get back from Jerusalem that day, and that Captain Nicholson was at liberty to make up a second party for the City of David.

Did n't we bustle around, and did n't we get off that very afternoon!

There were twenty-one of us, all active, nimble men. Each carried a brace of ship's pistols and a sword, and we felt equal to any predatory band we were likely to meet. We were to have had horses; but, alas! they could not be procured. Carriages were unknown in Palestine, and mules and asses were the best we could do.

It was much the same company that made such a fine display when on the pasha's horses in Cairo. How great the contrast!

Few of us had saddles. With bags of grain we improvised substitutes therefor, to which we attached rope stirrups. But we were a jolly crowd, for we were going to Jerusalem!

About sunset we got off, with a marine officer at our head. Originally twenty-one, our numbers had grown to threescore and ten.

Just outside of Jaffa one of our party got into a fuss with an Arab. High words and blows ensued, but we drove the man away. He vowed vengeance; and as our guide told us he was the captain of a strong band of rebels in the vicinity, we feared his party would attack us. We therefore formed a regular line of march, with the baggage in advance. Every one was on the watch; and if a bird rustled the foliage, or an affrighted lizard disengaged a stone from the roadside so as to bring to our attentive ears the sound of its fall, the noise was answered by the click of our pistols and the unsheathing of our swords. The guide said that our vigilance alone prevented an attack.

After leaving the pleasant gardens just east of Jaffa, we passed on to a sandy plain, which borders the east coast of the Mediterranean. The moon kindly lighted our way, and showed us that we were crossing a tract of land but poorly cultivated. Eleven o'clock brought us to a town of four thousand inhabitants, not counting fleas. At the date of our visit the latter had not been enumerated. The Arabs do n't like to take the census anyhow.

"This," said our friend, the chaplain (he had been here before), "is Ramleh. The ancient name is Arimathea."

"What! where Joseph lived—the Joseph who begged the body of Christ that he might bury it?"

"The same," said the chaplain.

"I respect it for his sake," said I, "and I will enter it with reverence. What an honor was Joseph's, to have given sepulture to 'Him who had not where to lay his head!'"

"And this place deserves high regard for another reason."

"Indeed! What is that, please?"

"It is the ancient Ramathaim-zophim (1 Samuel i, 1–20)—the birthplace of the prophet Samuel."

"I am glad you told me. I will enter it with uncovered head. I am glad it is such a nice place."

The distant view in the moonlight was indeed pleasing. It is on an extensive plain, in a grove of olive-trees; and dense masses of cactus adorn the gardens about the suburbs. Though beautiful without, it is like the rest within—dirty, mud-colored huts, filled with Arabs, lice, and fleas. Though I had uncovered out of regard for the memory of the old town, I put on my hat for protection from the modern.

Ramleh has some Turkish mosques and a Latin convent. These, with an occasional whitewashed house belonging to an Armenian or Turk, are all there are to relieve the monotony.

A Syrian, acting as American consul, had, by order of the governor, provided for us a house in which to lodge, with mattresses to lie upon. That was kind. We went in to get a little sleep.

> "Then all the fleas in Jewry
> Jumped up and bit like fury."

Sleep! Not a wink did I get. Thoms could go to sleep in about a minute. He did get into a doze; but all of a sudden he jumped so as to knock me almost off the mattress, which I was sharing with him.

"What's the matter, Thoms?" I asked.

"I think I must have put my knife in my pocket, with the blade open. I fear I have cut myself."

A dozen of us heard this answer, and we made the old house ring with laughter.

"Nothing to laugh at!" growled Thoms. "Somebody get a light."

Striking a light, I showed him that the blade which cut him was an immense *pediculus corporis*, or body-louse.

"I'm going to get out of this!" said he, striking for the fresh air. I followed him.

Shaking our garments, we sought rest under a tree some distance from any house. To our surprise, we found the chaplain there, and said:

"So you came out, too, did you?"

"No, indeed! I didn't go in. I've been here before."

By five o'clock in the morning, we were again on the road. The country about us now was most pleasing. At first level, it gradually became undulating, and finally attained the dignity of a hill.

"This," said the chaplain, "is the Plain, or Valley, of Sharon, so much mentioned in Scripture. It bounds the sandy tract on the east, and extends from Gaza on the south to Mount Carmel in the north. East of it is a range of hills, which extends from Mount Lebanon on the north to the desert south of the Holy Land. It used to be very fertile, but the rainfall is very light. It has lost much of its former beauty from neglect and lack of water; and now olive-trees and rose-bushes are about all with which nature relieves the scenery."

About eight o'clock we entered the mountain region, passing from the location of Ephraim, in which we had been journeying, into that of Benjamin, near the ruins of a castle supposed to occupy the site of Beth-horon. (Joshua xvi, 3–5.)

Our route now lay uphill, alongside the dry bed of a stream, whose source seemed to be in the vicinity of Jerusalem. It was terribly hot, and the ascent was hard for man and beast. We were thirsty, and, to our delight, saw what it was to find a well in a strange country. But alas! the well was deep, and we had nothing to draw with. We could only go on—a thing the animals, for a time, refused to do. We now passed through narrow defiles, where ambuscades would be very possible. Remembering the robber-captain, we moved with caution.

The country showed signs of former contention, the remains of old castles and defenses being numerous. The sun beat down painfully hot in these rocky defiles, and made some of the party regret having left the ship. Never did I suffer so intensely from thirst, save when traversing Sahara's sands.

After two hours among the hills, a grove of olive-trees told us of the proximity of a spring. Never will I forget that spring near the summit of a mountain in the "hill country of Judea." The Bible name is appropriate. The hills are of a conical shape and rise from valleys so narrow that their bases seemed to be merged one into the other. The water was delicious, and we made a long halt for breakfast.

Resuming our journey, we soon reached the

summit of this elevated country where we found the village of Jeremiah, and a valley of the same name. The view was very fine from this point. Not far away, on the apex of a hill, was a castle, one of the strongholds of the Maccabees; far off to the left was a city of Samaria— Shechem of the Scriptures.

We now began our descent by a rugged path down the valley. The whole country is extremely broken and rocky; the valleys are lined by precipitous cliffs, and the mountains rear their heads on all sides in such a manner as to convert the region into a vast labyrinth, so intricate as to render the assistance of a guide necessary. The wild olive abounds in the lower regions; the myrtle and terebinth on the acclivities, while dwarf-oak and laurel crown the summit, their verdant foliage breaking in pleasingly upon the grayish tint which the rocks and moss here give to the face of all nature.

Leaving the valley of Jeremiah, we entered the Valley of Terebinth, or Turpentine, the name being taken from both the tree and the product.

" Do you know any other name for this valley, Mr. Trumbull?" asked the chaplain.

" I do not, sir."

" In the Bible it is called the Valley of Elah,

and it was in this valley that David killed Goliath."

"Is it possible?"

"Yes, this is it, though it was not in just this part of the valley. This creek, now dry, is the one which separated the army of Israel from that of the Philistines, and from this creek-bed David took the five stones, with one of which he slew the giant."

"Then I am going to have some stones as souvenirs," said Thoms.

Off his mule he jumped, and I was going to, when the chaplain said:

"Wait and get them on the return. You will have enough to carry."

Good advice, that. We took it. This ancient and celebrated battle-ground has been the scene of a very recent conflict. Only a few days ago Ibrahim Pasha fought a battle right here, as the unburied bodies lying in plain view attested.

From the Valley of Elah we had to climb the mountains again. For an hour we climbed, being rewarded, when the summit was reached, by a fine view.

"Hello, Trumbull, look there!" said Mr. Thoms, as we passed onto a plain covered with sterile rocks and tufts of moss. "I wonder what that is."

"It looks like a wall with Gothic battlements and square towers. I did not think we would see anything like that. Where's the chaplain? Let's ask him about it."

The chaplain was near by, and had been an amused listener.

"Where are you going, Mr. Trumbull?"

"I am going to Jerusalem, sir!"

"And did n't expect to see anything like that, hey?"

I stopped my mule in amazement. "Is it possible," said I, "that it is Jerusalem?"

"You see before you the city of the Great King."

CHAPTER XXXIV.

APPROACH TO JERUSALEM—REMARKS ABOUT THE CITY—
OUR QUARTERS—THE RECENT CAPTURE OF THE CITY—
DEATH OF MRS. THOMPSON.

THE plain upon which we had entered was some three miles across. For some moments we rode in silence, filled with awe at seeing this sacred city.

"How old is Jerusalem?" asked Mr. Thoms. The chaplain replied:

"It is first spoken of as Salem, the king being Melchizedek. (Gen. xiv, 18.) He blessed Abram as he—Abram—was returning from war. That was about 1913 B. C. As this is 1834 A. D., this place is one of the oldest in history, having seen nearly thirty-eight centuries. Rome—self-yclept the Eternal City—is antedated by Jerusalem over eleven hundred years. Its history is thrilling, but too long for us to follow. For ages the center of Jewish worship,

VIEW OF JERUSALEM.

it has ever been loved and revered by this peculiar people. When in prosperity, they gladly gave their lives in its defense. Now that they are scattered, their veneration for these sacred localities has not in the least abated. Wherever situated, toward Jerusalem they turn their thoughts and faces in worship.

"Seventeen times have they seen Jerusalem wrenched from their possession. Twice have they beheld it razed to the ground. As surely as the deflected needle returns to the north, so surely do the Jews return to this the center of their worship.

"No other city upon earth has been the scene of such strife and contention; yet it has, to a degree, survived all the ravages of war. Babylon, Nineveh, Memphis, Carthage, Thebes, and many others, once the seat of sovereign power and glory of nations, have existed; but they have been utterly annihilated, and with difficulty can the ruins be identified which mark the site of their departed grandeur.

"With the coming of Christ this resilient city is made the nucleus of another religion—kindred to that of the Jews, yet different. Within the radius of a mile are concentrated the sacred spots of these two religions. The world has produced no parallel to this. Yet all has not been told. The Mohammedan also venerates Jerusalem. Second only to Mecca, he offers his body a willing sacrifice in its defense. To the grief of Jew and Christian alike, the Moslem power is in the ascendant in Jerusalem, and the Mosque of Omar covers the site of the Temple of Solomon.

"'Beautiful for situation is Mount Zion, the joy of the whole earth,' cried David, 'the sweet singer of Israel.' You will soon see that he was right. The city is situated amid the mountains, at an altitude of a little more than twenty-six hundred feet, upon a promontory of land somewhat lower than the mountains about it, but separated from them by deep valleys on the east and south, by a continuation of one of these at a less depth on the west, and partially by a spur of the other valley on the north. Only at the northwest can this promontory be attained without crossing a valley. For purposes of defense from ancient modes of warfare, this situation was beautiful.

"The valley to the east is known as that of Jehoshaphat, and down it passes the Brook Kedron. That to the south is called the Valley of Hinnom. Having traversed the south side of the promontory, it turns to the north almost at a right angle, and forms, for a distance, the west boundary. The Valley of Jehoshaphat sends a spur from the north part of its course to the west, also at an angle approximating a right angle. As the Valleys of Jehoshaphat and Hinnom come together at an angle of about ninety degrees, you see this promontory is almost a rectangular parallelogram.

"The sides of the Valleys of Jehoshaphat and Hinnom are very precipitous, and with strong and high walls built upon the crest of the declivity, would make the location of Jerusalem one of difficult capture. The northwest, near where we now are, would be the vulnerable point. As you can see, the surface of the promontory is not level. In fact, it is composed of several hills. The part to our left is called Akra, and is the northwest portion. South of it is higher ground. That is the southwest portion. It is at the apex of the angle the Valley of Hinnom makes when it turns from west to north. Its sides here are very steep, and strong walls made it almost invulnerable."

"But the walls," said I, "do not stand on the edge of the promontory. They are 'way back toward the north."

"Yes, but these are the walls of the modern city. The old walls were well-nigh on the edge. That part was called the 'City of David.' Josephus called it the upper city, Akra being styled by him the lower city.

"The 'City of David'—most of which is not

now in Jerusalem—was the citadel of ancient Jerusalem. It was separated from the lower city—Akra—by a wall, built along the edge of a precipice of moderate height, which divided these portions naturally. So defensible was this City of David that at many of the reputed captures of Jerusalem, this part was not taken, the victors contenting themselves with the other portions."

By this time, the chaplain, Thoms, and I, who were in advance of the rest of the party, had reached the Jaffa gate. While waiting for the others, that all might enter together, I said:

"The large building on the east side of town is, of course, the Mosque of Omar."

"Yes, that is it."

"Then, that is where Abraham came to offer up Isaac, and where Jacob saw the vision of the ladder, and about which he said: 'This is none other but the house of God, and this is the gate of heaven' (Gen. xxviii, 17); and where David bought the threshing-floor of Araunah the Jebusite, that he might offer sacrifice to the Lord (2 Samuel xxiv, 24); and where was built Solomon's Temple, with the Holy of Holies, in which glowed the divine manifestation of Deity in the Shekinah."

"Such are the traditions. Enough of them

are true to make this the most sacred spot in the world to the Jew, and scarcely less so to the Christian. Do you know what the Moslem says about it?"

"I do not."

"That from this very rock upon Mount Moriah—Sakhrah, they call the rock—Mohammed sprang through the seven heavens. They show the imprint of his foot in the solid stone, caused by the force with which he sprang. Now, the stone was going to follow him, and was only prevented from doing so by angels holding it down; in proof of which they exhibit the imprint of the angels' fingers, and claim, also, that the rock was tipped up somewhat, as one side got the start of the angels."

"I never heard that before," said Mr. Thoms.

"Now, Jerusalem, in her pristine grandeur, was a city of great magnificence. The Queen of Sheba, who came to learn of the wisdom of Solomon, was amazed at the elegance of his court. When she, who was used to royal surroundings, saw it, 'there was no more spirit in her.' (1 Kings x, 5.) For an idea of the elegance in Solomon's time, read the tenth chapter of 1 Kings. Now, in a few minutes, you will see how this is all changed; and when we have a favorable opportunity, we will talk about the prophecies foretelling the change."

About three o'clock, all the party being ready, we entered the city by the Jaffa gate. With feelings of great solemnity, I passed the gateway, though I did not kiss the dust, as the pilgrims proper are disposed to do. Having entered, an English gentleman, elegantly attired in a costume partaking of the style of both monk and Turk, met us, and escorted us to the best house in Jerusalem, which had been provided for us by command of the governor. How was it provided? By driving the owners out by force. This we did not know. Had we learned it ere our occupancy, we would have declined to enter. It had been cleaned up for us, but the key could not be found. So, after waiting an hour, the door was burst open, and we were at home. Cleaned? Yes, according to Syrian ideas; but out of a small room, which four of us occupied, our servants took more filth and rubbish than would be found in an average American pigsty of like size. At home? Not if old residents have any rights; for the fleas were there before us—yes, and behind us, and all about us. There was no escape; so we contented ourselves as best we were able, spending the remainder of the day in procuring cooking apparatus and food, and in resting from our fatiguing journey.

The house in which we were quartered was

reached by a long, narrow passage, leading back from the street through a range of stone and mud houses. It was a two-story building, the lower one being arched and having a dirt floor. The lower stories of Jerusalem dwellings are damp and unhealthy, being used as receptacles for lumber, apartments for cooking, dormitories for servants, and, at times, for stables. In the second story are the principal apartments. The roofs are flat or vaulted, and neatly plastered on the exterior. Stairs and floors are made of stone. Carpenter-work is rudely done. Wood is scarce, what is used being brought from Mount Lebanon or the valley of the Jordan. Chimneys are seldom seen, and the houses are poorly supplied with windows. Hence the houses look much like sepulchers or prisons. The house assigned to us had a flat roof, with a dome in the center thereof, which covered an inner court, beneath which was a cistern hewn from the solid rock. The streets of the city are narrow—from six to ten feet in width—crooked and uneven. Generally, awnings made of mats or planks, or arches, extend across the streets, their object being to exclude the sun. They often do it too well, leaving the passages damp and gloomy. As they are always filthy, a Jerusalem street is not a great joy.

The houses showed, on nearly every side, the

want of care, being dilapidated and almost in ruins. The inhabitants live as they can, and seldom make repairs. When the condition of a house is too ruinous to please an occupant, he moves out, and some one less fastidious moves in. Thus the occupants change as the house decays; but nothing is done for the preservation of the premises. At the time of our visit the city was in a condition more than usually forlorn; for within a few weeks it had sustained a shock from an earthquake, and been subjected to pillage. Each event had left marks.

The Egyptian Government had undertaken to disarm the inhabitants of Palestine. They resisted, and twenty thousand of them, coming from the mountains, drove the Egyptians into the city, which the mountaineers at once subjected to siege. Without artillery they could do little, owing to the walls, which are from twenty-five to seventy feet high, provided with Saracen towers, and some two and a half miles in circuit. From near the confluence of the Jehoshaphat and Hinnom Valleys a third but less deep valley extends a little west of north, right into the lower part of the promontory. It is called the Tyropœon Valley; also, Valley of the Cheesemongers. Upon its west side is Mount Zion, the location of the ancient city of David. Upon the east is Mount Moriah, the site of the Jewish temples in the olden time, and of the Mosque of Omar to-day. This Tyropœon Valley is full of subterranean passages, probably artificial water-conduits, hewn, in the time of prosperity, from the solid rock upon which Jerusalem is built.

The elements seemed to conspire with the mountaineers in the capture of the city; for one night, during the siege, a severe storm, accompanied with the earthquake already spoken of, opened up one of these passages which had been long closed. As the city walls cross the Tyropœon Valley, and as one end of the subterranean passage was upon either side of the walls, the assailants entered the city through it in numbers sufficient to overcome the guards at one of the gates, and admit their associates in force. Of course the city was captured, and the usual scene of bloodshed was expected, especially among the Christians. They were agreeably disappointed, as the mountaineers had no quarrel save with the Egyptians. These last, by shutting themselves up in the castle, largely escaped. The city was subjected to some pillage, marks of which we saw. The residence of Mr. Thompson, missionary from my adopted State of Indiana, was entered; but a present propitiated the intruders, and they did little harm. However, exposure to the storm, and excitement incident to the invasion of her home, aggravated the disease under which Mrs. Thompson was laboring. A few days before our arrival she passed to her reward, and was interred on Mount Zion.

CHAPTER XXXV.

Church of the Holy Sepulcher — Empress Helena, and Finding of the True Cross — The Moslem Guard Stone of Unction — The Ædicula — Impressions at the Sepulcher — Place of Apparition Chapel of the Armenians — Mount Calvary — Impressions — Other Localities about the Church.

AT breakfast the first morning in Jerusalem, Mr. Thoms asked the chaplain, whom we rather considered as heading our party, where we were to go first.

"To the Church of the Holy Sepulcher," was the reply.

"That is also the site of the crucifixion, is it not?"

"Yes, they are both beneath the same roof, as are also the graves of Joseph of Arimathea, Nicodemus, and Adam."

"What! the first man?" I asked.

"Yes. It is claimed by the crafty priests

that at the instant Christ gave up the ghost, Adam's grave gave up its dead."

"Do you believe that?" asked Mr. Thoms.

"Far from it, so far as the grave of Adam is concerned. And as to the location of the sepulcher and the identity of Mount Calvary, there is room for reasonable doubt. Still there is an honest belief among the people that these are the localities which saw the crucifixion, burial, and resurrection."

"The localities are of secondary importance," said I. "The grand facts are that Jesus died, was buried, and rose again. In the absence of proof to the contrary, I shall accept the traditionary sites as the real ones."

We reached the church about eight o'clock in the morning. It is a somewhat massive structure, presenting architecture of different ages, owing to its having been several times destroyed, or nearly so, and rebuilt. It was originally built by Constantine, in the fourth century, at the request of his mother, the Empress Helena. This royal lady made a pilgrimage to the Holy City, and was instrumental—as the credulous believe—in discovering the true location of Calvary and the sepulcher. Researches, made under her directions, disclosed a cistern in which were found three crosses, a tablet, and some large nails. Undoubtedly, it was claimed, they were the crosses of Christ and the malefactors; but which was that of the Savior? The question was indubitably settled by taking the three crosses,—one at a time—into the chamber of a noble lady of Jerusalem, who lay at the point of death. The presence of the first did not affect her; the second was alike impotent; but, when the third was brought to her bedside, her malady was at once stayed, and she sprang from the couch a well woman!

Such proof, said the priests, was conclusive that this miracle-working cross was that on which Christ died.

The court of the church is known as the "Mart of Holy Wares." As the name implies, a trade in trinkets, which the locality of their purchase renders sacred, is carried on with the many pilgrims who visit this sacred spot. Passing through this court, we entered the vestibule through the only door permitted to be open. The governor of the city keeps the key of the church, and opens it at the request of the occupants of the Latin, Greek, and Armenian convents, each of which controls a part of this edifice.

This is the most sacred spot on earth to the Christian, yet it is under the domination of an alien religion. The Moslem is in authority, and within this vestibule, upon a divan, surrounded by firearms, swords, and cowhides, sits a fierce Turk. He is the guard, and sees that the Christian worships in accord with the regulations of the Mohammedan. He is not loath to use his ready implements, the cowhide being his favorite.

A group of pilgrims were kneeling about a large marble slab—the stone of unction—upon which our Savior is said to have been washed and anointed for burial. We did not join them, but passed to the left into the body of the sacred edifice. It is a circular room, about a hundred feet in diameter, surmounted by a large dome. Galleries surrounded it, which, in common with the dome, are supported by an imposing colonnade. In the middle of the room, beneath the dome, is a beautiful though peculiar structure. It is of marble, and resembles somewhat a small church. It is the Ædicula, and contains the reputed tomb of the Lord of Life. It is perhaps twenty feet in length and height, and ten feet in breadth, being divided into two apartments. In the outer, really the antechamber, elevated upon a pedestal, is a large stone, said to be the one which the angel rolled away and sat upon, the morning of the resurrection. That the Armenians exhibit elsewhere a stone for which they claim the same identity, does not dampen the zeal of the average pilgrim.

Having inspected the outer apartment, we bowed our heads and entered the inner. All must bow who enter this sacred chamber, for the door is so low that ingress is denied, save in a posture of humility.

I bowed most gladly; for, though disgusted with much of the mummery about the hallowed spot, and somewhat distrustful as to this having been the sepulcher in which Christ lay, I wished to lay aside my distrust, and accept the tradition. With my whole manhood I recognized that Christ died and lay in a grave. That to me was the supreme truth, with which my whole being was possessed. With reverence, therefore, did I bow.

The apartment was so small that only three or four of us could enter at the same time. The sepulcher proper, which is a sarcophagus incased in marble, to prevent the zeal of pilgrims from carrying it off piecemeal as mementos, occupies the half of the chamber to the right. As my hands touched the cold marble my heart warmed to the memory of a Savior's love who had entered the grave for me. FOR ME! My familiarity with death had not been great. I remembered, when a child, having stood at the grave of my little sister Faith, when we laid her to rest after her tragic death, at Yellow Banks, Kentucky. She was my sister, my

Faith, and my heart warmed to her memory. In a few short weeks after that, I saw the body of my loved father placed in the silent earth. He was my father, my hope. With his death all that was bright in life seemed to fade. In the English Cemetery at Leghorn, I had stood beside the tombs of some officers of the American Navy. I knew them not as men; but they were fellow-officers, they were my countrymen, and most reverentially did I strew upon their graves such flowers as I could there command.

Now I stood at the sepulcher of the Savior! My Savior! For me he had died! Ay, more: for me he had voluntarily endured the cross upon Calvary but a few feet away!

What would I not have done for Faith, for father, for my fellow-officers, had aught been possible? What was I doing for Christ, who had done so much for me?

Thought is rapid, and, during the few moments I was permitted to remain beside the sacred tomb, these thoughts possessed me, and sank deeply into my being. Alas! the answer came also. I was doing nothing for my Savior!

A friar is ever present, day and night, to guard the welfare of the sacred mausoleum. Elegant lamps, the gifts of various European monarchs, illuminate it constantly. The sarcophagus is six feet long, three feet wide, and two feet two inches deep.

We were next conducted to the "Place of Apparition," where Christ, after resurrection, first appeared to Mary Magdalene. (Mark xvi, 9.)

Its location is indicated by mosaics in the floor. In another part of the building we were shown also the "Chapel of Apparition," where they claim Christ first appeared to his mother after his resurrection.

The Chapel of the Armenians—so called because they are in possession of it—next engaged our attention. It is an excavation in the rock, formerly a cistern, and here it was that the Empress Helena is said to have found the true cross.

Passing up a narrow staircase, we stood beside Mount Calvary. The stairs are said to be cut from the solid rock, but there is much masonry about them. The mount is also said to be natural rock. Many believe, however, that pious hammers and devout chisels have placed the marks of their religious zeal on this rock, as well as the stairs.

The place where the Savior was nailed to the cross was shown; also the holes in which the three crosses were erected, as also the rent in the rock which the earthquake produced at the supreme moment. The rent, to my mind, bore evidence of having been made by some great convulsion of nature.

I was deeply impressed with Mount Calvary. I did not like these sacred places being covered over with a roof. I believed that religious zeal—yes, religious fanaticism—had changed materially these consecrated localities, that, to the eye, they might conform to the Bible accounts. Yet all this did not alter that fact, gloriously paramount to all others, that "Christ Jesus came into the world to save sinners;" that he cheerfully—no, not cheerfully, for he sweat great drops of blood at the prospect—he willingly came as "a lamb to the slaughter," and died on a cross to save sinners.

As I stood there, I saw myself as the chief of sinners, and made of his death a personal application, as I had done at the sepulcher. Yes, it was for me he died.

I did not welcome these thoughts, but would gladly have thrust them from me. Like Banquo's ghost, however, they would not down, and I carried them with me from the church.

The "Pillar of Flagellation," to which Christ was bound when scourged, was also shown; likewise the "Chapel of the Crown of Thorns." As I remembered the account, the Savior was scourged and crowned with thorns ere reaching

Calvary. So these attempts to concentrate localities rather disgusted me.

In the quarter controlled by the Greeks is a small pillar, surrounded by a railing. Tradition says it is planted in the very center of the earth, in the identical spot from which the earth was taken to make the body of Adam—the first man. They call this pillar the "navel of the world;" and by an absurd freedom, which only their religious fanaticism will allow, they claim that Adam's skull is buried beside this monumental pillar, and at the same time exhibit his grave in another part of this church.

We studied this grave—as also those said to be the burial-places of Nicodemus and Joseph of Arimathea—with much interest; for, whether the tombs of these men or not, they showed much of the manner of sepulture in Christ's time. The sacred tomb had been so modified by recent masonry for its protection that it taught us little. These tombs were excavations from the solid rock. From the bottoms or sides of the excavations troughs or sarcophagi, large enough to contain the human body, are hewn from the rock. They are, at times, large enough to accommodate an entire family.

This Church of the Holy Sepulcher is not especially elegant, though it is rich in many of its furnishings, especially costly lamps, which the nations of Europe have given it. One part of it, occupied by a convent, we did not see, as, but a few weeks before our visit, nineteen out of twenty-two of its occupants had died of the plague. It was, of course, under strict quarantine.

After an hour and a half in the church, we went to our quarters, and prepared for a trip about the suburbs.

"Too bad," said the chaplain, after we had gained the street, "that these religious devotees overdo the matter so much!"

"Yes," said Mr. Thoms, "they have too much meat in one egg-shell."

"So say I," was my remark. "It is absurd so to concentrate these sacred localities. It staggers one's ability to believe. I want to accept the sepulcher and Mount Calvary, but some of the others are too much for my credulity; and the sepulcher is so different from what I expected, that I can not readily believe it is the real burial-place."

"I suppose," said the chaplain, "that you expected something more like the reputed sepulchers of Nicodemus and Joseph of Arimathea?"

"Yes, sir. As Joseph owned Christ's grave, it is reasonable to infer that it would be similar to the one he himself was buried in."

"Indeed it is, Mr. Trumbull, and I can tell you something which I infer you do not know. This sepulcher, said to be Christ's, used to be in the hillside—as are the others—'hewn from the solid rock.' Now, the rock composing the hillside has been cut away, all but a shell a foot or two thick. That shell has been covered by a layer of marble both inside and out, and constitutes the 'little church,' within which is the sepulcher."

"But, Chaplain," said I, earnestly, "how has this thin shell of limestone resisted the violence to which this massive church has so many times succumbed?"

"A hard question, my young friend. That the hillside was cut away is, I suppose, true. As to the preservation of the shell, I can only give you the legend. It is to the effect that the limestone resisted, miraculously, the violence, even the violence of heavy hammers, wielded with intent to destroy it. Fire, so hot as to crumble the marble columns about the church proper, affected not the limestone, usually less refractory under heat; and the sepulcher stood. Ay, more! Though the marble crumbled, and the metal lamps and hangings of the great building melted and ran down upon the sepulcher, the woolen and silk used in its adornment passed through the fire, and even the smell of fire did not attach to them! Such is the legend."

"Suppose," said I, "one doubts this legend, he must then believe that the limestone originally inclosing the grave was destroyed, and that the one now there is a substitution."

"Many so think," said the chaplain. "As you once said, the identity of the rock makes little difference. The grand truth is, that the Savior voluntarily died for you and for me, and for you, Mr. Thoms."

"Yes," said Mr. Thoms, "and was buried— if not in this identical tomb, in one in this vicinity."

Thoms could speak thus unimpassionately. I could not have done so; for the chaplain's personal application found ready lodgment in my heart.

CHAPTER XXXVI.

Via Dolorosa—Site of Saint Stephen's Martyrdom—Tomb of the Virgin Mary—Garden of Gethsemane—Mount of Olives—Magnificent View—Remarks about Sacred Places in Sight.

FOR the proposed trip to the suburbs we are to use our animals. As a rule, not the same with which we left Jaffa; for we have been on the watch, and procured, as we could, better traveling facilities. There are some horses; and grain-bag saddles and rope stirrups are no longer seen. I am fortunate in having an ambling mule, with a good saddle. A better riding animal I never mounted.

Before leaving the city, we passed along the *Via Dolorosa*—or Grievous Way—the street along which our Savior was led away to be crucified, and in which he fainted, if tradition is truthful, under the great weight of the cross which he was compelled to bear. The skillful guides indicate the spots most accurately; and where he is said to have fainted the third time, when Simon the Cyrenian was forced to take the load (Luke xxiii, 26), they point out the print of his hand as he leaned against the wall for support. Of course we looked at what they indicated; but as Jerusalem has been razed to the ground since Christ's time, we gave no credence to their story. They also showed us the residence of Dives, the rich man, and the door at which Lazarus lay, full of sores; also the house of Mary, and the house in which Jesus was buffeted and spit upon. How wonderful that these buildings should have stood through all the revolutions that Jerusalem had seen since the Savior's time! Believe it, ye who can.

Our destination was the Mount of Olives. It is east of the city, being separated from it by the Valley of Jehoshaphat, down which flows the Brook Kedron, though at our visit it was dry. We passed out the Gate of St. Stephen— named in honor of the first Christian martyr— and were shown the place, near by, of his martyrdom. The chaplain removed his hat, and said:

"This is a locality, gentlemen, about which I suppose there is little doubt. (Acts vii, 58.) From this gate, Stephen—the first martyr, the leader of that long procession of voluntary sacrifices—was cast out of the city. Near here, he was stoned to death. At this spot, Saul of Tarsus, who honestly thought he ought to do many things contrary to the name of Jesus of Nazareth, consented to this brutal stoning. Here the brief history of the sainted Stephen closes. Here the long history of the Apostle to the Gentiles opens. To me it is a sacred spot. Would that we, should occasion demand, had the spirit to emulate the example of either of these devoted men of God!"

The good chaplain was deeply affected, and so were we, his auditors. The sad truth that *I* was far from imitating the examples he so earnestly revered, struck home to my heart.

St. Stephen's Gate, the chief outlet from the city on the east, is about the middle of the wall on that side, and a little north of Mount Moriah, on which now stands the Mosque of Omar, upon which once stood the beautiful temple of Solomon. In the olden time, Mount Moriah was about the center of the east line of the city. Now it is the southeast corner, the city having moved so far north as to make this change, as also to leave a large part of the ancient and elegant City of David entirely without the walls of modern Jerusalem.

The descent from the city into the Valley of Jehoshaphat is very steep, in places almost precipitous, being from two to three hundred feet. Upon the east side the ascent is much more gradual, and quite pleasing to the eye, being covered with olive-orchards, gardens, and tombs. In fact, this valley has for centuries been used as a place of interment. To-day it is the wish of devout Jews to repose within it, especially the portion nearest the old temple site. If they so rest that the shadow of Mount Moriah will cover their graves as the day declines, sweet indeed will be that rest. The privilege is granted them; but the wily Moslem makes them pay well for it.

In the bottom of a deep grotto, which passes beneath the bed of the Brook Kedron, is the reputed tomb of the Virgin Mary. It is controlled by Roman Catholics, who guard it most closely, apparently thinking more of it than they do of the tomb of the Savior. Lamps are kept constantly burning, and monks are ever in attendance. A profusion of gold and silver embroidery surmounts it. Chapels for the Catholics, Greeks, Armenians, Copts, and Syrian Christians are near at hand.

The Garden of Gethsemane, which is about an acre in extent, is within a hundred yards of this tomb. It is partly at the foot of, and partly upon the ascent to, the Mount of Olives. The ready guides indicate the exact spots where occurred the bloody sweat and the betrayal of the Savior with a kiss by the hypocrite Judas. This garden, so sacred by association, is to-day but a grove of olive-trees.

Leaving it, our ride soon brought us to the summit of the mount, or rather, ridge; for the region known as the Mount of Olives is somewhat extended and rather indefinite, embracing several summits. It rises some seven hundred feet above the Brook Kedron, and nearly three hundred feet above the east wall of the city. As the ground of the city inclines from the west to the east some two hundred feet, a most satisfactory view of every house within the walls is obtained from this vantage ground. To the observer several hundred feet above the city, and only five furlongs away, it seems as though the city were tipped up for his especial gratification. The view from the mount is one of great extent and beauty. The lover of nature would be charmed with it. Though devoid of the verdure and variety of color incident to many landscapes, there is a solemnity of feature which these more vivid views lack. It is, however, to the Christian and Jew that this view is so transcendent.

After gazing in silence for some moments, the chaplain said:

"The world produces no parallel to what is

before us. There is but one Jerusalem; there can be but one, and that one can not be destroyed. Seventeen times captured and pillaged, several times almost annihilated, phœnix-like, it has risen from its ruins. Almost beneath our feet is the Mosque of Omar, a place of worship for the Moslem, upon the most sacred spot of Old Testament history to both the Jew and Christian."

"Is not its location there a terrible reflection against the true religion?" asked Mr. Thoms.

"To the casual observer, yes; to the student of prophecy, no. The Lord promised Solomon great things for the temple, if he and his descendants would serve him; but, 'if ye turn from following me,' he said, 'then will I cut off Israel out of the land which I have given them; and this house, which I have hallowed for my name, will I cast out of my sight; and Israel shall be a proverb and a byword among all people: and at this house, which is high, every one that passeth by it shall be astonished, and shall hiss; and they shall say, Why hath the Lord done thus unto this land, and to this house?' (1 Kings ix, 7, 8.) Could language more graphically describe the situation to-day of the Jews and of the site of their temple? And look at Mount Zion. David said: 'Walk about

Zion, and go round about her: tell the towers thereof. Mark ye well her bulwarks, consider her palaces; that ye may tell it to the generation following.' (Psalm xlviii, 12, 13.) And what said Josephus when speaking of this same Mount Zion, and the bulwarks erected by David and Solomon? 'For largeness, beauty, and strength, they are beyond all that are in the habitable earth.'"

"Mount Zion is mostly out of the city now," said I.

"Yes, it is; and it was predicted that it should be. 'For now shalt thou go forth out of the city, and thou shalt dwell in the field' (Micah iv, 10), is the prophetic language. Again, as the result of the base iniquity to which the inhabitants of Zion descended, the same prophetic voice declared: 'Therefore shall Zion for your sake be plowed as a field, and Jerusalem shall become heaps, and the mountain of the house as the high places of the forest.' (Micah iii, 12.) You have already observed that this, the site of the citadel in David's time and the very nucleus—aside from the temple—of the elegance and grandeur of Solomon's reign, is without the present city. Now look, and you will see that the husbandman is there at work, and that much of Mount Zion is cultivated ground. Another part is the English cemetery."

"What a wonderful fulfillment!" was the thought of all.

"Yes, this Mosque of Omar, which surmounts Mount Moriah, and is the one well kept and attractive feature of modern Jerusalem, is really a confirmation of Holy Writ; for were it not there, the Jews would endeavor to rebuild the house of the Lord. Success in such an attempt would negative the prophecy just quoted relative to the temple being cast out of sight of the Lord. You know the Emperor Justinian once offered to assist the Jews in rebuilding Jerusalem, but the Moslems rose in such force as to prevent it. Christ said: 'Jerusalem shall be trodden down of the Gentiles till the times of the Gentiles be fulfilled.' (Luke xxi, 24.) The time of the Gentiles is not yet fulfilled. When it will be we know not; but this we know, until it is, all the powers of earth can not restore Jerusalem and the Jews."

The next most conspicuous object in the Holy City was the Church of the Holy Sepulcher. Its massive architecture entirely erased Mount Calvary from the view, a fact we much regretted.

The general appearance of the city from Mount Olivet is most pleasing. As in David's time, it is "a city that is compact together." The climate being hot, and most of the year dry, there is little evaporation to cool the atmosphere. To obtain relief from the pungent sun's rays, the flat roofs of the houses are whitened. As most roofs are relieved from monotony by a dome, the distant view is one of beauty and purity. Alas! we were sufficiently familiar with the interior of these buildings to know that they, though beautiful without, were within full of all uncleanness, like unto whited sepulchers.

Casting our sight over the city to the west, we see the hill country. We admire its undulating beauty, and think of the times of David and Goliath, and the many, many conflicts there waged between the Philistines and the Israelites. Carrying vision to the south, the hills are seen to be continuous. Prominent among them is one about which I ask information of the good chaplain:

"What is that hill? It surely must have a history.

"It has. That is Beth-haccerem. (Jeremiah vi, 1.) You see how conspicuous it is. It was a signal-station in the olden time. We are now standing upon another. 'A sign of fire' upon either of these prominences would be instantly seen from the other. Thus was the country roused, in times of danger, by fires upon the hilltops. Do you see that opening in the hills to the south, through which the Brook Kedron makes its exit from these mountains?"

"Yes, sir. What is it?"

"It is the only point from which Mount Moriah can be seen from a distance. A traveler from the east can not see Jerusalem till he surmounts the crest of the ridge of Olivet. Should he come from the north, he will first see the Holy City from the hill Scopus, but a mile away. If, as we did, he journeys from the west, he will descry the sacred place from an elevation three miles away. Now, when Abraham, the father of the faithful, was making his sad journey to this vicinity, to immolate his loved, his only child, 'on the third day, Abraham lifted up his eyes, and saw the place afar off.' (Gen. xxii, 4.) Though pleasing to the natural eye, it was a sad, sad sight to the grief-stricken father.

"Since then thirty-seven centuries have passed, and the sight of the land of Moriah is still a sad one, though possessing most intense and sacred interest. Isaac was not sacrificed, but a willing sacrifice was here offered. Here was cruelly crucified the Lord of Life!

"Off to the south you also see the town of Bethlehem. 'But thou, Beth-lehem Ephratah, though thou be little among the thousands of Judah, yet out of thee shall he come forth unto me that is to be ruler in Israel; whose goings forth have been from of old, from everlasting.' (Micah v, 2.) Yes, that is Bethlehem!"

Our good chaplain was almost overcome with emotion, and so were the rest of us.

A little farther east were the plains where the angel appeared to the shepherds by night, and the heavenly host sang: "Glory to God in the highest, and on earth peace, good-will toward men!" (Luke ii, 14.)

Still farther to the east is that wonderful lake known in Scripture as the Salt Sea, or Sea of the Plain, but which we moderns call the Dead Sea. Over thirteen hundred feet below the level of the Mediterranean is the surface of this strange sheet of water. As we were nearly three thousand above the Mediterranean, we had a commanding view of this desolate locality, once teeming with life and animation.

Alas! it was the old story. Wickedness, the most intense, had compelled the Lord to annihilate the cities and people of this vicinity. Here had the population been so dense that four kings had gone out to fight with five. (Genesis xiv.) But in all this dense plain could not ten righteous men be found. Therefore the wrath of God overthrew them.

We associated the location of Sodom and Gomorrah with the lower end of the lake, and, in our imaginations, saw the fleeing family of Lot, and his wife looking back in her flight, when a destruction as great as that of the doomed cities came upon her. She ceased to move, and stood upon the plain a pillar of salt. (Gen. xix, 26.)

In our thought, the rain of fire and brimstone descended upon these places of abomination till they were destroyed; and, as with Abraham, we could see only the smoking plains, like to the smoke of a furnace. (Gen. xix, 28.)

Lifting our eyes from this desolate vale to the highlands beyond, we behold the land of Moab—the birthplace of Ruth, the ancestress of King David and the Messiah. Here were the Mountains of Pisgah, and, prominent among their peaks, Mount Nebo. There once stood the meek lawgiver of Israel. And yet he, after wandering in the wilderness forty years to gain possession of the land upon which we then stood, was compelled to die on its very threshold, and that for only one sin. (Deut. xxxii, 49–51.)

And where was this great Moses buried? No man knows. (Deut. xxxiv, 6.)

"By Nebo's lonely mountain,
  On this side Jordan's wave,
In a vale in the land of Moab,
  There lies a lonely grave;
But no man dug that sepulcher,
  And no man saw it e'er;
For the angels of God upturned the sod,
  And laid the dead man there."

Between us and this unknown though honored grave, the historic Jordan wends its way. Its serpentine and verdant course contrasts strangely with the barren, verdureless tract through which it passes from the mountains of the north to the Salt Sea. Shall we mentally do that which was denied the man who conversed face to face with God, and cross the Jordan? The waters, in imagination, are walled back upon the north, and fail upon the south. We pass over dry shod, and stand near the site of ancient Jericho, beyond which, near Gibeon, at the command of Joshua, the sun stood still. The ancient city we see in our mind; the modern Jericho we see with the literal eye.

Near here, also, is the wilderness in which John the Baptist preached, and in which the Savior was tempted. It is a rugged, barren labyrinth of hills; now, as in the olden time, the stronghold of robbers.

Far to the north are Samaria and Galilee, beyond our field of vision. Would that we might visit them, to see the places of the Savior's boyhood and much of his ministry! We have encircled our horizon. Impressed that in no other is so much that is sacred and sublime concentrated, we remember that we are on the mount from which the Messiah ascended to heaven.

CHAPTER XXXVII.

Mount of Olives, and Impressions received there—Bethany, and Tomb of Lazarus—King's Dale—Pool of Siloam—Moloch—Tophet—Valley of Slaughter—Gehenna.

"THE Mount of Olives! How blessed the associations connected with it! Here Christ came often, when desiring solitude and retirement for himself and his disciples," said the chaplain; "and from here occurred his ascension—the crowning *finale* to his physical manhood. The plan of Christian salvation, so efficient in its simplicity, was here perfected."

"I thought," said Mr. Thoms, "it was perfected when Christ said on the cross, 'It is finished.'"

"The sacrifice was then complete; but the grand culmination to the plan was yet to come. Thus far—that is, to the death upon the cross—Christ's life had, to a casual observer, been in many things a failure; for he was 'despised and rejected of men; a man of sorrows, and acquainted with grief.' (Isaiah liii, 3.) But having shown himself a willing and complete sacrifice by accepting death and descending to the grave, a course which to the same casual observer would be a brilliant success, is entered upon, and every step is victory. He arose from the dead! Well may we sing:

> 'Lift your glad voices in triumph on high;
> For Jesus hath risen, and man shall not die!
> Vain were the terrors that gathered around him,
>   In vain the dominion of death and the grave;
> He burst from the fetters of darkness that bound him,
>   Resplendent in glory to live and to save.
> Lift, then, your voices in triumph on high;
> For Jesus hath risen, and man shall not die.'

Abundant as was this sacrifice, it did not measure the fullness of the Savior's love, as evinced by his words, 'I go to prepare a place for you. And if I go and prepare a place for you, I will come again, and receive you unto myself, that where I am, there ye may be also.' (John xiv, 2 and 3.) That journey was to be the culmination. That journey was the ascension. Jesus is now gone to prepare these mansions for us. What, in the meantime, are we to do? The Savior's talk, just before he ascended, tells us plainly. He said: 'Go ye into all the world, and preach the gospel to every creature.' (Mark xvi, 15.) To whom was he talking?"

"To the disciples who were about him," said one of us.

"Was he talking to no one else? Did he not mean that those parting words should echo down the ages, and find lodgment in the hearts of thousands yet unborn? Were they not for me? I believe they were, and in a way so weak that I blush for my incompetency, I am heeding that voice. Are those words meant for you? Yea, verily! Are you heeding them? Your own consciences must answer."

Very solemnly our loved chaplain uttered these words. They struck me dumb with astonishment. At the tomb of the Redeemer—my Redeemer—I was impressed with the fact that I was doing nothing for him; and now, near the place from which he ascended to God, I was overwhelmed with the conviction that for me there was a special work; that the words 'Go ye into all the world and preach the gospel to every creature,' were for Samuel Trumbull. Was the thought pleasant? Far from it! It implied the abandonment of my life-work—forsaking the sea, which I loved almost as my own soul.

The necessity of being a Christian, which possessed me at the Savior's grave, was most unwelcome intelligence, but it was insignificant compared with this awful thought that "Go ye and preach" was meant for me. I was dumb with the overpowering conviction, and became oblivious to all surroundings. For how long, I knew not. This question, asked of the chaplain by Mr. Thoms, brought me to myself.

"Do you consider it every one's duty to preach?"

"Yes; but not all in the same way. All must preach by their lives and examples; but all are not called upon to become what, in common parlance, is termed a preacher. 'Actions speak louder than words,' and all must preach by their actions; but all must not be set aside as preachers, having no other vocation. A navy with nothing but chaplains in it would not do much execution."

That was such a comical idea that I joined in the laugh which it produced.

"No, Mr. Thoms; we need farmers and carpenters and merchants, and these should all preach by example and words spoken in private. I believe in a called ministry. We need preachers, and the Lord will let such as he means for chosen vessels know it. If such as are called will answer, we will not want for preachers."

Alas! alas! I, too, believed in a called ministry, and, to my infinite regret, recognized that I was called. To keep still was impossible. So I wandered away from the company, and began to cut some olive-branches for walking-sticks, intending them as mementos of the Mount of Olives. I had scarcely commenced cutting when a Turkish guard began screaming at me, and started for me in a run. He was some distance away, and had to come up hill. By the time he reached me I had several fine canes.

He was a fierce fellow, and could speak no English. I understood his pantomime, however, and stopped cutting. Had I been a civilian he would have arrested me. I was in full uniform, and that overawed him. There is that about a uniform which a private soldier can not resist. So, after doing his duty, by flourishing his sword and using much vociferation, he left me. Fortunately, he left the canes also; but I did not; I brought them away as trophies.

There are three prominent peaks on the Mount Olivet ridge. Upon one of them is an impression in the rock, said to be the imprint of the Savior's foot, made at the moment of his leaving the earth. Above this imprint were the remains of a Mohammedan chapel. We took no stock in the thought that this was the exact location of the ascension, or in the imprint. It was enough for us to know that Christ rose from Olivet.

Luke says (xxiv, 50) Bethany was the place,

and that village was on the eastern slope of the ridge, about two miles from Jerusalem (John xi, 18), and quite a distance from this traditional imprint. We preferred to think that the spot from which Christ rose was unsullied by a Mohammedan ruin.

We went to Bethany by a serpentine road, and found the village almost deserted, the inhabitants having gone to the city from fear of the rebels and robbers who infest the country between Jerusalem and the Dead Sea. The guide took us at once to the tomb of Lazarus, and the scene of the wonderful miracle in which the grave gave up its dead, and before which "Jesus wept." It was a cave, as in the Savior's time (John xi, 38), some forty feet deep, at the bottom of which was a sepulcher similar to those on Mount Calvary.

Leaving Bethany, we returned by a more southerly course, crossing that portion of Olivet ridge called the Mount of Offense. This is where Solomon kept his strange wives, and where he built altars for them to do their idol worship. (1 Kings xi, 7, 8.) It is "before Jerusalem," if we think of the ancient City of David, but not before the modern.

Descending again into the Valley of Jehoshaphat, we visited the tombs of Absalom, Zachariah, and Jehoshaphat. They are at the base of Mount Olivet, a few feet from and above the Brook Kedron, on the east side thereof, and opposite the site of the ancient temple. A portion—how much can not be definitely stated to-day—of this valley was called the King's Dale. Here Absalom made for himself a pillar. (2 Samuel xviii, 18.) Some regard this tomb as that pillar; others doubt it. It is square, perhaps twenty feet on a side, and resembles somewhat a small house. The roof is circular, and runs up to a point or spindle; in short, is a cone. The structure was made by removing portions of the native rock from about it, leaving a solid mass of the shape and size named. This was then hollowed out, leaving an apartment with sides and roof all of one piece, and anchored, as the Creator anchored it, to the everlasting rock.

The tomb of Zachariah is similar, save that the roof is a pyramid, and, judging by the appearance, never has been hollowed out. Jehoshaphat's tomb is a cave, hewn in the rock, with a sarcophagus like those already described.

A fourth of a mile down the valley, to the south, we came to the Pool of Siloam. That is not quite so; for the pool is really in the Tyropœon Valley, near its confluence with the Valley of Jehoshaphat, being at the base of the rock promontory formed by these valleys. This promontory is called Ophel.

The Tyropœon Valley commences by a broad depression in the ground, well to the north part of the city, and near the center, relative to the east and west boundaries. It becomes gradually deeper as it passes toward the southeast corner of the parallelogram already described, and finally joins the Valleys of Jehoshaphat and Hinnom at their point of confluence. Though much more shallow than either of the other valleys, it is of importance in a study of Jerusalem. It increases materially the level area of the low ground where the valleys unite.

Farther to the north it separates Mount Zion from Mount Moriah. In the olden time, when Mount Zion was surmounted with the royal palaces of the Jewish kings and Mount Moriah sustained the magnificent temple, this valley was an obstacle to easy passage from one to the other. Therefore, King Solomon built a bridge across it. It was very elegant, and built on scientific principles. The length was about three hundred and fifty feet; width, fifty-one feet; built of stone, arranged in the form of arches. This bridge was in use at the time of the visit of the Queen of Sheba to King Solomon. It was called "the Ascent," and was one of the many things which deeply impressed the queen with Solomon's magnificence. (1 Kings x, 5.) This was a thousand years before Christ, yet the arch is commonly said to have been introduced into architecture in the sixth century before Christ.

This triangular-shaped promontory of rock—Ophel—near the apex of which, on the western side, is the Pool of Siloam, embraces all south of the temple site and east of the Tyropœon Valley. The pool is about fifty feet long, fourteen and a half wide at the lower end, seventeen at the upper, and eighteen and a half deep. The sides are masonry. In the east face are six pillars of Jerusalem marble, poorly preserved, said to have supported some kind of a canopy. The water is reached by a stairway at the southwest corner. It is of easy descent, and evidently much used. Parched as we were with thirst, a draught from this celebrated pool was most refreshing, though the water is a little brackish.

The first seven verses of the ninth chapter of Saint John tell of one of Christ's miracles, in which this pool plays a prominent part. We there learn that the meaning of the word Siloam is *sent;* and the significance of the meaning is, that the water is *sent* from a fountain—Virgin's Fount; farther north in the rock Ophel—through a passage driven through the solid rock. The passage, leading most directly from the Virgin's Fount to the outer world, opens into the Valley of Jehoshaphat below—that is, south of—the temple site. It is spacious, and gives easy access to the fountain for pedestrians.

Our animals, too, were thirsty. We found water for them—though a scant supply—farther down the valley, at the outlet of a passage leading from the Pool of Siloam.

We were now at the junction of the Valleys of Jehoshaphat and Hinnom, a place of much historic interest. The latter comes into the former almost at a right angle, and the common valley passes to the south in the same direction as the Valley of Jehoshaphat, above the junction.

In this north and south valley was the Royal Garden of King Solomon. Its exact boundaries can not now be determined. Beyond doubt it occupied the locality where the valleys unite; but how far north or south it extended we do not know. It was, however, very extensive, and made an earthly paradise to correspond with Solomon's greatness. The side of the Olivet ridge called the Mount of Offense was in it, being almost opposite the mouth of the Valley of Hinnom.

Commensurate with the height of elegance and grandeur to which Solomon attained was the depth to which he fell. In early life an earnest worshiper of the true God, he built the first permanent edifice, the object of which was worship. The heathen, previous to this, knew nothing of temples and temple-worship; for their sanctuaries were groves. The Jews, though in advance of the heathen, had only the portable tabernacle.

Though of Divine approval, with the preliminaries of building greatly advanced by King David, to Solomon was allotted the glory of this great work. Well did he do it, making the structure surpass anything the world had yet seen. With earnest devotion he dedicated this temple to the worship of Jehovah. Yet he who had built this house for the Lord, of such magnificence that the whole earth could not produce a parallel, became in his later days enamored with strange women. He brought himself wives by the hundreds from Egypt, Moab, and the countries of the Ammonites, Edomites, Zidonians, and Hittites. And right here, on the side of the Mount of Offense, almost against this elegant temple to the Almighty God, did Solomon make homes for his idolatrous wives. Ay, more! Right here, in the open space created by the Valley of Hinnom joining that of Jehoshaphat—almost within slingshot of this same temple, where shone the cherubim—did Solomon declare his idolatry by building houses for the worship of "Chemosh, the abomination of Moab, . . . and for Molech, the abomination of the children of Ammon." (1 Kings xi, 1-8.) Both the Moabites and Ammonites worship fire, and the idols named are the respective tutelary gods of these people. To please these wives, whom he had taken contrary to God's commands, he joins them in their idolatry, and insults God by building houses for idolatrous worship, almost at the portals of the temple.

Within one of these houses, or high places, was the brazen image of Molech, or Moloch, the same as Chemosh, and identical also with Baal. (For proof of last see Jer. xxxii, 35.) This "horrid king," Moloch, as Milton calls him, demanded human sacrifices, and received them in vast numbers, especially children. The brazen monster was heated to an intense heat, and the bodies of his unfortunate victims were placed in the embrace of his fiery arms, which were partially extended, and ever demanding more. Their agonizing writhings caused them to disappear within the body of this gluttonous fire-fiend, whence they fell to the furnace below. Their distressing screams carried grief to the ears of the deluded but loving parents. To prevent them being heard, resort was had to the beating of drums; hence the name Tophet, by which this locality was known. (*Toph* means a drum.)

Could an abomination more detestable to the Jews be devised than thus polluting the vicinity of their sacred places? The good King Josiah thought not, and he, in turn, determined to further pollute it in such a disgusting way as to render it incapable of habitation. So he broke in pieces the images, and made Tophet the receptacle of the filth of the city, and the depository for dead men's bones. (2 Kings xxiii, 14.) God indorsed this action of Josiah when he declared: "Even so will I break this people and this city, as one breaketh a potter's vessel, that it can not be made whole again; and they shall bury them in Tophet till there be no place to bury." (Jer. xix, 11.) This prophecy referred to the destruction of Jerusalem by the Romans under Titus. Again Jeremiah says: "Behold, the days come, saith the Lord, that it shall no more be called Tophet, nor The valley of the son of Hinnom, but The valley of slaughter: for they shall bury in Tophet, till there be no place. And the carcasses of this people shall be meat for the fowls of the heaven, and for the beasts of the earth; and none shall fray them away." (Jeremiah vii, 32, 33.)

How complete the fulfillment of these prophetic words! Titus attacked and besieged Jerusalem at the time of the Passover, when it was densely thronged with people. It is said that a million and a half of people died at that siege within the walls. Josephus says, eleven hundred thousand. Six hundred thousand of them were thrown without the gates. To this very locality—Tophet—over one hundred and fifteen thousand dead bodies were carried, if the evidence of Josephus is to be taken. Verily, "*Valley of Slaughter*" is the correct name.

With such a history, it is a fit emblem of the place of torment. After Josiah's time, funeral pyres, to consume the dead bodies, were ever burning. This intensified the emblem; and "Ge Hinnom"—the Hebrew name of the place—became a synonym for the place of punishment, from which we get our word *Gehenna*.

> "First, Moloch, horrid king, besmeared with blood
> Of human sacrifice, and parents' tears:
> Though, for the noise of drums and timbrels loud,
> Their children's cries unheard that passed through fire
> To his grim idol.   . . . Nor content with such
> Audacious neighborhood, the wisest heart
> Of Solomon he led by fraud to build
> His temple right against the temple of God,
> On that opprobrious hill; and made his grove,
> The pleasant valley of Hinnom thence
> And black Gehenna called, the type of Hell."—*Milton*.

Yes, this abomination was hard by the temple of God; so near that the expression "From the temple to Tophet" has become proverbial.

CHAPTER XXXVIII.

HILL OF EVIL COUNCIL—MOUNT ZION—TOMB OF DAVID—BETHLEHEM—CHURCH OF THE NATIVITY.

THE south boundary of this Valley of Hinnom is quite precipitous, its eastern end being known as the Hill of Evil Council. Its rocky formation is perforated with catacombs, and upon its summit is the grave of Caiaphas. It is supposed that his palace was on a part of this hill, and that in that palace was held the council of the priests, scribes, and elders, the object of which was Christ's death. (Matt. xxvi, 3 and 4.) Hither he was brought as soon as the Judas kiss had effected his arrest. (Matt. xxvi, 57.) Tradition is sufficiently consistent with convenience to locate the tree upon which the traitor hung himself near by. It is a gnarled and homely specimen of arboriculture. I say *arboriculture* wittingly; for the tree has been trained to indorse, by its appearance, the detestation the Christian holds for Judas. This tree is comparatively modern. One used to be shown as the gibbet of Judas, which stood right upon the edge of the cliff. It was a better place; for had the rope broken, as we infer was the case, the wretch would have fallen down the precipice some thirty feet, and the effect described in Acts i, 18, would have followed. Moreover, he would have fallen in Gehenna, and, to all, that would have seemed appropriate.

Here also is Aceldama (Acts i, 19), the Field of Blood, bought with the proceeds of the Savior's betrayal. Not fit for the treasury, being the price of blood (Matt. xxvii, 6), it was taken to buy a potter's field. Yes, silver was counted out for the Savior's blood!

Leaving the Valley of Hinnom, we ascended Mount Zion, and again viewed the sacred surroundings from a height. This, once the stronghold of King David, is now mostly without the walls, and cultivated, as Micah predicted (iii, 12; iv, 10). In Christ's time, it was still an important part of the city. We were shown another house purporting to have belonged to Caiaphas— city residence, perhaps — now an Armenian church; the place where the Lord's Supper was held, now a Turkish mosque and hospital; and the tomb of David. At present the tomb is an obscure vault, with three or four tombs of dark-colored stone. Josephus says that Solomon buried his father David with much pomp and ceremony, and placed great riches beneath the tomb. He also states that a thousand years later, when Antiochus besieged Jerusalem, Hyrcanus, the high priest, opened one room of David's sepulcher, and took therefrom three thousand talents, with which he persuaded Antiochus to raise the siege. Josephus also says that the avaricious King Herod, years after, opened another room, and extracted vast sums. Yet neither of these despoilers found the king's remains, so artfully had Solomon effected their interment.

Yes, here, where once was the City of David, the Divine Messiah is believed to have instituted the sacrament commemorative of his death; here the Holy Ghost descended on the apostles; here Christ appeared, upon his resurrection-day, to the disciples; here Christ probably took his farewell of his followers, telling them to "preach the gospel to every creature," from here they probably took their departure, "without scrip or purse."

The chaplain told us of all these things. What he said about preaching the gospel was a theme of fire, which burned its way to my very heart. I wanted to think, but a squadron of noisy Arab cavalry was encamped upon the sacred spot.

army, at which time he heard the defiant challenge of Goliath, whom he slew for his impiety. (1 Sam. xvii.) This had been a pleasing story to me in my boyhood, and I greatly enjoyed the ride.

David seems to have done little for his native place. Only once, judging by the Scripture record, did memory revert to his birthplace. That was when he longed for a draught of water from the well which stood by the gate (2 Samuel xxiii, 15, and which three captains secured at the risk of their lives.

Just before our arrival at the town, we passed the head of a very beautiful valley, resembling in shape an amphitheater, and possessing some rich pastoral fields and gardens. It is the place where the angels appeared to the shepherds at night, and communicated the tidings of the Redeemer's nativity, and where the heavenly host sang, "Glory to God in the highest, and on earth peace, good-will toward men." (Luke ii, 8–14.)

We passed into the town under an old ruined arch, and found ourselves in a crowd of athletic Arabs. There are three thousand of them composing the population of Bethlehem; and all of them are Christians, save nine. We learned that the reputation of the town for better-looking women, more substantial houses, and more comfort than usually found in an Eastern town, was deserved.

The guide conducted us at once to the convent, built over the place of Nativity. It is a strong, castle-like building, erected by the Empress Helena in the fourth century. The roof, made of cedar brought from Mount Lebanon over fifteen hundred years ago, is in a good state of preservation. The monks had refreshments provided for us, of which we partook with good appetite. There are no hotels in Palestine, and entertainment, which is always extended with good-will, is the province of the monks in the various convents.

Having eaten, we were each provided with a taper, when we descended to the lower part of the church. There are, we may say, two churches, one above the other—of course beneath the same roof. The upper contains nothing remarkable except a star, inlaid in the floor, immediately under the spot in the heavens where, it is alleged, the star seen by the wise men in the East country became stationary; and, like it, directly above the place of the Nativity, which is an excavation in the rock—once used as a stable; now, fitted up and floored with marble.

We descended to this lower church through a long, narrow passage. As it receives no light from above, it is illuminated by thirty-two lamps, gifts of various princes of Christendom.

At the farther extremity of this small church is a recess, hollowed out into the form of an arch. Within the recess is the Altar of Nativity. It is supposed to occupy the exact locality where Immanuel, having laid aside his glory, first appeared in the garb of human nature. A circle in the floor, composed of marble and jasper, surrounded with radiating rays of silver, indicates the spot. An inscription in Latin, denoting that "Here Jesus Christ was born of the Virgin Mary," meets the observant eye of the visitor.

Adjoining the Altar of Nativity is the manger in which the infant Messiah was cradled. It is of marble, and resembles the rude furniture which alone the stable could supply. (Query: Was the original manger of marble?) Before it is the Altar of the Wise Men, the chief adornment of which is a valuable painting, in an elegant silver frame, representing their adoration.

These altars are controlled by the Catholics, Armenians, and Greeks. Much jealousy exists among them; and, at times, scenes most unbecoming to the place, and most diverse from the character of Him whom they worship, occur at the hour for mass. Bloodshed is not uncommon.

The same is true at the Church of the Holy Sepulcher in Jerusalem. At the latter place, tragedies are at times enacted, owing to the dense crowds who attend the services. A few months before our visit, when the Greek monks performed the service incident to the reception of fire from heaven, the air became vitiated, Ibrahim Pasha was carried out insensible by his guard, a panic occurred in the multitude, and three hundred persons were trodden to death in the rush for the door.

Leaving the convent, we went on foot a third of a mile to a cave, where, tradition says, the Virgin took refuge, with the young child, before the flight into Egypt.

From the mouth of this grotto we enjoyed another fine though less pleasing view than that from the Mount of Olives of the Dead Sea country and Beth-haccerem. We learned, in addition to our previously obtained information, that the latter place was the birthplace of Amos, and the site where lie the bones of the detested King Herod, who had a palace at Tekoa. (Tekoa was a town so near the signal-hill Beth-haccerem that the two are practically one. See Amos i, 1; and Jer. vi, 1.)

The Cave of Engedi, where David cut off the skirts of Saul's garment, is supposed to be near that same vicinity. Other points of interest were pointed out, but I do not remember them.

Retracing our steps, we again accepted the refreshing hospitality of the monks. Then we returned to Jerusalem, which we reached about three o'clock in the afternoon.

CHAPTER XXXIX.

STONES FROM SOLOMON'S TEMPLE—POOL OF BETHESDA—MOSQUE OF OMAR—JEWS' QUARTER—VISIT TO THE GOVERNOR—ORIENTAL JUSTICE—MISSIONARIES—FAREWELL TO JERUSALEM—ACCIDENTS.

MOST of the party were too tired after the return from Bethlehem to do more that day. But Thoms and I had muscles of steel, and we went out to steal some specimens of the stones formerly in the temple of Solomon. They now constitute a portion of the city wall where it skirts the brow of the cliff bounding the Valley of Jehoshaphat, just east of the Mosque of Omar. Going out through St. Stephen's gate, we turned to the right and walked along the brow of Mount Moriah, passing the Golden Gate. This gate has been closed, owing to an idle report that through it the Christians would one day enter and possess the city. So superstitious are the Moslems that they have deprived themselves of this convenient gate because of a vague story.

The stones for which we were searching are in the base of the walls, and are very large. We measured one that was twenty feet long by six wide. We watched our chances, and, when the guard was remote, broke off some pieces.

Near here a large stone projects from the wall, upon which the Mohammedans claim that their prophet will one day sit and judge the world, which is to be gathered in the Valley of Jehoshaphat below.

Re-entering the Gate of St. Stephen, we examined the Pool of Bethesda. It is within twenty paces of the gate, and due north of the temple site. It is one hundred feet long by sixty feet wide, and, I should think, forty in depth. It was empty of all save rubbish. We would call it a large reservoir. It is the best preserved of any relic of Jerusalem's former splendor. The plastering still adheres to the walls, and two of the original five porches remain. It was here that Christ cured the impotent man. (John v, 1–9.)

"Too bad, Trumbull," said Mr. Thoms, "that we can not visit the Mosque of Omar!"

"Yes, it is. But Jews and Christians are not admitted," I replied. "I think the commodore was right in deciding that we should not ask the

THE MOSQUE OF OMAR, JERUSALEM.

privilege of visiting it. They would not want to grant it, and as we are the guests of the Government they would not like to refuse."

"O yes! I know that to ask would be impolitic, and they won't ask. But, my boy, why can we not get onto the roof of Pilate's Palace and look down into the inclosure?"

A *buono mano* obtained us that privilege, and to the roof of the building we mounted. This palace has been repeatedly destroyed and as often rebuilt; only the original foundation remains.

Our view was a good one. The inclosure is the largest level space in the city; it is adorned with beautiful lawns and well-preserved trees, being made very attractive. The building is an octagon, surmounted by a dome. The minarets common to Mohammedan mosques are wanting, but this dome is said to be one of the most symmetrical in the world. To the Mohammedans Jerusalem is a sacred city, second only to Mecca. They revere the memory of Abraham, and especially of David. Our Savior they consider a great prophet, second only to Mohammed.

These feelings of the Moslem in common with the Jew and Christian have done much to secure the privileges of worship which the two latter classes enjoy in this Moslem city.

We returned to our quarters by crossing the upper part of the Valley of the Tyropœon.

Here is the Jewish quarter of the city. The houses are most inferior, and the people most miserable. The streets are the common slaughter-pens of the butchers. Here are their animals killed, and much of the entrails and offal left to putrefy in the hot sun. As we passed we saw the red-handed men at their bloody work. We hastened on, for it was a disgusting sight, and the stench was terrible.

The Jews have two "wailing places." One is on the brow of the precipice near where Thoms and I got the specimens an hour ago. The other is where some stones of sacred memory—having been in the old temple—compose part of the wall around the old temple area on the west side. When we recall how greatly they have fallen from their former high estate, and the awful surroundings in which these Jerusalem Jews live, wailing places seem appropriate. They are seldom vacant, for the Jews know their loss, and mourn it constantly.

The next day we paid a visit of ceremony to the governor of the city. He received us with great courtesy, and, at first, with much formality. After a time he laid aside his dignity, and descended to the level of social discourse. He wanted to know much about America, which the captain told him through an interpreter.

Though interested, he received many of the statements with a look of incredulity. He dismissed us politely when we rose to leave, but made some remark to the interpreter at the last moment.

Of course we wanted to know what it was he said; but the interpreter would not tell. We teased him, however, till he did. This was it:

"What they said about the length of the Mississippi River and the speed of the steamboats are lies, and what they said about the Falls of Niagara is another. I will always remember them as the lying Americans!"

How we did laugh at the captain, who had been our spokesman!

After having our laugh, we saw the character of Oriental justice. We had a young acting-midshipman in our party, a mere lad, not more than sixteen years old. The boy wore a very fine sword, which an Arab evidently coveted. Springing upon him, the Arab endeavored to wrench the sword from its scabbard. Fortunately, it was lashed to the scabbard. The youth's Yankee blood was up instantly, and he fought the man so desperately that he tried to run. Not so! The boy stuck like a Jerusalem bug. Our cavasse came and arrested the Arab, when the governor ordered his head struck off. That we thought entirely too severe, and, at the captain's request, the bastinado was substituted.

We met several missionaries while in Jerusalem. I was impressed with the fact that they were self-denying, God-fearing men, who had "left all and followed Him." Their example appealed loudly to me; for, most unpleasant as was the thought, I realized that it was my duty to preach; and my adopted State was to be the place, if I ever yielded. I did not mean to yield, but determined to fight this impression.

One of the missionaries, whom I did not meet, was a Mr. Nicholasin. When the *Delaware* arrived off Jaffa, this man was lying at the point of death. In response to a request for medical assistance, one of our surgeons was detailed to attend him. The doctor went to his house, and there remained as a member of his household. The remedies did the desired work, and Mr. Nicholasin recovered. This doctor was an avowed skeptic, but when he returned to the ship he bore this testimony:

"I have not believed in Christianity; but I have believed that these foreign missionaries are sharp, shrewd fellows, who want to see the world, and do see it, living on the fat of the land, and drawing upon the coffers of the people at home at their own pleasure. I learned from observation, while a member of Mr. Nicholasin's home-circle, that these missionaries are self-denying and God-fearing, eminent examples of the typical Christian, the very existence of which I had always denied, claiming that all such were hypocrites. They have abandoned all that is desirable in life, and are living in poverty, amid most boisterous surroundings. If religion prompts such zeal as this—and I know it does—there is something in religion! I believe it; and, as a result of the examples of these devoted people, I confess my belief in Christianity!"

This was powerful testimony from the former scoffer, and did us—me, at least—much good.

We did some shopping that last day in Jerusalem, buying some trinkets as mementos. The shops are poor, and the stocks meager.

When night came, I could not sleep. So I wrote up my journal. Fleas keep one stirring, and by two o'clock in the morning I had caught up in the record. At that time we mounted our animals, and started for the return to the ship, being favored with bright moonlight.

Jerusalem was indeed beautiful, as we left her, in the moonlight. Her Gothic battlements variegated the moonlit scenery about her in a most pleasing way. My sensations, as I took the last look at the sacred city, were a strange mixture:—regret, to leave the places hallowed by the footprints of the Redeemer; and gladness, to be getting away from the pest of fleas and vermin, as well as to be nearing again the ship and the sea. With these were the impressions received in Palestine, that the navy was not to be the scene of my life-work; and dearly as I loved my profession and the water, they were to be abandoned for a vocation wholly different. The thought was as gall; but it was there, and I feared it was there to stay. Try as I would, it was ever present with me.

Daylight overtook us as we were emerging from the Valley of Turpentine. While in the valley, we were beset by a band of robbers. They were big, vicious fellows, well mounted, but we were two to their one, and they speedily withdrew. Several shots were fired by each side; but none of our people were hurt, and, by the way the robbers rushed their horses down the rocky road we judge none of them were.

At the spring in the mountains we all stopped for refreshment. Some of the party started before the rest. I was with the rear division, for the baggage had been put under my especial care, as were also two seamen who were somewhat under the influence of Jerusalem rum when we left the city. By this time they were drunk. I had a big job on hand, for these men could scarcely hold on their donkeys. My good friend Thoms came to my relief, as also did Lieutenant Barker. The latter said:

"Trumbull, those men have some more liquor about them. You must get it, or you won't get them to Jaffa for days."

"Do you think so? I'll find out about it."

I searched them, and, sure enough, they each had a bottle, which they gave up reluctantly.

With the bottles went their little ambition to get along; they wanted to dismount and go to sleep. Taking the stirrup-straps we lashed their feet together beneath their animals' bodies, to keep the rascals from falling off. With no help from the men, traveling was slow work. In a fit of desperation I rode in front of them and showed them a bottle.

"Now boys," said I, "the first one here may have a drink."

That roused them up a little, and they tried to reach the whisky. Of course they did not succeed, for I was well mounted on an active mule; but I toled them along for miles as an Indiana farmer would tole a herd of swine.

We entered the valley of Sharon at a pretty fair pace. I was in front with the whisky-bottle in sight; then came the two sailors, each racing for it; then the sumpter mules with the baggage, and Thoms and Barker helping the mule-drivers to keep the calvacade stirring, for we wanted to overtake the first division. Suddenly Barker's horse shied, and he was thrown. To his and our dismay, his leg was broken. It was a terrible accident for any one of us, simply being of the party, but for Barker it was sad indeed.

Ramleh, the nearest place, was ten miles away. What should we do? We improvised a splint out of an umbrella, tying it on with our handkerchiefs; then we made a litter with some poles and boughs of trees, upon which we carried the poor man to Ramleh. This accident sobered up the drunken sailors, and they gave us good help. Thoms staid at Ramleh with Barker, while the rest of us pushed on to send a party with proper conveniences to convey the sufferer to the ship.

Toward evening we arrived under the walls of Jaffa. Suddenly my mule took fright—at what I never knew—and, as I was not suspecting trouble, threw me heavily to the ground. There I lay some time, unconscious. The first I remembered was a corona of anxious faces about me; then a severe twinge of pain in my shoulder, and next a feeling of chagrin that the Hoosier had let a mule throw him. No bones were broken, and I was soon on foot; but I carried a lame shoulder and hip for many weeks.

At eight P. M. we reported on board the

ship (the first company, which left us at the spring, had made the journey by ten A. M.), so very slow are these natives on whom we largely depended.

A surgeon, with assistants, was at once sent to rescue poor Lieutenant Barker from Ramleh and the fleas. He reached the ship next day, in fair condition, considering the circumstances.

CHAPTER XL.

MOUNT CARMEL.—PROPHECIES ABOUT PALESTINE AND THE JEWS—TYRE—SIDON—BEIRUT—SMALLPOX—CHOLERA—HOMEWARD BOUND.

THE tour of Palestine completed, I was wholly possessed with the desire to go home to America, as the commodore had promised me I should when the *Constellation* sailed. We were to meet her soon at Port Mahon.

My shoulder was very painful from the fall the mule gave me, and the record I kept of the next few weeks was meager.

We sailed from Jaffa on August 26th, bound north along the coast of Palestine. Saw the city of Cesarea from the deck. A southerly breeze took us close under the foot of Mount Carmel, upon the summit of which is a convent some centuries old. It was a desolate, dreary neighborhood as we saw it, but rich in memories to the Bible student, as the chaplain convinced us.

It was very warm down in Lieutenant Barker's quarters, and Thoms—good old Thoms!—with the help of some of the other officers, had carried the poor fellow up on the poop-deck, where he could have the air and see the coast. As "misery loves company," I sat near him, and nursed my shoulder.

"Gentlemen," said the chaplain, "do you know anything about Mount Carmel?"

"No, sir." "Not much." "Tell us."

Such were the answers.

Lieutenant Barker said:

"I believe it was on the top of Carmel that the prophet Elijah had the test of God's power, as compared with that of Baal, in setting fire to the sacrifices."

"Yes," answered the chaplain, "that is the place."

"Is it possible?" cried I. "That is one of the grandest incidents in Old Testament history. Let's read about it."

"A good idea. Get your Bibles."

We did so, and, as directed, turned to the eighteenth chapter of 1 Kings, and read, commencing at the seventeenth verse, the account of this test. We read in rotation, and the twenty-first verse came to me. I could scarcely get through it. In my thought, I saw Elijah on the top of the mount, and heard him say with the voice of divine authority: "How long halt ye between two opinions? If the Lord be God, follow him; but if Baal, then follow him."

"What's the matter, Trumbull?" asked Thoms.

"My shoulder," answered I.

It was not so great a falsehood as may at first seem the case. The thing that I must *shoulder* was what troubled me. The reading finished, the chaplain said:

"That was a glorious test and an overwhelming victory; for, you remember, Baal is another name for Moloch, the god of fire; and he could not answer by his own element, while God did. It was a most impressive lesson to these idolatrous people. The lesson for us is in the twenty-first verse. Decision is the point. 'If the Lord be God, follow him;' in other words, Do the right thing, and do it now."

I looked at the good chaplain with surprise and alarm. How much did he know of my life motto and of my present disturbance of mind? I could only rub my shoulder to hide my emotion. The good man went on:

"Now, this place used to be one of great fertility and beauty. When Solomon, in his song descriptive of the graces and beauties of the Church of God, wanted a simile for the head, he said: 'Thine head upon thee is like Carmel.' As he had compared other parts of the body (representing the Church) to the most pleasing things possible, that to which he likened the head—the crowning glory—must have been transcendent. That was Mount Carmel." (Sol. Song vii, 5.)

"I see nothing so fine about it!" said Mr. Thoms.

"No, you do not. Do you know why?"

"No, sir; only that there is nothing to admire. It is a dreary-looking mountain to me," said Thoms.

"Wait a little for the explanation, if you please, Mr. Thoms," said the chaplain. "When Isaiah is speaking of the joyful flourishing of Christ's kingdom, he says: 'The desert shall rejoice and blossom as the rose. . . . The glory of Lebanon shall be given unto it, the excellency of Carmel and Sharon.' Now, we know about the mountains and cedars of Lebanon, and of the great fertility of the plain of Sharon, in the olden time. Having been in such association, Mount Carmel must have been similar. But, Mr. Thoms, the voice of prophecy foretold a radical change. Amos cried, 'The top of Carmel shall wither' (chap. 1, verse 2), and so it is to-day."

"Chaplain," said Lieutenant Barker, "you promised us a talk on the fulfillment of prophecy about Palestine and the Jews when a good time came. Will not this time do?"

"First rate. Get the twenty-eighth chapter of Deuteronomy; and let us read, commencing with the fifteenth verse."

We read, and were powerfully impressed with the awful predictions there made. The chaplain said:

"Gentlemen, you have seen the city of the Jews, and you have seen their country. They are cursed in the city, and they are cursed in the field. Language can not describe their miseries; but word-painting more vivid than this chapter contains is not often produced; I think, never."

"Has the climate altered enough to explain all the changes in the fertility of Palestine?" I asked.

"I think not, Mr. Trumbull. It used to be a 'land flowing with milk and honey.' That statement implies prolific vegetation. Why the change? The rainfall is about the same each year as it was centuries ago, but in those times the land was *all* cultivated. That was made possible by terracing the hillsides, and keeping the dirt in place by stone walls. Thus the whole extent of the country was practically level, and rain was held upon it when it fell—first, because it was level; second, because the vegetable matter, both the living and the decayed, acted as a sponge, and retained the water long enough for the ground to absorb it. The roots of growing vegetation seem to attract moisture strongly, and they absorb it rapidly. Now, on cultivated land there is a layer of this vegetable mold several inches thick. Through it ramify millions of rootlets. These will take care of any ordinary rainfall, and keep the water where it fell. If there are trees, they help with the mulching their fallen leaves produce.

"Again, these same things prevent too rapid evaporation, and prolong the good effect of the rain. Such were the conditions in old Palestine. To which we must add that there were many reservoirs for storing water, and that much attention was paid to irrigation. But troublous times came—reservoirs leaked, and were not mended; walls, sustaining the terraces, decayed, and were not repaired; the beautiful level spaces were thus converted into slopes, over which the fallen rain rushed rapidly, carrying with it the vegetable mold or soil, which was collected in the valleys. A thing of this kind grows ever worse. To-day the hills of Palestine are sterile, the soil which should cover them being in the valleys; which, as we know, are fertile. The rain falls upon these hills as in days of yore, but not a moment does it remain. Away to the valley it hastens, and the hillside is not much benefited by its fall.

"The uncertain tenure of property has aided in this; for the country has been so oppressed that nothing was sure about the Government, and the farmers did not feel safe in keeping up improvements. For the same reason houses are never repaired in the city, and both city and field are feeling this curse.

"Wars are predicted in this chapter (verse 52). Surely they have had them. Seventeen times Jerusalem has changed masters, and twice has she been prostrate; namely, at the captures by Nebuchadnezzar and by Titus. But this is not all. The prophecy declares that the Jews shall be scattered 'from one end of the earth even unto the other' (verse 64), and that they shall have no rest."

"That surely has been fulfilled," said Lieutenant Barker, "for they are everywhere, and everywhere abused."

"Yes; the thirty-seventh verse declares that they shall be 'an astonishment, a proverb, and a byword among all nations.' How true is that! Balaam declared: 'Lo, the people shall dwell alone, and shall not be reckoned among the nations.' (Numbers xxiii, 9.)"

"That's accomplished," said I, "for the Jews have no place amid the nations."

"Amos gives his prediction thus: 'Lo, I will command, and I will sift the house of Israel among all nations, like as corn is sifted in a sieve, yet shall not the least grain fall upon the earth.' (Amos ix, 9.)"

"I don't think I quite understand that," said I.

"It is not wholly adverse to the Jews. It means that, though the Jews shall be scattered, the good in them will be recognized, and that not one of their good deeds should go unrewarded."

"I see!" said I. "Looking toward their final restoration, I suppose?"

"Yes, I suppose so. With that in view, the Lord had promised that, though they should be scattered and afflicted—a very byword among men—'I will not cast them away, neither will I abhor them, to destroy them utterly.' (Lev. xxvi, 44.) Death to the Jews as a people would have been a great blessing, but it was denied them. They were not permitted to die. They had rejected the worship of Jehovah, and served idols. They had killed the Prince of Life, and cried, 'His blood be upon us and our children!' It is upon them, and they may not die. Strangers in their own land—strangers in foreign climes—

strangers they must ever remain. They have, in turn, been ejected from almost every land under the sun. Persecutions have followed them; kings have endeavored to exterminate them; but all in vain. They have thriven amid their miseries, all because the Lord said he would not destroy them utterly.

"Christ predicted the downfall of Jerusalem under Titus, in the twenty-first chapter of Luke. 'When will it be?' they asked him. 'This generation shall not pass away till all be fulfilled,' was his answer. (Verse 32.) It seemed improbable, for Jerusalem was then at peace. But the Roman war began in the year 66 A. D., and soon the sacred city was razed to the ground. The Romans aimed to preserve works of art, and Titus intended to save the temple, but he could not do so. It was utterly destroyed, and the very foundations plowed up. 'Not one stone was left upon another,' as Christ had predicted."

"Will Jerusalem never be restored?" asked Mr. Thoms.

"Luke xxi, 24, says: 'Jerusalem shall be trodden down of the Gentiles until the times of the Gentiles be fulfilled.'"

"When will that be?"

"When the Gentiles are converted. The date we can not give."

"Will Jerusalem then be restored?"

"Some think so, basing their belief largely on Zechariah xiv, 11, in which it says: 'Jerusalem shall be safely inhabited.' That the Savior's prediction of Titus's siege and capture, and Micah's prediction that Zion—the nucleus of Jerusalem in David's time—should be plowed as a field (iii, 12), and that it should go forth out of the city and dwell in the field (iv, 10), are so abundantly fulfilled, leaves little room to doubt the truth of prophecy, so far as Jerusalem is concerned. Add to this the prediction the Lord made as to the temple—viz., that he would cast it out of his sight, and that those passing by the site should hiss—and you make it stronger." (1 Kings ix, 7, 8.)

"It is strong enough! It is convincing!" said I. "There go the bells, and the watch changes. Thank you, Chaplain."

All joined in the thanks, and the company dispersed.

Anchored off St. Jean d'Acre on the 27th. The officers went ashore; but I did not, owing to my lame shoulder and hip. Next morning we were off Tyre. Here I went ashore; but it was unwise, and I suffered keenly for it. Tyre is a mass of ruins. We wanted to see the fishermen spreading their nets, as prophesied in Ezekiel xxvi, 14. The top of the rock was there all right, but not a fisherman or a net did we see. Sidon, but twelve miles away, we also visited, finding nothing of interest, save the best figs I ever ate.

On August 29th we were off Beirut, where we filled our water-casks. While here a man on the *Delaware* came down with smallpox. Consternation was on every face when the disease was recognized. "Will it keep me from sailing on the *Constellation*?" was the question with me.

The poor man—think of being left in Palestine with the smallpox!—was sent ashore, and placed in the charge of the American consul at Beirut, and of the good missionaries, who promised to care for him.

September 19th found our anchor atrip, and our good ship headed for Malta.

Going home! Going home! The thought was ecstasy. To see my loved wife! To see my darling boy! How could I wait? Why was the *Delaware* so slow? She used to be a clipper.

On the 4th of October we fell in with the frigate *United States*, and the next day we made the Island of Malta in her company. A day or two at Malta, and away we sped for Port Mahon, where the *Constellation* had been for some time, fitting for the homeward voyage across the Atlantic. I was to go on her. I would have danced with glee at the thought, only my hip was sore yet, and it would not be dignified.

We arrived off Mahon in a storm, and no pilot came out. Would we have to lie to till that storm saw fit to stop, thus delaying the start for home? No. The blessed captain said: "I know this entrance well, and I am going in." In we went in great style, much to the chagrin of the harbor pilots.

Where was the *Constellation?* I knew the good ship well, and she was not there. Alas! She had sailed, a week before for America. I was dumb with surprise and disappointment at this intelligence. It seems that the cholera had been raging in Mahon, and the *Constellation* had suffered much, twelve seamen and one officer having died. She lay off and on before the harbor for some days, but no relief came. To secure a radical change of air, she hastened her departure.

I had my baggage all packed to go on board her, but I now most sadly unpacked it.

A few days after arrival here the dread disease, cholera, broke out on board both the *United States* and the *Delaware.* The prospect was most doleful. To relieve matters all possible, the commodore—God bless him!—decided to send the *United States* to the United States. Was not that glorious? I was to be a passenger on board of her. She got away, homeward bound, on October 26th.

We had nearly one hundred and fifty cases of cholera on the ship, all told, five of which died. We buried several of them at sea. In due time we reached New York harbor, and went into quarantine—a tedious necessity for a homesick sailor on the threshold of his native land.

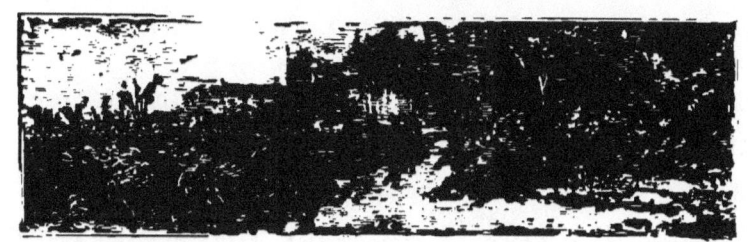

CHAPTER XLI.

HOME AND FRIENDS—PERFECT HAPPINESS—CONVERSION—
SHALL I PREACH?—PROMOTION—CAMP-MEETING—"I
YIELD."

AFTER release from quarantine I remained in New York a day to do a little shopping; among other things, to have a gold head put upon one of the canes of olive-wood I had cut, in spite of the guard, on the Mount of Olives. It was a fine stick, and I went to this expense that I might have a cane second to none. Then off I hastened for home in Madison, Indiana, with a furlough for three months in my pocket. There was some staging to be done in crossing the Alleghanies. When we alighted from the stage I had my cane, but the head was gone. Some rascally passenger had wrenched it off and pocketed it.

Dear old Madison! How happy was I to walk her streets again! Hastening to the house which held my dear ones, I saw my wife while yet some distance away, but did not notice a little boy whom I met running upon the sidewalk. We had passed each other, when the thought occurred to me that the little fellow was my Philip. In an instant I had him in my arms. He struggled for release, and cried: "No! you are man; I want father."

Poor child! Nearly two years old, and did not know what a father was! A moment more and we were with my dear Harriet. Wife, child, and father again together. And the good mothers, both my own and my wife's, were there to join in the welcome home to the wanderer.

About this time the Internal Improvement Bill was passed in Congress. Railroad building was at once commenced, and surveyors and civil engineers were wanted. They were scarce. My naval studies had taught me much of this science. The State of Indiana solicited my services, and, with the consent of the Government, I entered the State employ; the naval authorities kindly extending my furlough.

My work was to be on the preliminary survey of the Madison, Indianapolis and Lafayette Railroad, and I began it early in 1835. I was to have good pay from the State, and the usual salary of my naval rank when waiting orders.

"Now, Harriet," said I to my wife, when all was settled, "I am going to enjoy perfect happiness. At home for many months with you and Philip and the mothers; good pay and pleasant work."

"How nice it will be! I am so glad!" said my wife.

"Yes, perfect happiness! It has been a pet theory with me for years, as I walked the quarterdeck, and now it is to be attained."

"My dear husband," said my wife somewhat sadly, "there is no perfect happiness unless religion is a part of it. Be a Christian, and perfect happiness is possible, but never without!"

I then told my dear wife what I had never before mentioned to a soul, of my impression received at the tomb of the Savior that I should be a Christian; but I did not tell even her of the other impression, that I must preach the gospel. She urged me strongly to do the right thing, knowing well the significance of that word with me; but I would not yield.

Several months passed. We were very happy; but the fact that I was not doing *right*—not serving Christ—marred perfect happiness.

The State of Indiana wanted me a year longer than my leave covered, and application had been made for an extension. Would it be granted? Full of anxiety, I went one day to the post-office. O how I wanted that leave! Stopping in my walk, I said to myself: "If I get a year's leave, I will seek religion."

The leave was at the post-office. In my happiness, I forgot the decision I had made; but it came forcibly to memory when I reached the point in the walk where I had made it.

"Trumbull, will you back down?" asked a voice within me.

"No, I will not!" was my audible reply. "I will do right!"

My wife was in Michigan City, on a visit. I wanted to unburden my soul to her, but, of course, could not. Got my Bible, to study and to see what religion was. Thursday night I went to prayer-meeting, but said nothing to any one. Sunday night an invitation was given to any desiring to join Church. I wanted to, but my feet would not take me forward. Four stanzas of a hymn were sung while the invitation lasted, during each of which I was determined to go; but each time I failed. Keenly disappointed, at the close of the last stanza, I whispered to a friend:

"If they had sung another time, I would have gone."

The friend at once went forward and whispered to the preacher, who said:

"There is a young man who says he will

come forward if we will sing again. So let us all sing."

Every one was alert to see who it was. I was in for it, and went forward. Having broken the ice, it was my desire that every one should know that I meant to be a Christian. I went into the altar—which was quite elevated—and faced the audience, that every one might see.

The next morning, when breakfast was announced, I said to the girl:

"Please set the things where they will keep warm; we will have family prayers."

That statement was an astonishment to the household. My wife had not yet returned; and the old ladies had not been to church the evening before, so I said in explanation:

"I have concluded to be a Christian, and hereafter we will have family prayers."

Oral prayer was new to me, but my soul was in it. The happiness of the mothers, I can not and will not attempt to describe. Though conscience approved my course, I was in great distress of mind. "What is religion?" and "How is Christ to help me?" were the questions in my mind. All day Monday and Tuesday I sought answers in vain. Wednesday, I took up a Methodist Discipline belonging to Mrs. Goode—my wife's mother—and read in it the expression, "Christ was both God and man."

"Just as a marine is both soldier and sailor," thought I. "If a soldier had a fuss with a sailor, the best person to settle it between them would be a marine; for he is both soldier and sailor. Just leave it to him. Now, Christ is both God and man, and the best possible mediator between God and man. He is my mediator. I will leave it all to him."

The thought gave me infinite comfort. How glorious to have some one to rest upon, on whom you can rely!

"That rest is *faith*," thought I. "I accept Christ for *my* Savior."

At that instant my mental burden was gone, and peace took quiet possession of my soul. What it meant, I knew not; but I was happy to think that I had taken Christ as my Mediator and Savior.

"Why, Trumbull, that acceptance is religion," said a voice within.

"Can it be possible? It is! It is! So simple I had not seen it!"

I told the mothers, and we had a love-feast then and there.

My conversion made considerable impression on the community; and several of my associates followed my lead, and started upon a religious life, much to my delight. Soon my wife returned, and shared with us this great joy.

There was much in my position with the railroad management which I did not like. The public moneys were not spent wholly for the best interests of the people, but to aid some individual by locating the track near his land.

"This is iniquitous!" I had often said to my wife, who helped me with my topographical drawings.

"Then, why do you do it?"

"How can I help it, Harriet? I am only obeying orders."

Having become a Christian, I knew how I could help it; but I wanted to confer with my wife before action. I had only a day or two to wait. During those days, "Touch not, taste not, handle not the unclean thing" kept sounding in my ears, as I was at my work.

Having conferred with my wife, and found that she would indorse my action, I resigned my position as civil engineer. It was a radical move, and left me for a year without employment, as the navy would not want me till my leave was expired a year hence. Only "waiting-orders" pay would I have; and the perfect-happiness scheme, so far as financial matters were concerned, was severely knocked. Was I happy? Yes, at first, for conscience approved; but soon the impression received on the Mount of Olives came to me with vivid distinctness.

"Go ye into all the world, and preach the gospel to every creature," was ever sounding in my ears. I could not banish it; but for a time I told no one, not even my wife. To yield necessitated a terrible sacrifice. I loved the navy so dearly! My prospects were very bright. No one stood better than I in my chosen profession. Must I give it up? Conscience said, "Yes;" the man Trumbull said, "No."

"What is right? Decide by your life-motto," said an inward monitor.

"O," cried I, in my grief, "that concedes the whole point!"

"But you must!" said the monitor.

In my distress I made a confidante of my wife. To my surprise she did not want me to become a preacher.

"You a preacher, Samuel! I am surprised! O, this is awful!" cried she, bursting into tears.

"Yes, it is!" said I, adding my tears to hers.

"It is not awful for you; it is awful for me!" she said. "You are all right!"

"I do not understand you," said I.

"It is plain enough! I am not a proper person for a preacher's wife; and if you preach, I will have to die, and leave you and Philip; and you will get another wife!"

This doleful picture was so comical that I had to laugh; but Harriet was in solemn earnest, and could not enjoy the laugh. She verily believed that my preaching implied her death.

My conversion occurred on the 6th of October, 1836, and this battle with the "woe-to-me-if-I-preach-not-the-gospel" impression was waged till the springtime of 1837. I was weary with the conflict, and much worn in body, and about to yield, when my warrant promoting me to the rank of lieutenant in the United States Navy was received. This so revived my love for my profession that I decided to stay in the navy.

"Woe to me if I preach not!" sounded still in my ears in spite of the decision.

I bought some theological books, and studied them under the direction of Edward R. Ames (afterward a bishop in the Methodist Episcopal Church) and William Daniels. I got no help, and the time was near when I must report in New York for duty.

My wife had a brother—William H. Goode—a Methodist minister, then living in New Albany, Indiana. Mr. Goode was a man of great decision of character, and the thought came to me that perhaps he could help me. One day I said:

"Harriet, let's go to New Albany, and see your brother William?"

"There is nothing I would like better," said my wife.

So we jumped on a steamboat, and went down to New Albany. Mr. Goode was in the midst of a camp-meeting, held a few miles out of town. We went out to it, but I could not enter into the spirit of the services. My load was too heavy. I could not support it.

"Why not give up?" said that persistent monitor.

"I can not make the sacrifice! It is too great! Just as I have been promoted!"

I fled to the woods to escape observation. Day after day I sought the solitude, but there was no relief. The still small voice, "Woe is me if I preach not!" was alike in the camp and the solitude.

"Is there no escape?" I cried aloud, in agony.

The voice within replied:

"Whither shall I go from thy Spirit? or whither shall I flee from thy presence? If I ascend up into heaven, thou art there: if I make my bed in hell, behold, thou art there. If I take the wings of the morning, and dwell in the uttermost parts of the sea; even there shall thy hand lead me, and thy right hand shall hold me."

"The sea, then, will afford no escape?" cried I, in my misery.

"It will not! You learned your duty beyond the sea, on the sacred spot from whence your loving Savior ascended to heaven; you brought a keen knowledge of that duty across the broad expanse of the Atlantic; it has been ever with you, and there is no escape! This is the supreme moment of your life, Trumbull. Be a man, and decide for the right! Not because there is no escape, but because it is right. Your life-motto is part of you, and by it you must decide. '*Do right!*' Assert your manhood, and 'DO RIGHT!'"

I sank upon the ground with the violence of my emotion, exclaiming:

> "Nay, but I yield, I yield!
> I can hold out no more!
> I sink, by dying love compelled,
> And own Thee conqueror."

CHAPTER XLII.

My Wife's Distress—Licensed to Preach—Resignation as Lieutenant—Join the Indiana Conference—Become a Chaplain in the Navy—Resignation.

"PEACE, like a river," flowed into my soul as I lay there submissive to God's will. But it was action God wanted. I arose and went into the camp. The altar was surrounded with mourners. Entering the altar I began to work with them, hoping to help them find Him under whose banner I had just enlisted for the war. My wife knew all in a minute.

"I must get Mr. Trumbull away from this meeting, sure, or he will be a preacher," she said to herself.

After service, my wife and I went with some friends to Dr. Leonard's tent.

"Well, Brother Trumbull," said the doctor, "how does this compare with the deck of a man-of-war?"

"I will never again walk the deck of a man-of-war!" was my reply, an enigma to all but my wife. It confirmed her worst fears. She said:

"Mr. Trumbull, I must go to town. The 'bus starts in a few moments."

"Go to town! I am surprised. But if you must go, of course I will take you in."

We entered the 'bus, and in due time were at Mr. Goode's door. Assisting my wife to alight, I said:

"I will be back to-morrow evening, Harriet," and jumped into the vehicle, which took me back to the camp-ground.

I knew not the sad heart I left, till Harriet told me afterwards. She really thought that if I preached she must die to make place for a more fitting preacher's wife, and felt justified, therefore, in trying to dissuade me from leaving the navy. To get me from religious influences she had adopted the ruse of asking me to take her to town. I had cheerfully done so, and she thought her object attained. Imagine her distress when I returned to the camp-ground. She was inconsolable, and shut herself in her room, absolutely holding her breath, that she might die, and thus promote God's plans.

On Friday, the Quarterly Conference of Mr. Goode's Church met, and recommended me for license to preach.

On Sunday, I was sent to a colored congregation to make my maiden effort as a pulpit orator. It was to me a pleasing coincidence that to this same Negro audience, in the same church, had my brother-in-law preached his first sermon. God was with me, and I enjoyed the service, whether the auditors did or not.

On the Tuesday following, having already sent to Washington my resignation as an officer in the United States Navy, I went with my brother-in-law, Mr. Goode, to the Indiana Conference, of which I was made a member, and appointed, as assistant preacher, to Lawrenceburg Circuit, Rev. James Jones being the senior preacher.

In a week myself and family were in the parsonage at Manchester, Indiana. How wonderful a change had a few short weeks made in our affairs! Then, a favored officer in the United States Navy, with a most flattering prospect for the future; now, a humble itinerant preacher, on the frontier of Indiana, with no prospect of earthly prosperity.

My wife, having become convinced that she was not to die, and was to share my lot for better or worse, entered into my work with enthusiasm, and made a most desirable wife for a preacher, as she had done for a sailor. She always insisted, however, that she had married a sailor and not a preacher.

Yes, we had both made sacrifices; but we would not have left the little parsonage in Manchester for the glitter of a naval position.

That God accepted our sacrifices was shown, during the first year of my ministry, by an extensive revival of religion.

Many of my friends asked me if I did not think I had made a mistake in exchanging a lucrative position for that of a humble itinerant. My reply was:

"As duty and God called, it was right for me to obey. The awards of eternity will far outweigh the temporal sacrifice. I will be far happier and more useful in traveling a circuit in modest garb than pacing, in uniform, the deck of a man-of-war, desirable as the latter may be."

Others tried to dissuade me. To them I replied:

"It is needless to urge! I have nailed my colors to the masthead, clinched the nails, and thrown the hammer overboard."

Notwithstanding these positive answers, some of my friends could not abandon the belief that a person with a naval education should work among sailors. They believed that I could preach more acceptably to seamen than to landsmen, and sought for me the position of chaplain in the navy. They were successful; and a warrant as chaplain in the United States Navy, dated September 8, 1841, was sent me from Washington. With doubt as to the wisdom of doing so—for God had given me many souls for my hire—I accepted the position, and was assigned duty as chaplain of the Brooklyn Navy-yard. It was eminently a desirable position. My familiarity with the sea enabled me to illustrate my discourses by nautical facts and incidents, much to the pleasure of my auditors. The trouble was that my audience was ever changing. Seldom would I have the same listeners two consecutive Sabbaths, and conversions were not numerous. To see men converted was what I wanted. In Indiana, the sight was almost constantly present; and I longed for the frontier. Moreover, the voice that told me on the Mount of Olives that I was to preach, told me also that Indiana was to be the field.

At the end of the year I therefore resigned the chaplaincy, and returned to the itinerancy, ambitious only to be a preacher of the gospel.

NOTE.—Many have asked why the hero of this narrative, having been educated by the Government, did not serve his country during the recent Civil War. The question is pertinent. These are the facts: A few weeks prior to the session of the Indiana Conference for 1862 (the first session of the same after the magnitude of the conflict was recognized), father, through Oliver P. Morton—the "War Governor" of Indiana—tendered his services to the General Government, with the provisos that, if desired, they be accepted previous to the session of Conference then approaching; and that he be given rank with his classmates who were still in the service.

It was distinctly understood that failure to accept father's proposition before Conference met would imply that his services were not wanted; in which case, he would take work from the Conference for another year.

Anxiously were the mails watched for word from Governor Morton, but it came not. Only one conclusion was possible; and, with reluctance, father accepted ministerial work for another year.

A few days later, came a communication from Washington, forwarded by Governor Morton, gladly accepting father's proposition. Why was the acceptance late? Governor Morton was peremptorily called from home. He left word with his secretary to forward at once to father any mail relative to this subject. The boy who took the communication from the post-office carried it in his pocket for a week. In the meantime Conference met, and father took work. Having done so, it seemed to him right to continue in the pastorate.

THE END.

www.ingramcontent.com/pod-product-compliance
Lightning Source LLC
Chambersburg PA
CBHW022137300426
44115CB00006B/231